The Rivals

THE BOSTON RED SOX VS.
THE NEW YORK YANKEES

An Inside History

The Baseball Writers of
The New York Times* and *The Boston Globe

DAVE ANDERSON

HARVEY ARATON

JACK CURRY

GORDON EDES

TYLER KEPNER

JACKIE MACMULLAN

DAN SHAUGHNESSY

BOB RYAN

GEORGE VECSEY

with Introductions by
ROBERT LIPSYTE AND
DAN SHAUGHNESSY

ST. MARTIN'S PRESS ❧ NEW YORK

Frontispiece: The Yankees and Red Sox in a 1973 brawl sparked by catchers Thurman Munson and Carlton Fisk (Handout/*The Boston Globe*)

www.stmartins.com

Book design by Michael Collica

Library of Congress Cataloging-in-Publication Data

The Rivals: the Boston Red Sox vs. the New York Yankees: an inside history / the New York Times and the Boston Globe.—1st ed.
   p. cm.
ISBN 0-312-33616 0
EAN 978-0312-33616-5
   1. New York Yankees (Baseball team)—History—Sources.
2. Boston Red Sox (Baseball team)—History—Sources.
3. Sports rivalries—United States—History—Sources.
I. New York times. II. Boston globe.
GV875.N4R47   2004
796.357'64'097471—dc22
                                2004049747

First Edition: September 2004

10 9 8 7 6 5 4 3 2 1

Contents

The **Rivals**

Introduction

Dan Shaughnessy of The Boston Globe

Rivalry. It's an interesting word. Here in Boston, the Hub of the Hardball Universe, we think that the "rivalry" between the Red Sox and Yankees is the greatest rivalry in all of sports—better than Dodgers-Giants, Cardinals-Cubs, Celtics-Lakers, Cowboys-Redskins, Ali-Frazier, Texas-Oklahoma, Russell-Chamberlain, Michigan-Ohio State, Seabiscuit-War Admiral, and even Harvard-Yale.

But it's a little provincial of us to think this way. I'm not sure who first said it, but the "rivalry" between the Yankees and the Red Sox could best be likened to the eternal contest between the hammer and the nail. Since 1918, when the Red Sox won their fifth and thus far final World Series, the Yankees have won 26 baseball championships to Boston's none. That's 26-0.

The rivalry, therefore, is more about tradition than competition. It's not so much a match of equals as it is Boston's obsession with all things New York. New Englanders grow up trained to hate pinstripes. The Yankees are bullies, buying championships and steamrolling everything in their way. They don't play fair, they always win, and we spend our lives thinking about how to conquer this team that stole Babe Ruth from under our noses.

Like many regions of America, my hometown has a self-contained Little League with teams of 11- and 12-year-old boys playing for teams named after big-league ballclubs. The Newton North Little League plays its games at Murphy Field and annually features the Orioles, Cardinals, Indians and Yankees. The kids wear replica uniforms. One of my neighbors has a son who played for the Yankees and she admitted, "I just have a hard time looking at him sitting there in the kitchen before games, eating his cereal, wearing that uniform with the pinstripes."

In New England, we are obsessed with the Yanks. We like to think that the feeling is mutual, and that the Yankees live in fear of their rivals from Boston, but truthfully, that hasn't been the case most of the time. There's an arrogance to the Yankees, a smug contentment owed to decades of dominance. The Yankees in most years have merely thought of the Red Sox as another team they'd beat en route to the World Series. It's maddening for us. New Englanders carry all the frustrations and near-misses, blaming the hated Yankees for every slight while the Yankee fans sit back and dismiss the Bostonians, secure in the knowledge that the Sox will fold in the fall and the Yankees will win another baseball championship. It is the natural world (Series) order.

When I think of the emotional disparity of this regional baseball rivalry, I am always reminded of a favorite scene from *Casablanca*, a famous flick which has taken on new meaning in Red Sox Nation. The movie was written by the Epstein twins, Philip and Julius, and one of their better lines comes when a nervous Peter Lorre sits across a table from Humphrey Bogart and says, "You despise me, don't you?" Bogey's response, "If I gave you any thought, I probably would."

In many ways, this exchange demonstrates more than eight decades of the alleged Red Sox-Yankee rivalry. And who could have known that in 2002, Philip Epstein's grandson, 28-year-old Theo, would take over the Red Sox as the youngest general manager in baseball?

Young Theo was at the controls in 2003 when this century-old rivalry reached new levels of intensity. On and off the field, the Sox and Yankees battled as never before and going into 2004 the Red Sox think they're finally ready to overtake the Yankees and win their first World Series since 1918.

Nineteen eighteen. It is the Yankee answer to any taunt a Sox fan can muster. The Red Sox can sweep the Yankees in a five-game series, winning every game by ten or more runs and the Yankee fan can diffuse all the Boston bravado by whispering, "1918." Just as Bogey and Bergman will always have Paris (there go those Epstein twins again) the Yankee fans feel they'll always have 1918.

George Herman Ruth was the Red Sox ace left-handed pitcher in 1918, and he was a pretty fair hitter as well. He set a record, pitching 29.2 consecutive scoreless innings, and was on three of Boston's World Series championship teams. A charter franchise of the upstart American League in 1901, the Red Sox won the first World Series and five of the first 15 that were played. The Yankees, who came to New York from Baltimore and were originally known as the Highlanders, were regularly buffeted by the Bostons in those first

two decades of the American League. For Boston, all the trouble started when the Sox were owned by a Broadway producer and theatre owner named Harry H. Frazee. It was Frazee who colluded with fellow New Yorker Jacob Ruppert in the transaction that changed the course of baseball history and permanently altered the fortunes of both the Red Sox and the Yankees.

The transfer of Ruth was only the beginning. Ruppert hired Edward Barrow, who was the field manager of the 1918 Red Sox, and made him general manager of the Yankees. Barrow proceeded to strip the Boston franchise of all of its talent and Frazee was only too happy to stock the Yankees with players in exchange for more cash. Frazee, remember, was the carpetbagger who bragged that the best thing about Boston was the train to New York. After Ruth, the Sox sent Waite Hoyt, Harry Harper, Wally Schang and Mike McNally to New York. Everett Scott, Sam Jones and Joe Bush were next. When the Yankees won their first World Series, in 1923, in the shiny new House That Ruth Built, 11 of the 24 New York players were former Red Sox.

There was another aspect to the Ruth deal which played to the deep-seated fears of all Yankee-hating New Englanders. When Frazee collected his cash for the Babe, he borrowed another $300,000 from the Yankees in the form of a mortgage on Fenway Park. For the ensuing 15 seasons, as the Yankee dynasty took over the American League, the Yankees actually owned Fenway Park. It wasn't until millionaire Thomas Yawkey bought the Sox in 1933 that the note was finally paid. And Yawkey didn't fork over the entire sum until Jake Ruppert demanded to be paid after his

Yankees were uncharacteristically swept by the Red Sox.

While the Yankees went about winning championships, the Red Sox bottomed out in the 1920s and '30s and didn't start to challenge New York again until a young man named Ted Williams came along in 1939. Striving to be "the greatest hitter who ever lived," a goal he may have realized, young Ted went about his work, winning batting titles and triple crowns. By the time Ted arrived in Boston, the Yankees already had his counterpart—a graceful outfielder who could do it all. Patrolling center field in Yankee Stadium was Joltin' Joe, a man known to Ernest Hemingway's Santiago as "The Great DiMaggio."

Ted and Joe. They were the centerpiece players in the Boston-New York rivalry from 1939 until 1951. They inspired debate at both ends of the Boston-New York corridor: Which one is better? Who would you take first if you were starting a team? What would have happened if Ted had played in New York and Joe in Boston? The individual rivalry was hottest in the summer of 1941 when DiMaggio captured the nation with his 56-game hitting streak. Ted's answer was to hit .406. Williams would be the last man ever to crack the .400 barrier, but in that magical summer it would be DiMaggio who'd walk away with the MVP award.

In 1999, when I called Ted Williams to ask him about Pedro Martinez getting robbed in the MVP election (a New York Post scribe was one of only two writers who failed to place Pedro anywhere in the top ten), Ted said, "Hell, I hit .400 one year. I thought that was pretty good, but I didn't win it."

Joe and Ted. In April of 1947 Yawkey and Yankee owner Dan Topping toasted one another long into the night and agreed to swap superstars. In the light of the morning, Yawkey realized this was a bad deal (Williams was in his prime while DiMaggio was breaking down) and the deal was off. "Scotched" might be a better word.

The personal rivalry between the two never waned. In old age, Williams—who had battled with the media throughout his career—became the outgoing, generous ambassador for the game. Thomas Boswell of the Washington Post called Ted the "Father Christmas" of baseball. DiMaggio, who had been cool but cooperative with the press during his playing days, became a virtual recluse. But the fierce pride remained. Joltin' Joe insisted on being announced as "baseball's greatest living ballplayer" any time he made an appearance. This no doubt annoyed Ted Williams and Willie Mays (to name a couple of contenders), but DiMaggio would have it no other way. The Ted-Joe controversy and competition carried over after their deaths. Both were estranged from specified family members and postmortems stripped much of their dignity, particularly in the case of Williams, whose remains were frozen in a lab in Arizona.

Dominic DiMaggio perhaps had the best look at the Yankee-Red Sox dynamic during the golden years of Ted and Joe. Young Dom, dubbed "The Little Professor" because of his glasses and scholarly demeanor, was in a unique position. He got to be Ted's outfield partner for 11 years and Joe's brother for life. It must have made for interesting Christmas conversations at the DiMaggio family home in the North Beach section of San Francisco.

Ever-dignified, Dom played second banana to Ted in the Boston lineup and went though a lifetime of being Joe's little brother. To this day, he has tremendous regard for both.

Playing in the shadow of Joe was tough enough, but playing for the Red Sox in the long shadow of the Yankees broke the spirit of many a ballplayer. Dominic played in only one World Series. He played on teams that rarely finished ahead of his brother's Yankees. He was, alas, a Red Sox. "I feel quite privileged," Dominic said in December of 2003. "My brother was, in my opinion, the greatest all-around player I've ever seen and my friend, Teddy Williams, was the greatest hitter. Even Joe knew that. They usually finished ahead of us, but he didn't rub it in. But in 1948 we knocked them out of the race and still had to win the last day to make the playoff. I was getting married then and the whole family was there. We got in the car after we beat the Yankees and there was silence for two-thirds of the drive to Wellesley Hills. Then Joe said, 'You guys beat us today, but I will personally take care of you tomorrow.'"

Joe DiMaggio cracked four hits the next day at Fenway and even his mom wondered, "Why is Joe doing this to Dominic?" Dom hit a homer and the Sox won, but Boston lost the next day's playoff against Cleveland. Some blamed Joe DiMaggio. The Yankee Clipper's tour de force had forced Boston manager Joe McCarthy to wear out his pitching staff with pitchers warming up in the bullpen.

Dom DiMaggio and the Sox trailed the Yankees for most of the summer of '49, then got hot after the All-Star break and went to New York for the final two games of the season needing only one victory to advance to the World Series. Alas, the hated Yankees won

both games, denying Sox fans and setting the stage for near-misses which would torture New England minds for more than a half-century. Crushed by the double-dip at the end of '49, Tom Yawkey would not return to Yankee Stadium for 19 years.

There wasn't much of a rivalry in the two decades after the 1949 pennant race. The Yankees kept winning pennants and World Series and the Red Sox annually finished near the bottom of the American League. I was born in 1953 and grew up watching the Yankees beat our brains out every summer. The Yankees of the early 1960s had Mantle, Maris, Berra and Whitey Ford. Maris's record-breaking 61st home run came against (naturally) the Red Sox. Those Sox had clown princes like Gene Conley, a right-handed pitcher who got drunk after losing a game at Yankee Stadium and went on a two-day bender in New York City. The Crown(Royal)ing moment came when Conley went to Idlewild Airport and bought a plane ticket to Jerusalem. He was denied boarding because he didn't have his passport. When he finally returned to Fenway, he had to go see owner Tom Yawkey to accept his punishment. Seeing the contrite Conley in his office, the Sox owner offered his pitcher a cocktail. "No, sir, I don't drink." said Conley.

Those were the Red Sox of my youth and that was the extent of our rivalry with the Yankees.

When the Red Sox returned to respectability in the late 1960s, the Yankees were free-falling and it wasn't until the 1970s that both teams were good at the same time. We saw a surge in fighting on the field, much of it involving catchers Carlton Fisk and Thurman Munson, who emerged as the de facto cap-

Catcher Thurman Munson of the Yankees slides safely home past Boston Red Sox catcher Carlton Fisk in the sixth inning at Yankee Stadium in August 1978, reminiscent of their collision at home plate on a failed Yankee squeeze back in 1973. (Associated Press)

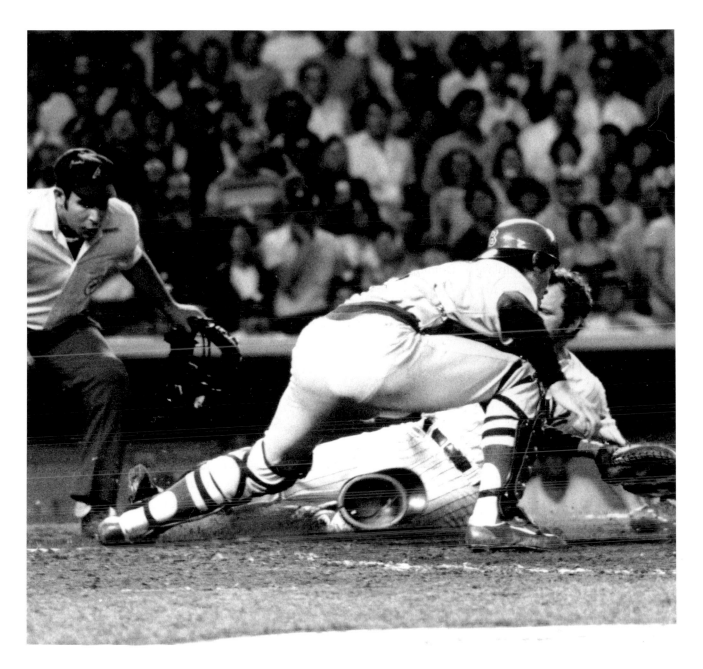

tains of the respective rivals. A generation after Ted and Joe embodied the rivalry, the young catchers picked up the torches and ran headfirst into one another. Early on, Munson was probably the better all-around player, but it was a close call and the grubby Yankee backstop was wildly jealous of his Boston counterpart. Fisk was tall, handsome, graceful and powerful—all things Munson was not. It had a Jack Kennedy-Richard Nixon feel to it. In 1973, the two collided at home plate, sparking a memorable brawl.

At the height of the catchers' rivalry, former Yankee public relations director Mickey Morabito put together a pregame stat sheet featuring comparative stats on Munson and Fisk. At that particular juncture of the season, the Yankee catcher was leading Fisk in batting average, homers, RBI, runners caught stealing and every relevant statistic. Fisk had two more assists than Munson. Morabito remembers Munson seeing the numbers before the game and mumbling something to himself. That night, Munson dropped third strikes the first three times Boston batters struck out. Each time, Munson would retrieve the ball, and fire to first for the official "K, 2-3." Each intentional drop earned Munson an assist. He turned and shook his fist toward the press box after the third assist gave him a lead over Fisk.

Now *that's* a rivalry.

With Fisk, then Munson behind the plate, the Red Sox and Yankees represented the American League in the 1975 and '76 World Series. Both lost to the powerful Big Red Machine from Cincinnati. The Sox and Yanks went eyeball to eyeball in '77 with New York finishing two and a half games ahead, en route to another World Series win. This set the stage for the 1978 pennant race, one which would torture Boston and solidify the notion that no first place lead is ever safe. The '78 Sox were an All-Star cast and led the Yankees by 14 games on July 20. But the Yankees were the defending World Champs and made a crucial move, replacing Billy Martin with Bob Lemon as manager in midsummer. As New York surged, the Sox faltered and on the first weekend of September the Yankees came to Boston and swept four straight by an aggregate count of 2-9. It would forever be known as the Boston Massacre and it left indelible scars in the Boston psyche.

The Sox eventually recovered, winning their last eight regular season games to force the second one-game playoff in American League history. Yankee players convened at Daisy Buchanan's saloon on Newbury Street in the Back Bay the night before the playoff. "We always knew we could beat Boston when he had to," Reggie Jackson said later.

And so they did. On the fateful afternoon of October 2, 1978, the Sox watched a 2-0, seventh inning lead vanish into the left-field netting as Bucky Dent's soft fly feathered over the wall and into the screen. The Yanks eventually won when Rich Gossage got Carl Yastrzemski to pop up with the winning runs in scoring position, but the signature blow of that loss is Dent's homer and to this day he is known as Bucky (expletive) Dent throughout New England.

The Yankees endured a championship drought after '78, but the Red Sox were unable to capitalize. There was little competition from New York in 1986 when Boston made its strongest bid to win a championship. The '86 Sox teased New England as never before and appeared to have beaten the New York Mets to win their first World Series in 68 years before an unlikely chain of events again conspired to thwart the Red Sox. The October collapse of 1986 produced probably the most memorable gaffe in baseball history, the Mookie Wilson grounder that skipped between the legs of Sox first baseman Bill Buckner. The Charlie Brown moment has come to symbolize eight decades of Sox frustration.

The 1986 World Series—in which the Red Sox came closer to winning a World Series, without actually winning, than any team in baseball history, gave birth to the cult of the Curse. The *Times's* George Vescey penned a column about the Red Sox bad luck beginning with the sale of Babe Ruth to the Yankees, and two years later I went to work on a hardover book entitled *The Curse of the Bambino* which was first published by E. P. Dutton in 1990. In the years since the book's publication, the Curse has taken on its own life and it is now used to explain anything that goes wrong for the Red Sox.

Cursed or not, it was the 1986 Red Sox team that put fear into the heart of Sox fans everywhere. No lead would ever be safe again.

The fact that the '86 collapse came at the hands of a New York baseball team only underscored the Boston-New York dynamic that is so much a part of the Red Sox-Yankee rivalry. In the years after '86 Boston was again made to feel inferior when several of its institutions were engulfed by New York. In 1996, the Hub's venerable Jordon Marsh department store was bought out by Macy's, a New York giant. Closer to home for this typist, *The Boston Globe*, which had been owned by the Taylor family since 1873, was bought by *The New York Times* in 1993. The purchase expanded a complicated loop: the Taylors had once owned the Boston American League franchise and were the ones who named the Red Sox and built Fenway Park—which had once been owned by the Yankees as part of the Ruth deal.

On the ball field, the Yankees returned to championship glory in 1996 while the Sox drought continued, magnifying the pain of the near-miss of '86. After 1995 the Red Sox started a run of eight consecutive finishes behind the Yankees (a streak still active going into 2004). This annual, futile chase expanded the cult of the Curse and pushed the vile New England mantra of "Yankees Suck" into the mainstream.

"Yankees Suck." It started sometime in the 1970s and took off in the 1990s. The indelicate couplet has become the New England sports fans' equivalent of "The British Are Coming." Yankee fans, if they bother to respond ("If I gave you any thought, I probably would"), might retort with "Boston sucks," but it doesn't carry the passion or bitterness of "Yankees Suck."

On the surface, of course, the charge makes no sense whatsoever. The Yankees, most decidedly, do not suck. They do not stink. They are not a bad baseball team. It's like calling Cameron Diaz ugly. You can say it, but that does not make it so. It just makes you jealous. And that is what we are here in New England. Can you blame us?

In the 1970s Fenway fans would hurl darts at Yankee center fielder Mickey Rivers, while those at Yankee Stadium would toss batteries at Dwight Evans. Chants were more civil, even in college dormitories where students from both regions mingled and taunted one another. But somewhere along the way, late in the 20th century, the word "sucks" lost its sexual connotations and became okay on prime time television and talk radio. Kids got away with saying it in school without being suspended.

By the time the Red Sox reached the 1999 playoffs, eventually facing the Yankees in the American League Championship Series, "Yankees Suck" was practically a cottage industry. Bandit T-shirts bearing the phrase were sold all around Fenway Park on game days, and the phrase also appeared on bumper stickers and posters. It's not unusual to see suburban New England parents standing outside Fenway, holding hands with grade-schoolers who are wearing "Yankees Suck" T-shirts. Meanwhile, the chant is ubiquitous. Weddings, bar mitzvahs, graduations—anyplace in which two or more Sox fans are gathered, there's potential that "Yankees Suck" will break out. I have heard it at a spring training game in Kissimmee, Florida, between the Red Sox and Astros, while filing out of a Crosby, Stills, Nash and Young concert at the Fleetcenter, and at high school football games in Greater Boston. There was a bomb scare at my childrens' high school the day after 9/11. While all students were herded into the football stadium as the school was being swept, a "Yankees Suck" chant broke out in the bleachers. When Chinese basketball sensation Yao Ming made his first trip to Boston with the Houston Rockets, he was asked (through a translator) if he'd ever heard "Yankees Suck." When a half million fans crammed Boston's City Hall Plaza two days after the Patriots won the 2002 Super Bowl, New England player Larry Izzo started a "Yankees Suck" chant from the stage.

The Red Sox lost the 1999 playoff to the Yankees in five games and the series did little to diminish Boston's obsession with the Yankees. In two of the games, umpires made erroneous calls which went against the Red Sox. In both instances, there were published apologies from the men in blue. When the Sox were losing Game 4 at Fenway, fans littered the field with debris and action was stopped for several minutes after the Yankees were pulled from the field. Yankee owner George Steinbrenner accused Boston manager Jimy Williams of inciting a riot. Williams called Steinbrenner "Georgie Porgie."

The only satisfaction for Red Sox fans was the rout of Roger Clemens in Game 3 at Fenway. According to Ma Clemens, Fenway fans treated her son "like Hitler." Clemens won three Cy Young Awards and a franchise-best 192 games for the Red Sox, but New Englanders resent Clemens for getting himself traded to the Yankees. Like Wade Boggs before him, the Rocket assembled a Hall of Fame résumé with the Red Sox, but went to the Yankees to win his World Series ring. Ouch.

After the 2001 baseball season, the "Boston/New York/Ruth/Fenway/*Times*/*Globe*/Red Sox/Yankee" loop was completed when *The New York Times* joined billionaire John Henry as the second-largest investor in a group that purchased the Red Sox from the Yawkey Trust. Perfect. More than eight decades after the Bambino debacle, Boston's baseball team again was (partially) owned by New Yorkers. It didn't make Sox fans any more comfortable to learn that Henry still had a one-percent ownership of the New York Yankees and owned a couple of Yankee championship rings.

But those fears were quickly allayed when the Red Sox new ownership made it clear that beating the Yankees would be the top priority. New Sox CEO Larry Lucchino was an old Steinbrenner enemy. Lucchino worked for Edward Bennett Williams when the great trial attorney purchased the Orioles in 1979. The O's and Yanks jousted for AL supremacy in the early 1980s and the combative Lucchino took on Steinbrenner headfirst. Big George never forgot and was ready for a battle when he learned that Lucchino would be running the Red Sox for Henry and Co.

In 2003 the Red Sox-Yankee rivalry reached new heights and it was Lucchino who set the tone. In the winter after 2002, both clubs went to Nicaragua in hopes of signing Cuban free agent righty Jose Contreras. It was reported that the Red Sox bought up all the available hotel space in an effort to box out the Yankees. When Contreras wound up signing with New York, Epstein was rumored to have broken hotel furniture while Lucchino called the Yankees, "the Evil Empire." Offended by the remark, Steinbrenner lobbed insults at the feet of Lucchino and comissioner Bud Selig issued a gag order, silencing both houses. But the off-field activity continued as the Yankees got involved in an Expos-White Sox trade for the sole purpose of keeping righty Bartolo Colon out of Boston. When the Red Sox traded for Jeremy Giambi, New Yorkers smirked. As with the DiMaggios, the Yanks already had the superior brother.

In the present climate of competition and distrust, it's impossible to imagine the Sox and Yankees working together on a trade. Past deals certainly would discourage the Red Sox from trading with New York. The Ruth thing didn't work out too well and in 1972 the Red Sox dealt reliever Sparky Lyle to the Yankees for first baseman Danny Cater. Lyle went on to win a Cy Young Award with the Yankees. Cater did nothing. In 1986 the Sox traded Mike Easler to the Yankees and acquired Don Baylor at the end of spring training. It turned out to be a good deal for Boston, but there aren't likely to be any more Red Sox-Yankee swaps in the immediate future.

In 2003 the Red Sox and Yankees wound up playing one another a record 26 times, including seven pulsating playoff games. The Yankees won 10 of 19 regular season contests and four of seven in the American League Championship Series. The season-long battle, which included beanballs and young Theo's author dad ripping Steinbrenner by mentioning an old felony conviction, culminated in a seven-game American League Championship Series for the ages. A century of acrimony and New England angst came to a head on the Saturday afternoon of Oct. 11 at Fenway when Pedro Martinez (the same Pedro who once said, "Wake up the damn Bambino and I'll drill him in the ass.") went head-hunting and wound up tossing 72-year-old Yankee coach Don Zimmer to the ground during a bench-clearing melee. That was the same day that two Yankees and a Red Sox groundskeeper got into a fight in the visitors bullpen. As ever, the Yankees won the game. And the series.

Sox fans forever will hang black crepe around Oct. 16 because that was the date of the seventh game of the 2003 ALCS. The Red Sox routed Roger Clemens, led, 4-0, in the fifth and 5-2 in the eighth. And then manager Grady Little joined Bill Buckner, John McNamara, Mike Torrez, Denny Galehouse, Johnny Pesky and the other busts which adorn the Boston Baseball Hall of Shame. Grady left Pedro on the hill as the Yankees cracked four straight hits, good for three runs and extra innings. It all ended at 12:16 a.m. in the 11th inning when Aaron Boone hit a walkoff homer off Sox knuckleballer Tim Wakefield. The loss joined the Buckner game and the Dent game as one of Boston's three most painful. Gold, silver or bronze. Didn't matter. It was on the medal stand before Boone's ball landed in the left-field stands.

It was exhausting and when it was over Yankee manager Joe Torre said that the 2003 Red Sox were the best team his Yankees had faced in their championship run, which started in 1996. Didn't matter. Back in the Hub, this collapse of biblical proportion—ghoulish even by the lofty standards of Boston baseball lore—made the Red Sox and their fans more obsessed than ever with beating the Yankees.

Indeed, as this book goes to press, the scorched earth still smolders in both cities. Fueled by more than a century of hard history, reenergized by Lucchino's remark and Boston's torturous near-miss in October 2003, the Red Sox and Yankees went to work for 2004 with the distrust and fever we'd normally associate with global superpowers. It was the baseball equivalent of the Cold War and the nuclear arms race between the United States of America and the Soviet Union. Former All-Stars and future Hall of Famers were courted, acquired and traded at a dizzying pace. The Sox signed Curt Schilling while the Yankees lost Roger Clemens (retired, then signed as a free agent with Houston) and Andy Pettite (free agent, signed with Houston). The Sox attempted to trade Manny Ramirez for Alex Rodriguez, but the deal fell through at Christmas. The Yankees traded for Expos righty Javier Vazquez and acquired former All-Stars Kevin Brown, Gary Sheffield, Tom Gordon, Kenny Lofton and Paul Quantrill. The rest of baseball looked on in amazement as the Sox and Yankees threatened to spend themselves into oblivion. Vegas bookmakers created a new line, inviting gamblers to bet on which team would win the majority of the 19 regular season games in 2004.

Schilling, Boston's top acquisition in the hyperactive off-season, spoke to the rivalry at his introductory press conference when he donned a Red Sox cap and jersey. Speaking for an entire Red Sox Nation, the big righty looked into the cameras and said, "I guess I hate the Yankees now."

Introduction

Robert Lipsyte of The New York Times

There is no rivalry.

How could there be? A true rivalry implies a certain level of parity, the possibility that on any given day either side might win; think Muhammad Ali vs. Joe Frazier, David Letterman vs. Jay Leno, Athens vs. Sparta.

The New York Yankees vs. the Boston Red Sox is a Potemkin Village of a rivalry, more like the 20th-Century Cold War between the United States and the Soviet Union, a psycho-political construct that gave both countries a reason to impose economic and social controls on its people and whip them into paranoid frenzies whenever it seemed necessary to divert them from, say, a White House scandal or a Moscow meat shortage.

As it turned out, the Reds were the Red Sox, dogma without bite. Someday, a betrayed people will rise up in Fenway Park and tear down the Green Monster with the same angry passion a betrayed people tore down the Berlin Wall.

I don't want to beat up on Boston, which has an important place in the early historical narrative of my fellow Americans, who are known throughout much of the rest of the world, funnily enough, as Yankees. It was here, of course, that the Boston Tea Party took place, in which a group of locals cravenly disguised themselves as Native Americans and vandalized ships in their harbor. They tend to do the same sort of thing these days after a major victory or loss.

Boston, which still calls itself "The Hub," is a lovely boutique city despite its vicious history of racism (the Red Sox were the last major league team to hire an African-American player, Pumpsie Green in 1959) and classism (the term Brahmin originally referred to Boston families that spoke only to each other or God).

I'm always amused when Red Sox fans attack the Yankees as "arrogant." My goodness. Boston's primary legacy—after the banning of slightly smutty books, helping sales elsewhere—is the invention of arrogance, at Harvard.

Gifted Harvard writers, most notably John Updike, '54, David Halberstam, '55, and John Cheever, who received an honorary degree in 1978, have been instrumental in the concoction of the Bosox mystique. It was Cheever who wrote: "All literary men are Red Sox fans. To be a Yankee fan in literary society is to endanger your life."

It was a literary woman, actually, a Harvard classics professor quoted in *The Official Retrospective* of the Red Sox, who may have best encapsulated this sensibility. This was in response to the so-called "greatest game ever played," which, of course, the Yankees won, 5-4, to clinch the 1978 pennant. Emily Vermeule wrote in *The Boston Globe*: "The Red Sox did not fail, they became immortal. They were worthy of the Sophoclean stage, actors in the traditional and poignant myth, the long conflict between the larger-than-life hero and inexorable time, native brilliance and predestined ruin, the flukiness of luck, tyche, set against the hardest strivings of the individual."

Having been born in the Bronx and graduated from Columbia, I can only assume that literary people like to blame luck, tyche, when recognition and fulfillment slip away, and so find writing about the Red Sox a form of identification and catharsis. On the other hand, the explanation for their output may be simpler. There are always better stories in the losers' locker room, and a writer can feel superior, even nobler, by patronizing the doomed. It's more romantic. The editor of *The Red Sox Reader,* Dan Riley, wrote: "Has there ever been an also-ran in history that's inspired as much sympathetic passion as the Red Sox? Maybe Robert E. Lee."

But while the exquisitely painful pleasure of losing is the primary strand in the Red Sox mystique, it is not the only one. There is also the painful pleasure of being scorned. The Red Sox' iconic superstar, Ted Williams, was arguably the greatest pure hitter in the game, as well as the most disdainful of his city's players, press and fans. In 1940, his second year with the club, he told Austen Lake of the *Boston American* that he wanted to be traded because, "I don't like the town, I don't like the people," and as for the newspapermen, "I don't like 'em and I never will."

The writers in particular seem to have found an almost sensual agony over Williams's contempt for them. Did they spin that contempt into proof that he was aware of them, that they indeed existed? Red Sox fans seemed to love the idea that the Splendid Splinter signaled to them with insulting fingers, even spat on them. Ah, recognition! If only he could have beaten them with his bat, might that have signified repressed love?

And Teddy Ballgame, in death, is still a splendid example of Boston's ongoing ignominy. This man of prickly independence and pride became a late-night joke as relatives fought over his quick-frozen remains. His head was separated from his body, a metaphor too obvious to belabor.

But I digress in a way that I hope doesn't appear mean-spirited. After all, I liked Ted Williams almost as much as I liked Joe DiMaggio, the beau geste of the Yankees. Williams was a bona fide war hero. Astronaut-Senator John Glenn was proud to have had the Splinter on his wing in Marine air combat over Korea. Amiable after his playing days were over, Williams was also an unobtrusive philanthropist. He had a far more humane spirit than the Yankee Clipper, whose most current biographer portrayed a stingy, suspicious recluse who might have been abusive to Marilyn Monroe.

But this isn't a discussion of matchups; games between all-time, all-star teams of Yankees and Red Sox would probably yield the same score as the Yankees-Red Sox World Series championships won since 1918—26-0.

There. I've dropped the bomb, which should be enough to end what seemed to be a discussion of this nonexistent "rivalry." Now we can move on to what's truly important here, the story behind the story, why the *idea* of a rivalry is so useful, even essential to our understanding of the two teams, their cities, their fans, perhaps the Pastime and its nation. In many ways, it is similar to that Cold War rivalry between those other Reds and Yankees. It may even have been the model for it.

There are five critical points to be made, all underlining the positive value of the rivalry, even though it doesn't exist.

1. The idea of a rivalry helps us understand the Boston state of mind.

It's almost too pat to use the sociologists' term "borrowed prestige" to explain this insistence on a rivalry. That would suggest a community scheme to attach the Hub to the Apple in an attempt to bask in reflected glory. Boston is too fragmented a society to conspire. Beyond class and race is the youth-age divide. After cod and beans, Boston is best known for processing and shipping college graduates. All those institutions of higher learning in the Boston area mean there is an enormous and ever-changing population of young people, their energy and promise constant reminders of Professor Vermeule's "inexorable time."

For those stuck in Boston, the basic choices are the New Englanders' stereotypical bitter crankiness or the enthusiastic acceptance of "predestined ruin," which is a main symptom of Red Sox fandom. It would take a far more astute observer than I (browse in this volume and you will find them) to sort out the chicken-egg question here. Are Red Sox fans always prepared for defeat because their team is mediocre or are the Red Sox perennial also-rans because their fans need that role modeled for them? I suggest the latter, which seems like a more radical theory than it is; if a team does not satisfy the need of its fans, it will not survive. The Red Sox ultimately lose because they have to. How could their fans live with their own mediocrity while rooting for a team

that was successful? This theory also explains why the Yankees have to win.

2. The idea of the rivalry helps us see New York's endearing neediness.

Obviously, Boston could not create and maintain this idea of rivalry on its own. New York is an accomplice in this fantasy, if not the prime mover. New York has some deep-seated need to feel less alone, you might even say less feared and hated. New York has never felt as comfortable as it should at the summit. The old line, "If you can make it in New York you can make it anywhere," is unassailably true. Yet it also implies an enormous pressure and responsibility.

Two old saws—"It's lonely at the top," and "It's harder to stay at the top than to get there"—apply here. New York and its Yankees need at least the illusion of something climbing up to knock them off, a dangerous contender, in order to stay focused. The Red Sox are handy straw men. Of course, there is always the concern that the Yankees could conjure up an apparition that could freeze their knees. Luckily, enough of those young people educated in Boston have come to New York. Used to having their hearts broken at Fenway Park, they have spread just enough of that tough tyche to keep the Yankees from being beaten by their only true rivals, themselves.

3. The idea of the rivalry helps pave over the real schisms in American society.

The only way to even justify rooting for any team other than the Yankees is to make some profound yet sentimental point about a childhood sense of place. Imagine growing up in St. Louis, the fine hot red clay dust of summer in your eyes as you watched Stan Musial's corkscrew stance at the plate. Think of learning to drink beer and curse fate with Grandpa and his useless cronies in the bleachers at Wrigley Field. Remember driving from the oil patch with Dad to fight the mosquitoes at Houston's first major-league park to watch the Colt 45's. A new generation will recall the retrograde charm of Camden Yards and Cal Ripken refusing to take a day off.

Those are psycho-geographical reasons, and they are comforting. They preclude the issue of meritocracy—isn't sports supposed to be about objective standards of who is best?—that should compel us all to be Yankee fans. Far, far more important, however, is it rules out the issues of race, religion and ethnicity that spoil fandom in, most glaringly, the so-called "beautiful game." In his brilliant *How*

Soccer Explains the World: An Unlikely Theory of Globalization, Franklin Foer visits with the Serbian hooligans of Red Star Belgrade (who have their own office in the club's headquarters) and the warring Glasgow fans, the Protestant Rangers and the Catholic Celtics, before setting off on an amazing trip linking futbol with terrorism, oligarchy and political corruption that leaves the vilest of our baseball owners looking like harmless naifs and the Yankees-Red Sox rivalry as a national down comforter.

4. The idea of the rivalry helps us accept Fate.

By Fate I don't necessarily mean Professor Vermeule's "predestined ruin," but rather the recognition that what Pete Rose calls "the big umpire in the sky" may be making decisions

(Left) The jubilant
Yankees swarm
over the field, Oct.
2, 1978, to cele
brate their victory
over the Red Sox
at Fenway.
(Associated Press)

(Right) Babe Ruth
was a winning
pitcher for the Red
Sox when they
won the World
Series in 1918.

before the play is complete. What else but a Sophoclean deus ex machina could have caused the Red Sox to lose the World Series in '46, '67, '75 and '86? When a ball skitters between the wounded legs of a courageous hero like Bill Buckner, a veritable Hector of Troy (another losing city), and, conversely, when a 12-year-old reaches out of the right-field stands to turn a Derek Jeter fly-out into a home run that leads to the pennant, we have to believe that some higher power is playing the universe like a video game.

The big umpire in the sky is a Yankee fan. How else can you explain four World Series titles for Joe Torre, who had never appeared in a post-season game as a player and had been a mediocre manager with three previous major-league teams. Something touches journeymen when they put on the Yankee pin-stripes. How else can you explain Don Larsen's perfect game in the 1956 World Series, Bucky Dent's 1978 home run? This metamorphosis is even more striking when the changeling is a former Red Sox. In mid-season, 1932, Boston traded the veteran right-hander Danny MacFayden to the Yankees after a seven-year career in which he won 36 and lost 66 for the Bosox. Danny won seven games for the Yanks that year, helping them to hold off the A's and win the pennant (and the World Series.)

5. The idea of the rivalry helps keep alive a fabulous myth.

The so-called Curse of the Bambino, first named, I believe, in Dan Shaughnessy's 1990 book of that name, has been seized on by both Yankee and Red Sox fans, although for different reasons.

For Yankee fans, the belief that a spell was placed on the Bosox after owner Harry Frazee sold Babe Ruth to New York for $100,000 (a steal, it turned out, but record dough then) is part of the magical aura that surrounds the Bronx Bombers and thus their fans. Even the Stadium's infamous "bleacher creatures" can feel like Hobbits on a quest.

For Red Sox fans, the presence of a spell is both alibi and sign of hope. So many events can be blamed on the dark powers.

How else can you explain the famous "try-out" in 1945, when Red Sox brass looked over Jackie Robinson, Sam Jethroe and Marvin Williams and dismissed them as not major-league material. Legend has it that an official's voice boomed from the Fenway grandstand, "Get those niggers off the field!"

How else can you explain the dreadful beaning that cut short the career and the life of Tony Conigliaro, among the team's greatest all-time prospects, or the talent drain that sent Cy Young, Tris Speaker, Sparky Lyle, Wade Boggs and Roger Clemens to star on other teams, the last three on the Yankees.

And, of course, add Babe Ruth to that list. Perhaps it was less of a curse than systemic disease. In 1918, a year before he sold Ruth, owner Frazee was in financial trouble despite having won three of the past four World Series. How inept can you be? In his Yankee encyclopedia, Derek Gentile calls it "The Curse of Many Dumb Red Sox Executives." He then recounts how Frazee sold pitcher Carl Mays to the Yankees, where he became a winner. Ruth, who made it clear he wanted to be traded, was sold the following year. For the next few years the Frazee fire sale blazed on—among the new Yankees were future Hall of Fame pitchers Waite Hoyt, Herb Pennock and Red Ruffing, and third baseman Jumpin' Joe Dugan. Dean Chadwin, author of *Those Damn*

Yankees, points out that by 1923 almost half the Yankee roster had been members of Boston's old championship teams. They made the Yankees into a dynasty as the Red Sox slipped into the league basement.

But belief in a spell implies belief that a spell can be broken. Another radical theory: For Red Sox fans, the end of this Curse and beginning of a true rivalry would be a burden while for Yankee fans it would be a blessing.

For the Red Sox, battling the Yankees under the Curse may seem like struggling with a juggernaut, with Leviathan, locked in a losing match with the Force of Destiny. But to shake free of this shroud would mean taking responsibility for bold and intelligent management, spending money on good players, acting like a business instead of a quaint regional treasure, the old mill village of baseball.

For the Yankees, the end of the Curse and the beginning of a true rivalry with the Red Sox (or any other team, truth be told) would be a liberation. For almost a century now, the Yankees have played gallantly despite the crushing pressure of their real rivalry with their own history.

Can you conceive what it must be like to wrestle with ghosts? Each new Yankee team is held up to its ancestors, every player measured against the immortal who left his footprints on the field. How can the Yankees derive total satisfaction from swatting back the Red Sox when they are being fitted to the shadows of the Babe, the Iron Horse, the Clipper, the Mick, Mr. October, every lineup found wanting compared to Murderers' Row?

Yet then again, lifting the spell, closing the Curse, might also mean the end of the most powerful mystique in sports. The Yankees start every game with a lead just by showing up. Perhaps, without the fantasy of the rivalry, their advantage might be gone and they would be just another team, like the Red Sox.

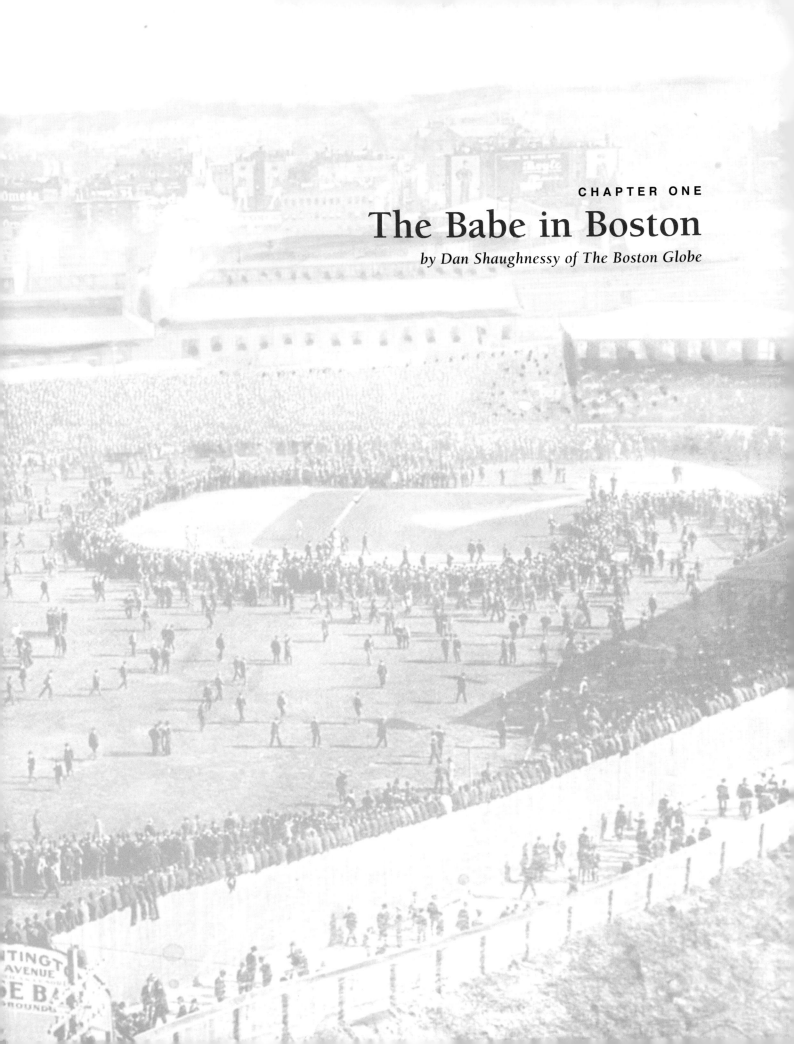

CHAPTER ONE

The Babe in Boston

by Dan Shaughnessy of The Boston Globe

The Boston Red Sox were established as the American League's signature franchise when 19- or 20-year-old (there's some dispute) George Herman Ruth arrived at Fenway Park in July of 1914. The 1914 Sox were a struggling team when Ruth arrived, but they had many players who'd been on the 1912 World Series champs, including future Hall of Famers Tris Speaker and Harry Hooper, plus Smokey Joe Wood, who went 34-5 in 1912. The veterans were in no mood for a big cocky kid from Baltimore who wanted to pitch *and* hit. The brash youngster even demanded to take batting practice, which was unheard of for a pitcher. After a brief stint in the majors, the Sox sent Ruth to Providence of the International League in August but called him back up for the final week of the big-

league season. He beat the Yankees at the end of the year and cracked his first major league hit, a double off Leonard (King) Cole. It was a rather unremarkable beginning to a career that would make Ruth the most famous athlete in the world.

In Ruth's rookie year he also met a 16-year-old waitress named Helen Woodford. They were married in October of 1914.

Ruth went to spring training in Hot Springs, Arkansas, with the Sox in March of 1915. Manager Bill Carrigan did not have the Babe in the Sox starting rotation early in the season, but when star righty Carl Mays sprained an ankle Carrigan turned to his large southpaw. Ruth quickly impressed the brass, pitching 13 innings and hitting his first big-league homer in a 4-3 loss to the Yankees

(who else?) at the Polo Grounds. It was an eye-opener for Carrigan and Company. In July, at Sportsman's Park in St. Louis, Ruth hit a single, two doubles and a prodigious home run while hurling the Sox to a 4-2 victory. The Red Sox finished first with a 101-50 record and Ruth wound up going 18-8 with a 2.44 ERA and 28 complete games in 32 starts. He also hit .315 with four homers in 92 at bats. Carrigan opted not to use Ruth on the mound in the World Series against the Phillies. The Sox won the championship in a tidy five games and Ruth's only appearance came as a pinch hitter. The Babe grounded out to first base. Some players never get another shot at the Fall Classic. This was not the case with Babe Ruth.

In 1916 Ruth went 23-12 for the defending World Champs and led the American League with a 1.75 ERA and nine shutouts. He start-ed 41 games, completed 23, and fanned 170 batters in a whopping 323.2 innings. He hit three more homers and batted .272. The Sox won another pennant and faced the Brooklyn Dodgers in the World Series. These were heady times for Boston's American League franchise.

Ruth finally got a chance to pitch in the Series and won the second game, pitching 14 innings in a 2-1 victory. It was the longest World Series game ever played at the time and Ruth told Carrigan, "I told you a year ago I could take care of those National League bums, and you never gave me a chance." The Sox won the Series in five games and Carrigan retired when it was over.

After the Red Sox won the Series in 1916, the club was sold to Harry Frazee, a New York theater producer. Frazee and partner Hugh Ward bought the team for $675,000 and pledged to spend whatever it took to bring another championship to Boston. Frazee was the sixth owner of the Red Sox, following Charles W. Somers, Henry J. Killilea, John I. Taylor (of the *The Boston Globe* Taylors, who built Fenway and named the Red Sox), James R. McAleer and Joesph J. Lannin. Born in Peoria, Illinois, in 1880, Frazee financed and

CHAMPIONS 1912
RED SOX
WORLD'S SERIES
FENWAY PARK·BOSTON·
Souvenir Biography and Score Book.

Price. 10 Cents

(Top) 1912 Red Sox World's Series championship souvenir booklet. (John Tlumacki/ *The Boston Globe*)

(Right) Babe Ruth was 19 or 20 when he signed up with the Red Sox in 1914. He pitched only four games that year for them, but the next year he won 18 games and lost only 8.

built theaters in Chicago and New York before buying the Red Sox. On the day the sale was announced, Frazee said, "I have always enjoyed the game and now I think that I shall have a chance to show what I know about handling a baseball club." After the press conference, he took the midnight train back to his home in New York. It was a sign of things to come for Boston fans.

In 1917 Ruth went 24-13 with an ERA of 2.01 and led the league with 35 complete games. He hit two homers and batted .325, but it was not enough to help the Sox to another pennant. Boston finished in second place, nine games behind the White Sox. This was the year in which Ruth became more difficult to handle, on and off the field. The respected Carrigan was gone and Jack Barry had trouble handling his star pitcher. In addition to running around on Mrs. Ruth and getting into car accidents, the Babe wanted his salary doubled to $10,000.

After the season, Barry was called to active duty and Frazee hired Ed Barrow to manage Ruth and the rest of the Red Sox.

In 1918, Barrow and Ruth led the Red Sox

to their fifth and thus far (through 2003) final World Series championship. The Yankees, meanwhile were still in search of their first World Series win.

Frazee was actually accused of buying a pennant in 1918, an odd charge given what later happened. Unsatisfied with the runner-up finish in 1917, he bought Stuffy McInnis, Amos Strunk, Wally Schang and Joe Bush. Ruth won the season opener and hit his first homer in his fifth start of the season—against the Yankees at the Polo Grounds. Notice the pattern. The Bambino made a lot of noise in Boston-New York jousts. He always seemed to come up big against the Yankees and he would later specialize in torturing the Red Sox.

The '18 Sox were a fairly light-hitting team, and outfielder Harry Hooper urged Barrow to play the Babe every day. On May 6, three years to the day after hitting his first big-league homer, Ruth started at first base and batted sixth in the lineup . . . against the Yankees. Other than pinch-hitting appearances, it was the first time Ruth batted anywhere other than ninth in the lineup.

Naturally, he hit a home run. Yankee owner Jacob Ruppert watched the blossoming of a superstar with great box office appeal. Five of Ruth's first 11 big-league homers were hit against the Yankees at the Polo Grounds.

Ruth was batting cleanup by the time the Sox moved to their next stop on the road trip in Washington. By this time, the Babe had decided he wanted to be an every day player, not a pitcher. He finished the season with 11 homers and 64 RBI, batting .300 in 317 at bats. He started only 18 games on the mound and went 13-7 with a 2.22 ERA. Meanwhile, he ignored signs from his manager and jumped the club in July to join a barnstorming team. Making $7,000, he temporarily left the team in July, signing with the Chester

Shipyards of the Delaware Shipbuilding League. He was AWOL from the Sox for only two days, but Frazee was beginning to think that his young star might be too much to handle.

Ruth beat the Cubs, 1-0, in the first game of the 1918 World Series. He also won Game 5, extending his Series scoreless streak to 29.2 innings, and cracking his first World Series hit, a two-run triple at Fenway Park. The Red Sox won the Series in six games and Ruth retired as a World Series pitcher with a life-time record of 3-0 (all one-run wins) and an ERA of 0.87. It's still incredible to think that the best hitter of all time started out by being one of the finest pitchers of his day.

The Boston Globe • September 6, 1918

McINNIS' SMASH BEATS CUBS, 1-0

Ruth Hurls Superbly

By Edward F. Martin

Chicago, Sept. 5—To be at home when that excising old codger, Mr. Opportunity, drops around is not only the proper caper in the matter of etiquette, but a swell move from a diplomatic angle. Well, the Red Sox were waiting for the old boy in the vestibule when he brushed in today at Comiskey Park, and that is why they trimmed the Cubs so skillfully in the opening battle of the World's Series.

They passed up nothing in the way of opportunities. They made hay while the sun was on the job, did not stop anywhere for a drink and sneaked in the stitch in time, while the Cubs

On his first trip to the plate Babe soaked the apple to center, Paskert getting under it after flopping around the pastures for a while. The next two times that the Oriole boy faced Hippo he fanned and he looked stupid, as he was missing bad balls. The fans applauded him every time he stepped to the plate and he was a picture even when he was striking out, but the kind of picture that no Boston artist would seek to paint.

The Boston Globe • *September 6, 1918*

TITLE SERIES FEELS HEAVY HAND OF WAR

Chicago, Sept. 5—War made its hand felt in the attendance and receipts of the first game of the World's Series.

The attendance today of 10,274 was nearly 13,000 less than a year ago. The receipts, $30,348, were less than half the amount taken in for the first game a year ago, as the prices this year were reduced, the choice box seats selling for $3 as compared with $5 in 1917.

The figures on the opening games today and a year ago are:

	1918	1917
Attendance	19,270	32,000
Receipts	$30,349.00	$73,152.00
Players' share	6,387.92	39,502.08
Each club	5,462.64	13,167.36
Commission	3,034.80	7,315.20

Indeed, he can rest on his pitching laurels. He worked out of a number of tight holes so artistically that many wanted to know if he ever hung around with Houdini.

---

threw Mr. Opportunity down flat, turning their backs on him as they would on a professional manhandler.

Ruth Hurls Superb Game

It was a battle of southpaws, Babe Ruth being pitted against Hippo Jim Vaughn and while the National League champion outhit the Red Sox, Babe proved himself to be a master workman. There were times when he had to be there to avoid disaster, and the world should know that he was there. On the attack, the Oriole Adonis was just about as useful as an umbrella which has been given the Kayo by the wind.

Established as a champion and a star, the Babe wanted more money. He wanted $30,000 spread over two years. Frazee wasn't interested. These were war years, baseball attendance was down, and money was tight. Rather than accommodate Ruth's demand, the Sox owner shipped three solid players (including leftfielder Duffy Lewis) to the Yankees in exchange for four marginal talents and $50,000. Yankee owners Ruppert and Colonel Tillinghast Huston were happy to give the Sox cash if it would improve the championship-starved Yankee ballclub.

By this time Ruth had settled in Sudbury, Massachusetts, where he lived on a farm with cattle, pigs and hens. He stayed home when the defending World Champion Red Sox reported to spring training in 1919, threatening to become a heavyweight fighter, but eventually agreed on a three-year deal worth $30,000. When he got to Florida he hit a tape-measure home run in Tampa and moved into Lewis's spot in left field. Conversion to the outfield was virtually complete. In 1919 Ruth smashed 29 homers, a big league record, and hit .322 in 432 at-bats while starting only 15 games on the mound. He also became a big draw at the gate. Ruth was on his way to becoming the Great Sultan of Swat.

Meanwhile, he ran into more trouble off the field. He was suspended after a curfew battle and almost got into a fistfight with Barrow. Late in the year, he embarrassed Frazee, claiming that Mrs. Ruth had to pay her way into Fenway for "Babe Ruth Day." Despite Ruth's record slugging, the Sox slumped to sixth place and the Babe left a bad taste when he

bolted the team to play in a lucrative exhibition on the final weekend of the season in Washington. Then he said he wanted $20,000 for 1920.

Frazee was fed up with his star. Ruth was for sale and the Yankees were the logical buyers. Former 20-game winner Carl Mays (he'd win 53 games for the Yankees in the next two seasons) had already been sold to New York in the latest cash deal and it was only logical that Ruth would be next.

In recent years, much has been made of the "fallacy" that Frazee sold Ruth to the Yankees in order to finance a play titled *No, No Nanette*. The debunkers point out that the Ruth deal was struck in 1919 and that the hit play didn't debut until 1923. The Frazee family has embraced these facts as proof that Big Harry did not sell out Boston in order to produce a hit play. It's also been pointed out that American League president Ban Johnson didn't like Frazee and the Sox owner dealt almost exclusively with New York as part of an alliance against the league president. While the limitations of Frazee's options are certainly a factor, and the cause-and effect of the Ruth sale and the timing of *Nanette* are open to argument, the fact remains that Frazee cared more about his Broadway shows than about his baseball team and struck a deal which was good for him and bad for the Boston ballteam.

On Monday, January 5, Frazee announced that Babe Ruth had been sold to the Yankees for cash (it was $100,000 with $300,000 more going to Frazee in the form of a mortgage on Fenway Park).

Mr. and Mrs. Babe Ruth on their farm at Sudbury, Massachusetts, before her 1929 death in a fire. (Associated Press)

The Boston Globe • January 6, 1920

THE RED SOX SELL RUTH FOR $125,000 CASH

Demon Slugger of American League, Who Made 29 Home Runs Last Season, Goes to New York Yankees

Frazee to Buy New Players

By James C. O'Leary

"Babe" Ruth, home-run hitter extraordinary of the Red Sox, has been sold to the New York American League club for a cash price of probably $125,000 and probably more.

Pres Frazee in announcing the sale at Red Sox headquarters in the Carsay Building late yesterday afternoon declined to state the amount.

. . .

"With this money the Boston club can now go into the market and buy other players and have a stronger and better team in all respects than we would have had if Ruth remained with us.

"I do not wish to detract one iota from Ruth's ability as a ball player nor from his value as an attraction, but there is no getting away from the fact that despite his 29 home runs, the Red Sox finished sixth in the race last season.

"What the Boston fans want, I take it, and what I want because they want it, is a winning team, rather than a one-man team which finishes in sixth place."

Ruth Popular in Boston

Ruth was very popular in Boston, and for sentimental reasons the fans may be first inclined to regard his transfer to the Yankees with disfavor, but if they withhold judgment until they have thoroughly sized up the affair, the chances are that they will agree with Pres Frazee and others that the sale of "Babe" will, eventually, redound to the welfare of the Boston club.

"Cy" Young, Tris Speaker and other stars were let go and the Red Sox still won championships. Ruth and others came along and helped them to win, and it may reasonably be expected that the club will again do without Ruth what it did without Young, Speaker and the others.

Considering what the club received for its rights in him: the risk of carrying such a valuable player, and all the other circumstances, it is hard to see how Frazee could have turned down New York's offer for the star, and it looks as if he had made a good bargain.

If "Babe" should hold up for a couple of years, the Yankees will undoubtedly get their money back and much more, but, if, for instance, he should be injured while at the training camp next Spring, he would prove a costly buy for them. His weak knee makes him susceptible to injury and no insurance can be bought against a ball player being hurt on the field.

With the money the club has received, it should be able to buy three or four great players and go into the race next season with a much stronger team than it would have if Ruth were retained, and no new talent was secured.

. . .

The price was something enormous," Frazee said. "But I do not care to name the figures. It was an amount the club could not afford to refuse. I should have preferred to have taken players in exchange for Ruth, but no club could have given me the equivalent in men without wrecking itself, and so the deal had to be made on a cash basis. No other club could afford to give the amount the Yankees have paid for him, and I do not mind saying I think they are taking a gamble."

Frazee's statement is baseball's equivalent of Neville Chamberlain's prediction that the Munich agreement of 1938 would bring, "peace in our time." Certainly Ruth was hard to handle and there was no way of predicting that he'd blossom into the greatest slugger the game has ever known, but Frazee's baseball transactions after the sale of Ruth indicate that his interests were not in concert with those of Red Sox fans.

After the sale of Ruth was announced, an editorial appeared in *The New York Times*, under the heading, "The High Price of Home Runs."

Indeed.

Harry Frazee sold the Red Sox in August of 1923, less than six months after the first performance of *No, No Nanette*. Since that day, the New York Yankees have won 26 World Series, the Boston Red Sox 0.

CHAPTER TWO

The Babe Captures New York

by Dave Anderson of The New York Times

If Babe Ruth had been sold to the Yankees in today's world, he would have been introduced to New York at a glitzy news conference at Yankee Stadium, if not Times Square or City Hall, with television cameras rolling, photographers clicking and George Steinbrenner gloating. But this was 1920 and the Babe didn't arrive in New York until nearly two months after the Jan. 5 announcement that inspired his opinion of H. Harrison (Harry) Frazee, the Red Sox owner who had sold him, so to speak, down the Boston Post Road.

"Frazee is not good enough to own any ball club, especially one in Boston," the Babe growled between rounds of golf in California where he was pursuing a movie deal. "He has done more to hurt baseball in Boston than anyone who was ever connected with the game in that city."

How prophetic. But at the time not even the Babe realized how prophetic that statement would be. More than eight decades later, the pain of the Babe's departure not only still hurts in Boston, but the name Harry Frazee still lives in infamy to anyone with a connection to Fenway Park.

"Because I demanded a big increase in salary, which I felt I was entitled to, he brands me as an ingrate and a troublemaker," the Babe said, alluding to Frazee. "The time of a ballplayer is short, and he must get his money in a few years or lose out. Any fair-minded fan knows that my efforts last season warranted a larger salary, and I asked him for it. If my playing last year did not merit a raise, then it never will and I would go along in a rut.

"I like Boston and the Boston fans," he added. "They have treated me splendidly and

if not for Frazee, I would be content to play with the Red Sox to the end of my baseball days. Boston seems more or less like my hometown, and with a regular man at the head of the club, I would prefer to remain there. Frazee sold me because he was unwilling to meet my demands and to alibi himself with the fans, he is trying to throw the blame on me."

The New York Times — January 6, 1920

RUTH BOUGHT BY NEW YORK AMERICANS FOR $125,000—HIGHEST PRICE IN BASEBALL ANNALS

Yanks Buy Babe Ruth For $125,000

Acquisition of noted Batsman Gives New York Club the Hard-Hitting Outfielder Long Desired.

Babe Ruth of the Boston Red Sox, baseball's super-slugger, was purchased by the Yankees yesterday for the largest cash sum ever paid for a player. The New York Club paid Harry Frazee of Boston $125,000 for the sensational batsman who last season caused such a furor in the national game by batting out twenty-nine home runs, a new record in long-distance clouting.

Colonel Ruppert, President of the Yanks, said that he had taken over Ruth's Boston contract, which has two years more to run. This contract calls for a salary of $10,000 a year. Ruth recently announced that he would refuse to play for

$10,000 a year next season, although the Boston Club has received no request for a raise in salary.

Manager Miller Huggins is now in Los Angeles negotiating with Ruth. It is believed that the Yanks manager will offer him a new contract which will be satisfactory to the Colossus of the bat.

President Ruppert said yesterday that Ruth would probably play right field for the Yankees. He played in left field for the Red Sox last season, and had the highest fielding average among the outfielders, making only two errors during the season. While he is on the Pacific Coast Manager Huggins will also endeavor to sign Duffy Lewis, who will be one of Ruth's companions in the outfield at the Polo Grounds next season.

Home Run Record in Danger

The acquisition of Ruth strengthens the Yankees club in its weakest department. With the added hitting power of Ruth, Bob Shawkey, one of the Yankee pitchers, said yesterday the New York club should be a pennant winner next season. For several seasons the Yankees have been experimenting with outfielders, but never have been able to land a consistent hitter. The short right field wall of the Polo Grounds should prove an easy target for Ruth next season and, playing seventy-seven games at home, it would not be surprising if Ruth surpassed his home-run record of twenty-nine circuit clouts next Summer.

Ruth was such a sensation last season that he supplanted the great Ty Cobb as baseball's greatest attraction, and in obtaining the services of Ruth for next season the New York club made a ten-strike which will be received with the greatest enthusiasm by Manhattan baseball fans.

Ruth's crowning batting accomplishment came at the Polo Grounds last Fall when he hammered one of the longest hits ever seen in Harlem over the right field grandstand for his twenty-eighth home run, smashing the home record of twenty-seven, made by Ed Williamson way back in 1884. The more modern home-run record, up to last season, had been held by Buck Freeman, who made twenty-five home runs when a member of the Washington club in 1899. The next best home-run hitter of modern times is Gavvy Cravath, now manager of the Phillies, who made twenty-four home runs a few seasons ago.

Ruth's home-run drives were distributed all over the circuit, and he is the one player known to the game who hit a home run in every park on the circuit in the same season.

The New York Times — January 5, 1920

FRAZEE DISCUSSES SALE.

"Red Sox Were Fast Becoming a One-Man Team," Says Owner.

Harry H. Frazee of the Boston Americans said tonight that he has sold "Babe" Ruth to the New York Americans because he thought it was an "injustice" to keep him with the Red Sox, who "were fast becoming a one-man team." He did not make public the purchase price.

Ruth, who is the world champion home run hitter, recently returned his three-year contract, which called for a payment of $10,000 a year, without his signature, demanding a much larger salary. Mr. Frazee said he would use the money obtained from the New York Club for the purchase of other players and would try to develop the Red Sox into a winning team.

Largest Sum on Record for Purchase of Ball Players

Babe Ruth, Boston to Yankees	$125,000
Tris Speaker, Boston to Clevelend	*50,000
Eddie Collins, Athletics to Chicago	50,000
Carl Mays, Boston to Yankees	*40,000
Art Nehf, Boston to Giants	*40,000
Frank Baker, Athletics to Yankees	*40,000
Joe Jackson, Cleveland to Chicago	*31,500
Benny Kauff, Feds to Giants	30,000
Lee Magee, Feds to Yankees	22,500
Strunk, Schang and Joe Bush Athletics to Boston	*60,000
Alexander and Killger, Phillies to Boston	*60,000

*and players

About six weeks later the Babe returned to Boston where he promoted his investment in a 5-cent cigar, sometimes sitting in a store window and smoking three simultaneously. He also was honored at a Hotel Brunswick dinner, although he really went to Boston to wangle a percentage of the money Frazee got for him from the Yankees: $125,000 plus a $300,000 loan for the Fenway Park mortgage. But when he tried to talk to Frazee, he was rebuffed.

"The son of a bitch wouldn't even see me," he growled.

On Feb. 28, the Babe finally arrived in New York to join the Yankee players and officials on a train to Jacksonville for spring training and the start of a Yankee career that popularized baseball as never before while polarizing the Yankee-Red Sox rivalry to this day. As the Babe carried the Yankees to six American League pennants and three World Series championships in his first nine seasons, the Red Sox thudded to the depths of the second division. When he hit a record 60 homers in 1927, the last-place Red Sox hit a total of 28.

The Babe was not merely a good player who got away from Boston, he remains arguably the best player in baseball history. He not only hit 714 homers, he had been the American League's best pitcher with the Red Sox (89-46 record, 3-0 in the World Series with an 0.87 earned-run average).

Over the years, Hank Aaron has surpassed the Babe's home run total, hitting a record 755, and Barry Bonds has approached it in recent years, but the Babe was much more. Had he remained a left-handed pitcher, he almost surely would have been voted into the Hall of Fame as a pitcher.

For all of the Babe's outbursts as a Yankee, his emergence as a baseball idol was all the more galling to Boston's fans because it coincided with the Red Sox' descent to disgrace. If he had been sold to another A.L. team, Red Sox fans might not have resented his loss so much. But as a Yankee, his success was now neighboring New York's triumph and Boston's loss. That stung. No wonder Red Sox devotees eventually would describe their team's frustrations into the 21st century as "The Curse of the Bambino"—the nickname for the Babe that developed when that era's New York immigrant Italians used the Italian word for baby, "bambino," at what amounted to his New York baseball baptism.

While the Yankees prospered financially throughout the Babe's 15 seasons, the Red Sox staggered in red ink. When Frazee, a New York theatrical producer who was mostly an absentee Red Sox owner, sold out to Robert A. Quinn in 1923 for $1.25 million, not one player remained from Boston's 1918 World Series champions.

To salt the wounds of the rivalry, of the 24 Yankee players eligible for the 1923 World Series (the Yankees' first of their record 26 Series triumphs), 11 were former Red Sox players that Frazee had supplied, mostly for cash—the Babe, right-hander Waite Hoyt, catcher Wally Schang and outfielder Mike McNally in 1921; third baseman Joe Dugan, shortstop Everett Scott, right-handers Joe Bush and Sam Jones in 1922; left-hander Herb Pennock and right-hander George Pipgras in 1923, as well as right-hander Carl Mays, who had arrived in a 1919 trade. If so many deals strengthening one team while weakening another were to occur today, the Commissioner's office, if not Congress, surely would be asking questions. But back then, the Boston Post Road was a one-way street to the beginning of baseball's most successful franchise.

"The Yankee dynasty," said right-hander Ernie Shore, who had been dealt by the Red Sox to the Yankees in 1918 before leaving after the 1920 season, "was the Red Sox dynasty."

Or what should have been the Red Sox dynasty. Hoyt and Pennock joined the Babe in the Hall of Fame. Except for right-hander Bob Shawkey, Red Sox alumni started every one of the Yankees' World Series games from 1921 to 1926. And in 1930 the Yankees acquired another Red Sox pitcher, Charles (Red) Ruffing, who also earned a bronze plaque in Cooperstown. Over the Babe's 15 seasons with the Yankees, they had a 224-99 record against the Red Sox; only in 1922 did the Red Sox win the season series, 13-9. And every so often, the Babe would return to Boston, not merely to haunt the Red Sox at Fenway Park. His first wife Helen was from Boston; they owned a farm in suburban Sudbury, and later she would die in a house fire in Watertown. He was always a cruel reminder of what might have been for the Red Sox had he (and so many other Red Sox players) not been sold to the Yankees. No wonder that one day when Frazee was about to pay a cab fare in Boston, the driver stared at him. "Are you Harry Frazee?" the driver asked. When Frazee nodded, the driver slugged him.

Maybe the driver remembered the 1922 season. Frazee sold Dugan, then baseball's best third baseman, to the Yankees on July 23 for $50,000 plus four journeymen, prompting Judge Kenesaw Mountain Landis, then in his first year as baseball's first Commissioner, to create the June 15 trading deadline. On the next-to-last day of the season, with the Yankees still needing one victory to clinch the pennant after the last-place Red Sox had won the first two games of the weekend series, Red Sox manager Hugh Duffy wanted to start Pennock, but Frazee ordered Duffy to use right-hander Alex (Cousin) Ferguson, picked up from the Yankees on waivers during the season. Ferguson never got anybody out and the Yankees won. Three months later, Frazee traded Pennock to the Yankees for three obscure players and $50,000.

After leaving Boston, Hoyt, Pennock,

Jones, Mays, Pipgras and Bush combined for a total of 873 victories for other teams, mostly the Yankees—873 victories that surely would have kept the Red Sox in contention instead of in the cellar. Hoyt had six Series victories, Pennock five, Mays and Bush each one.

To add to Boston's distrust of Frazee, he lived in New York to be closer to his theatrical ventures and often socialized with the Yankees co-owners: Jacob Ruppert, rich from his family's booming brewery even with Prohibition's arrival five days after the Ruth deal, and Tillinghast L' Hommedieu Huston, an Ohioan who made a fortune in construction in Cuba after the Spanish-American War and later served in World War I. Ruppert was president, Huston vice-president. When Yankee Stadium opened in 1923, Frazee even marched to the flagpole with Ruppert and Huston behind John Philip Sousa and the 7th Regiment band, then sat with Ruppert and watched the Babe hit a three-run homer in the Yankees' 4-1 victory.

Ruppert and Huston, who had purchased the Yankees in 1915, paid $600,0000 for a shabby plot of land along the Harlem River in the Bronx where Yankee Stadium was built at a cost of $2.5 million. But then as now, it was the House That Ruth Built, girder by girder and seat by seat, from the moment he started hitting home runs for the Yankees in 1920 at the Polo Grounds.

"Ruppert's wealth enabled him to make the big loan to Frazee, which made the deal possible," the Babe wrote in his autobiography, "but I have always believed the idea originally was Huston's. He was downright impatient over the failure of the Yankees and I believe it was he who first got the inside on Frazee's financial condition. Frazee was one of his

favorite drinking companions and I believe that it was over a few glasses of beer that Huston first learned of Frazee's need and that if the amount was right he could obtain me."

Until the Babe arrived, the Yankees, the former Baltimore Orioles franchise that moved to New York as the Highlanders when the A.L. began in 1903, had never won a pennant. They had never even been close except for the 1904 race with Boston, then known as the Pilgrims. On the final day of that season at the Highlanders' park in Washington Heights in upper Manhattan, Yankee right-hander Jack Chesbro's wild pitch enabled the Pilgrims to finish first; they went on to win the first of Boston's five World Series titles in the first 15 Series.

As the Red Sox' ace left-handed pitcher, the Babe had a 17-5 record against the Yankees, winning nine in a row at one stretch. With the Yankees in 1920, he was strictly a slugger and, at age 25, relatively svelte. While batting .376 and knocking in 137 runs, he hit 54 homers. No other major-leaguer had more than 19 that season; the Red Sox, as a team, hit only 22.

With the Babe on display, the Yankees attracted a major-league record 1,289,422 attendance at the Polo Grounds in 1920, outdrawing their landlords, the previously more popular Giants, by 350,000 customers. John McGraw, the Giants' thorny manager and part owner, was so annoyed, he ordered the Yankees to build their own ballpark. The sooner the better.

The Babe was more than just an attraction as a ballplayer; he was a New York celebrity. In the late summer, he found time to appear in a movie, *The Babe Comes Home*. He would drive from the Ansonia Hotel, at Broadway

and West 73rd St., where he lived with his wife Helen, to nearby Haverstraw, New York, do that day's filming, then drive back for the three o'clock game. On road trips, he maintained his reputation for drinking, eating and wenching, often staying away from the Yankees' hotel until breakfast, where he once reportedly ate an omelet of 18 eggs with three big slices of ham.

When outfielder Ping Bodie was asked what it was like being the Babe's roommate, he said, "I don't room with the Babe. I room with his suitcase."

One of the Babe's few disappointments in 1920 occurred in his return to Fenway Park. He had a double and two singles, but the Yankees lost both games of a Patriots Day morning-afternoon doubleheader. When the "Ruthless Red Sox" arrived at the Polo Grounds, their 10-2 record was leading the league. On May 1 the Babe walloped his first homer as a Yankee at the Polo Grounds, a mighty blast over the right-field roof in a 6-0 rout. The Red Sox eventually skidded to fifth as the Babe lifted the Yankees to a third-place finish, only three games behind the Cleveland Indians.

Not long after that 1920 season ended, the Babe hired a business manager, Christy Walsh, a former newspaper cartoonist who acted as his agent for non-baseball income, notably ghostwritten stories during the World Series for newspapers and news services. Walsh also tried to polish the Babe's image while acting as his financial adviser. He convinced the Babe to put much of his money into annuities that eased his later life.

During the last week of that 1920 season, eight members of the second-place White Sox

(notably hard-hitting outfielder Shoeless Joe Jackson, ringleader and first baseman Chick Gandil, third baseman Buck Weaver, and ace pitchers Eddie Cicotte and Lefty Williams) were suspended by A.L. president Ban Johnson after having been indicted by a Chicago grand jury for conspiring to dump the 1919 Series to the Cincinnati Reds.

Those White Sox players were persuaded by gamblers to throw the Series because they were being shamefully underpaid by Charles Comiskey, the White Sox owner. The Babe wasn't underpaid. He not only still had another season on the record three-year contract worth an eventual $41,000 that he had signed with the Red Sox, he played on a tour of October exhibition games for $1,500 a game, then sailed with his wife Helen for Cuba and another series of exhibitions reportedly worth $40,000, although he supposedly lost most of it betting at the Havana racetrack.

The Yankees, meanwhile, hired another Frazee employee, Ed Barrow, as their new general manager. Barrow, who had been the Red Sox' dugout manager when the Babe was there, had been unhappy with Frazee's cost-cutting and when Frazee recommended Barrow, he quickly moved to the Yankee offices. He soon swung the trade for Hoyt and Schang.

When the eight White Sox players were suspended from baseball for life and Landis was installed as Commissioner, it shook the public's confidence in the game. But when the Babe continued to hit home runs in 1921, baseball's popularity rebounded as the Yankees won their first pennant. That season he hit 59 homers in what was arguably his most dazzling season: .378 average, 171 runs batted in, 177 runs scored, 204 hits, 44 doubles, 16 triples, 144 walks, .846 slugging percentage. And he was more popular than ever. When he was nabbed for speeding one day on his way to the Polo Grounds, he went to court, was fined $100 and then the police escorted him to the ballpark in time to play the last few innings.

In the Yankees' first World Series, a best-five-of-nine confrontation with their Polo Grounds landlord, John McGraw's Giants, the Yankees won the first two games but the Babe, while stealing third base in Game 2, scraped an elbow on the infield dirt. Even though it became infected, he played in the next three games, but then had to sit out the last three as the Giants won.

Days later, the Babe was about to leave on another lucrative October exhibition tour with leftfielder Bob Meusel; he was expected to make about $25,000. "I heal quick," he said, alluding to his elbow. "I always heal quick." But in 1911 baseball had passed a rule forbidding World Series players from participating in exhibition games after the Series, so he had to ask Landis's permission.

"If you do it," Landis told him in a telephone conversation, "it will be the sorriest thing you've ever done in baseball."

The Babe did it. The next day he played in Buffalo, then in games in upstate New York at Elmira and Jamestown, then on to Scranton, Pennsylvania, where Huston warned that if the Babe and Meusel were suspended by Landis at the start of the 1922 season, the entire Yankee team would be affected. The Babe agreed. He had lined up a 16-week vaudeville tour that opened in Boston and a week later played the Palace on Broadway.

The vaudeville tour was in Washington on Dec. 5 when the Babe learned that Landis had not only fined him and Meusel the amount of their World Series share, $3,362, but had suspended them for the first six weeks of the 1922 season.

In his Washington hotel suite, the Babe had no comment. When the vaudeville tour ended in Feb. in Milwaukee, he retreated to Hot Springs, Arkansas, then a fashionable winter resort, to consider, despite the suspension, how much he should ask for in his new Yankee contract. The Yankees had drawn the remarkable total of 2.5 million fans to the Polo Grounds in 1920 and 1921. And now, as the primary drawing card, he expected a substantial share of the anticipated future attendance.

When Huston offered $40,000, the Babe snorted. When Huston offered $50,000 a year in a five-year contract, the Babe suggested $52,000. Why? "There are 52 weeks in the year," he said, "and I always wanted to make a grand a week."

To appreciate the magnitude of the Babe's deal, consider that Frank (Home Run) Baker was the second highest salaried Yankee at $16,000. Schang made $10,000, three-time 20-game winner Bob Shawkey $8,500, Pipp $6,500. Consider too that a Yankee fan earning $80 a week (about $5,000 a year) could comfortably raise a family in his own home with a car parked outside. But the Babe, also appointed the Yankee captain, understood baseball was a business long before free agency in 1976 proved it.

"A man who knows he's making money for other people ought to get some of the profits he brings in," the Babe said. "Don't make any difference if it's baseball or a bank or a vaudeville show. It's business, I tell you. There ain't no sentiment to it. Forget that stuff."

While the Babe was doing vaudeville, Ed Barrow fleeced Frazee of right-hander Joe Bush, who would be 26-7 in 1922, and short-stop Everett Scott, who would play 1,307 consecutive games, a major-league record until Lou Gehrig shattered it. But the suspension sapped the Babe's style for what would be a combustible season. Although he had played in a few exhibition games, when he returned on May 20, he went 1 for 12 before he hit a home run.

On May 25, he tried to stretch a single into a double but when he was tagged out, he flung a handful of dirt at umpire George Hildebrand and was ejected. Booed on his way to the dugout, he stopped, took off his cap and offered a deep bow. That's when a fan bellowed, "You goddamned big bum, why don't you play ball?"

Hearing that, the Babe hopped onto the dugout roof and rushed into the stands. The heckler fled, but the Babe was ejected from the game. On his way to the center-field club-house at the Polo Grounds, the boos were louder. Many fans had to be thinking, *$52,000 a year for a guy who gets himself suspended for six weeks and then can't hit when he comes back.* And after the game, the Babe wasn't sorry for his behavior.

"I didn't mean to hit the umpire with the dirt," he said, "but I did mean to hit that bastard in the stands."

Ban Johnson fined him $200 and the Yankees took away his captaincy; it had lasted six games. He later was suspended for three games for insulting umpire Bill Dineen with what Johnson called "vulgar and vicious" language. When he confronted Dineen the next day under the stands and had to be held back

by three Cleveland players, Johnson banned him for two more days—his fourth suspension of the season. On Sept. 1, he had his fifth, a three-day ban for objecting to a called third strike by umpire Tom Connolly.

The Babe's wild behavior on the field reflected his and his teammates' wild behavior off the field. Bootleggers, bookmakers and friendly women were everywhere the Yankees were. Landis even traveled to Boston to scold both the Yankees and the Red Sox for betting on racehorses. But the Yankees won the pennant again, by one game over the St. Louis Browns. In only 110 games, the Babe batted .315, drove in 99 runs and scored 94. His 35 homers were third to Ken Williams's 39 and Tilly Walker's 37.

In the World Series sweep by the Giants, the Babe was a woeful 2 for 17 with one double, one single, one run batted in, one run scored and one burst into the Giants club-house to confront benchwarmer Johnny Rawlings, who had shouted insults at him. No punches were thrown and the Babe finally left quietly, but this was another wild scene in a wild year.

To polish the Babe's image, his business manager Christy Walsh arranged a dinner party attended by James J. Walker, the future mayor. When Walker asked the Babe if he was going to "keep letting down" all those kids who idolized him, the Babe promised not to drink until the following October. He returned to his Sudbury farm outside Boston for the winter, then arrived at spring training weighing 215, a significant drop. When Yankee Stadium opened, the Babe hit a home run that thrilled a crowd announced at 72,217, but what Barrow later acknowledged to be an "estimate," not the actual attendance.

The New York Times — April 19, 1923

74,200 SEE YANKEES OPEN NEW STADIUM; RUTH HITS HOME RUN

Record Baseball Crowd Cheers as Slugger's Drive Beats Red Sox, 4 to 1.

25,000 Are Turned Away

Gates to $2,500,000 Arena Are Closed Half an Hour Before Start of Game.

Governors, generals, colonels, politicians and baseball officials gathered together solemnly yesterday to dedicate the biggest stadium in baseball, but it was a ball player who did the real dedicating. In the third inning, with two team mates on the base lines, Babe Ruth smashed a savage home run into the right field bleachers, and that was the real baptism of the new Yankee Stadium. That also won the game for the Yankees, and all the ceremony which had gone before was only a trifling preliminary.

The greatest crowd that ever saw a baseball game sat and stood in this biggest of all baseball stadia. Inside the grounds, by official count, were 74,200 people. Outside the park, flattened against doors that had long since closed, were 25,000 more fans, who finally turned around and went home, convinced that baseball parks are not nearly as large as they should be.

. . .

Shawkey Pitches Fine Game

It was an opening game without a flaw. The Yankees easily defeated the Boston Red Sox, 4 to 1. Veteran Bob Shawkey, the oldest Yankee player in point of service, pitched the finest game in his career, letting the Boston batters down with three scattered hits. The Yankee raised their American League championship emblem to the top of the flagpole—the chief feature of an opening-day program that went off perfectly. Governor "Al" Smith, throwing out the first ball of the season, tossed it straight into Wally Schang's glove, thus setting another record. The weather was favorable and the big crowd was handled flawlessly.

Only one more thing was in demand, and Babe Ruth supplied that. The big slugger is a keen student of the dramatic, in addition to being the greatest home run hitter. He was playing a new role yesterday—not the accustomed one of a renowned slugger, but that of a penitent, trying to "come back" after a poor season and a poorer world's series. Before the game he said he would give a year of his life if he could hit a home run in his first game in the new stadium. The Babe was on trial, and he knew it better than anybody else.

He could hardly have picked a better time and place for the drive that he hammered into the bleachers in the third inning. The Yankees had just broken a scoreless tie by pushing Shawkey over the plate with one run. Witt was on third base, Dugan on first, when Ruth appeared at the plate to face Howard Ehmke, the Boston pitcher. Ruth worked the count to two and two, and then Ehmke tried to fool him with one of those slow balls that the Giants used successfully in the last world's series.

The ball came in slowly, but it went out quite rapidly, rising on a line and then dipping suddenly from the force behind it. It struck well inside the foul line, eight or ten rows above the low railing in front of the bleachers, and as Ruth circled the bases he received probably the greatest ovation of his career. The biggest crowd in baseball history rose to its feet and let loose the biggest shout in baseball history. Ruth, jogging over the home plate, grinned broadly, lifted his cap at arm's length and waved it at the multitude.

. . .

But the game, after all, was only an incident of a busy afternoon. The stadium was the thing. For the Yankee owners it was the realization of a dream long cherished. For the fans it was something they had never seen before in baseball. It cost about $2,500,000 to build, and eleven months were spent in the construction work. It is the most costly stadium in baseball, as well as the biggest.

First impressions—and also last impressions—are of the vastness of the arena. The stadium is big. It towers high in the air, three tiers piled one on the other. It is a skyscraper among baseball parks. Seen from the vantage point of the nearby subway structure, the mere height of the grandstand is tremendous. Baseball fans who sat in the last row of the steeply sloping third tier may well boast that they broke all altitude records short of those attained in an airplane.

. . .

Early in that 1923 season, Huston sold his share of the Yankees to Ruppert for $1.5 million. Huston had wanted to fire Miller Huggins after the manager's dispute with right-hander Joe Bush in the 1922 World Series, but when Ruppert stood by Huggins and Ed Barrow, whom Huston had hired, also stood by Huggins, Huston decided to depart.

The Yankees, bolstered by left-hander Herb Pennock's arrival from the Red Sox, ran away with the pennant, winning by 16 games with a 98-54 record. The Babe batted .393 with 41 homers, 205 hits, 170 walks, 17 stolen bases and virtually no bad scenes. In the World Series against the Giants, he hit .368 with three homers, a triple, a double and three singles as the Yankees won in six games over their former landlords. After two decades as New York's other team, the Yankees had dethroned the Giants as champions and the Babe ruled the Roaring Twenties.

Boston mourned. Reduced by Frazee to a ragamuffin lineup, the Red Sox finished last for the second straight season, 37 games behind the Yankees.

In 1924 the Babe, resuming his drinking and carousing, slugged 46 homers and batted .378, but the Yankees finished second, three games behind the Washington Senators and their Hall of Fame righthander Walter Johnson (23-7, 2.72 ERA), who would win 417 games. And in 1925, the Yankees never recovered from what was known as "the bellyache heard round the world." Described as an ulcer by one doctor, it flared on the trip north from spring training and required surgery in St. Vincent's Hospital. His personal physician, Dr. Edward King, blamed the Babe's eating and drinking habits for the illness. When he returned to the lineup on June 1, the Yankees were mired in seventh place. That June 1 would also be a historic date; Lou Gehrig, their young first baseman up from the Hartford farm team, pinch-hit that day, the start of his 2,130 consecutive-game streak.

The Yankees finished a dreadful seventh as

the Babe, still carousing, had his worst season. In only 98 games, he batted .290 with 25 homers, 66 runs batted in, and two life-changing quarrels, one with his wife Helen, the other with Miller Huggins, the little 5-foot-6-inch, 140-pound manager he disrespectfully called "The Flea."

The Babe's marriage had not been the same since he met Claire Merritt Hodgson, a brunette beauty from Athens, Georgia, in 1923 while on his vaudeville tour. In the summer of 1925, Helen and their daughter Dorothy retreated to the Sudbury farm outside Boston. In late August, the Babe was late arriving at Sportsman's Park in St. Louis after being out all night when Huggins confronted him.

"Don't bother getting dressed, Babe," the manager said. "You're not playing today. I'm suspending you and I'm fining you $5,000."

The Babe blew, growling obscenities and saying that if he were "even half Huggins's size, he would have punched the manager, prompting Huggins to bark, "If I were half your size," he would have punched the Babe.

"I'll tell you something else, mister," Huggins said. "Before you get back in uniform, you're going to apologize for what you said. And apologize plenty."

On his way home, the Babe declared he wouldn't play for the Yankees in 1926 if Huggins were still the manager, saying, "Either he quits or I quit." But when the Babe met with Ruppert in New York in the hope of gaining his support, the Yankee owner stood by Huggins.

"I told Ruth," Ruppert told reporters, pronouncing it Root, "he went too far. I told him Miller Huggins is in absolute command of the ball club and that I stand behind Huggins to the very limit. I told him it is up to him to see Huggins and admit his hotheadedness."

Turning to the Babe, who was standing outside the owner's office at the brewery on the Upper East Side, Ruppert scolded the now 30-year-old slugger.

"Your heart is in the right place," Ruppert said, "but your head has run away from you. You must look forward to the day when you are no longer able to play ball. You must guard your name and your reputation for the time when they are the only assets you have. I think you are big enough to go to Huggins and admit your error. We want you in New York and we need you, because we want to regain the championship next season. We are ready, willing and able to pay you your big salary, but the fan who pays his dollar at the ballpark expects a full measure from you. Think it over, then go see Huggins. I will do nothing for you. The matter lies in his hands."

When the Babe, properly chastised, was asked if he now would see Huggins, he replied, "Maybe we can get this settled."

Huggins made him suffer. When the Babe knocked on the door of Huggins's office the next day, a Wednesday, the manager told him, "Call me Friday afternoon." When the Babe called on Friday, a Yankee open date, Huggins told him, "See me Saturday." When they finally met, Huggins demanded that the Babe apologize to him in the clubhouse Sunday before the entire Yankee team. The Babe did, saying, "I'm hotheaded." On Monday he was in the lineup for a Labor Day doubleheader in Boston.

Humbled as never before, the Babe, as Robert W. Creamer wrote in *Babe: The Legend Comes to Life*, his classic biography, "never again challenged Huggins's authority . . . he

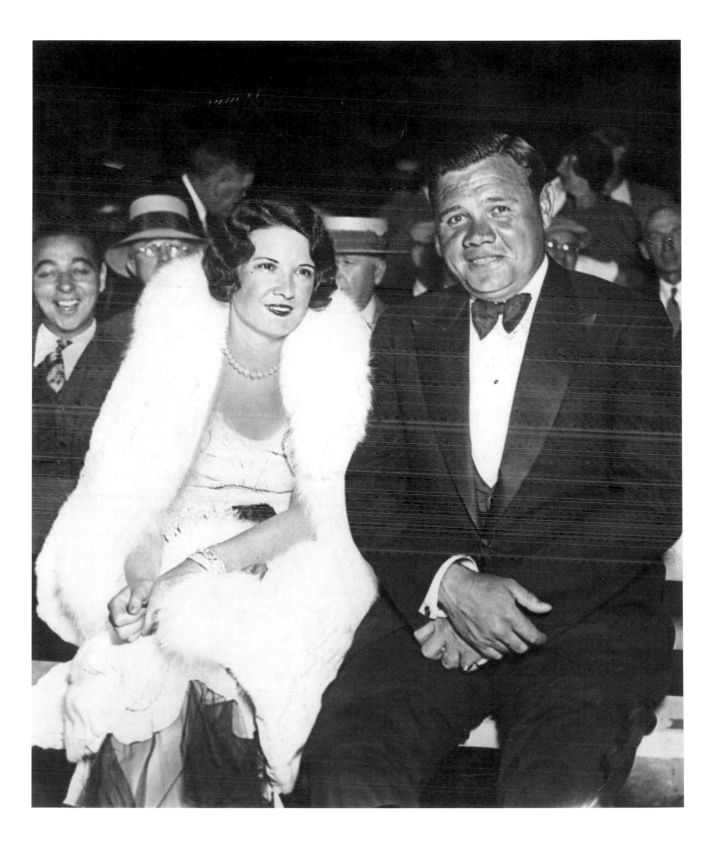

was never again seriously out of shape." And he was never better.

Over the next six seasons, from 1926 to 1931, the Babe averaged .354 with 50 homers, 155 runs batted in, and 147 runs scored. After the 1925 season, he even spurned $25,000 for a Canadian exhibition tour. His personal life also changed. With their marriage disintegrating, the Babe and Helen separated. They would never reconcile, but since both were Catholics in a stricter religious era, neither filed for divorce. When the Babe was in New York, he spent more and more time with Claire Hodgson. After his winter workouts, he reported to spring training weighing 212, his lightest since his days with the Red Sox.

With the Babe batting .372 with 47 homers and 145 runs batted in, the Yankees, bolstered by rookie second baseman Tony Lazzeri and rookie shortstop Mark Koenig, rebounded to win the 1926 pennant as the ragamuffin Red Sox finished last for the fifth time in six seasons. In the World Series against the St. Louis Cardinals, the Babe hit a record four homers but wound up making the strangest last out in Series history; he was thrown out trying to steal second base.

In 1927, after signing a new three-year contract for $72,000 a year, the Babe reported overweight and was drinking more. When he struck out twice in the opener against Bob (Lefty) Grove, the Philadelphia Athletics' ace, Huggins benched him for a pinch hitter. Huggins explained that the Babe was suffering from a "billious" attack, meaning he was drunk. When the Yankees arrived at Fenway Park in late April, he had hit only three homers and driven in only three runs. His only ambition, he said, was to eventually hit

500 home runs—"a pretty big assignment," he said, "considering that I'm 33 and I only have 359 so far."

That day the Babe hit another homer. By the end of the Yankees' next visit to Boston, he had 24. Gehrig, the muscular son of German immigrant parents, hit three in the series finale for 21. In a July 4 doubleheader against Washington before 72,641 at the Stadium, Gehrig hit two to jump ahead of the Babe, 28-26. Their duel was on. During a series in Boston, Gehrig went one ahead with his 45th, but the Babe responded with three for 47; the next day he hit two more for 49—only 10 away from the record 59 he had hit in 1921.

Gehrig suddenly stopped hitting homers; he finished with 47, but the Babe hit 17 that September. When the Yankees clinched the pennant in Cleveland, he hit two. When his 57th created a ninth-inning victory at the Stadium, he held on to his bat as he rounded the bases. As he turned past third, a youngster jumped out of the stands and tried to grab the bat, but the Babe, laughing, dragged the boy and the bat across home plate. He hit his 57th against Grove, a grand slam. The next day, against the Senators at the Stadium, he hit 58 and 59. On Saturday, he pulled Tom Zachary's pitch down the right field line for 60 and the record. In the clubhouse, he celebrated.

"Let some son a bitch try to break that," he roared.

What a season. With their 110-44 record, breaking the 1912 Red Sox record of 105 victories, the Yankees won the pennant by 19 games and batted .307 as a team as the ragamuffin Red Sox finished last, 59 games out. The Babe hit .356, Gehrig .373, centerfielder Earl Combs .356, Meusel .337, Lazzeri .309. Gehrig drove in 175 runs, the Babe 164. Hoyt

Babe Ruth and his 4-year-old daughter Dorothy in 1924 on his farm in Sudbury, Massachusetts. (World Wide Photos)

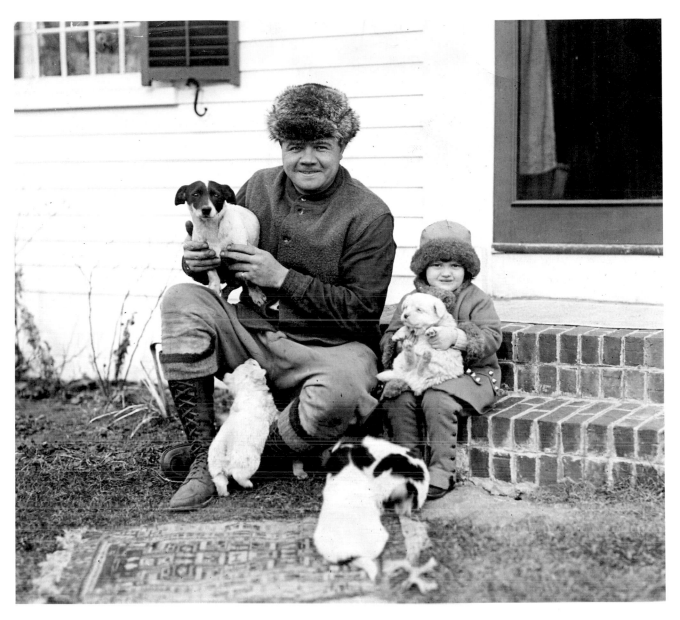

was 22-7, Pennock 18-8, Wilcy Moore 19-9, Urban Shocker 18-6. In the World Series, they swept the Pittsburgh Pirates in four straight as the Babe hit .400 with two homers. No wonder that Yankee team is still considered by many baseball historians to be the best ever. And no wonder it was another reason for Red Sox fans to suffer, then and now—the Babe, third baseman Joe Dugan and three of the four winning pitchers in the Series (Hoyt, Pennock and George Pipgras) had been shipped to the Yankees by Harry Frazee.

The Yankees won again in 1928 as the Babe hit 54 homers. In their sweep of the Cardinals in the World Series, Gehrig hit four homers and drove in nine runs, but the Babe upstaged him, batting .625 with three homers, all in the 7-3 finale during which he held up two fingers while playing left field and waved at the fans in Sportsman's Park. "I told those friends of mine in the bleachers I'd hit two," he grinned later, "and I hit three."

For all his fame and glory, the Babe soon was confronted with real life. On Jan. 11, 1929, his wife Helen, from whom he had been separated for three years and who had been hospitalized with a nervous breakdown three months earlier, died at 31 in a fire that consumed the home in Watertown, Massachusetts, where she had been posing as the wife of a dentist, Dr. Edward Kinder, for nearly two years. At the time of the fire, which was attributed to faulty wiring, Kinder was attending the fights at Boston Garden.

Told of Helen's death, the Babe took an overnight train to Boston, where he issued a statement to reporters. "My wife and I have not lived together for the last three years," it read. "During that time I have seldom met her. I've done all that I can to comply with her wishes. Her death is a great shock to me." When the Babe took questions, he said, "We were married Oct. 17, 1914, in Ellicott City, Maryland." But when asked about their 8-year-old daughter Dorothy, he said, "I'd rather not say anything about the little girl." Dorothy, who had lived with her mother and Dr. Kinder for two years, was away at boarding school at the time of the fire.

Helen's death now freed the Babe to marry Claire Hodgson in a Catholic ceremony. Not long after dawn on April 17, Opening Day, the Babe, 35, and Claire, 28, were married at St. Gregory's church on West 90th St. Dorothy soon was adopted by Claire, whose daughter Julia was adopted by the Babe.

The 1929 Yankees made a fashion statement that remains their symbol. To slim the Babe's belly, Ruppert ordered pin-striped uniforms. Ruppert also put numbers on the backs, the first baseball team to do so. In accordance with the batting order, Combs wore 1, Koenig 2, the Babe 3, Gehrig 4, and so on.

Another death haunted the Yankees and Red Sox that year. Harry Frazee died of Bright's disease at his Park Avenue home. For

all his theatrical failures, he had struck it rich in 1925 with *No, No, Nanette,* a Broadway musical that toured London, Paris and Berlin and earned more than $2.5 million. He was buried in the Kensico cemetery in Valhalla, New York, not far from where the Babe would be buried nearly two decades later.

Even with a 13-4 start and the Babe's 46 homers, the Yankees finished 18 games behind the Philadelphia Athletics' powerhouse that featured first baseman Jimmie Foxx, leftfielder Al Simmons, catcher Mickey Cochrane, third baseman Jimmy Dykes and pitchers Lefty Grove, George Earnshaw and Rube Walberg.

On Sept. 25, the Yankees were in Fenway Park when the news arrived: Miller Huggins was dead from blood poisoning. For all of the Babe's disputes with Huggins in previous years, he had grown to respect the little manager. When the reporters surrounded him after the game, he broke down. "It's one of those things you can't talk about much," he said. "You know what I thought of him and you know what I owe him."

With the Yankees needing a manager in 1930, Ed Barrow hired Bob Shawkey, who had been one of Huggins's coaches and had also managed in the minors. Although the Babe wanted the job, he was more concerned with demanding $100,000 a year for three years. When Col. Ruppert offered $75,000, the Babe was a holdout for the first time since 1919.

In a letter (composed by Christy Walsh) to the Yankees and the New York newspapers, the Babe, referring to the annuities Walsh had arranged, insisted, "I'm good for $25,000 a year for life even if I quit baseball today." But he soon agreed to $80,000 a year for two years. Ruppert, now that Huggins was dead,

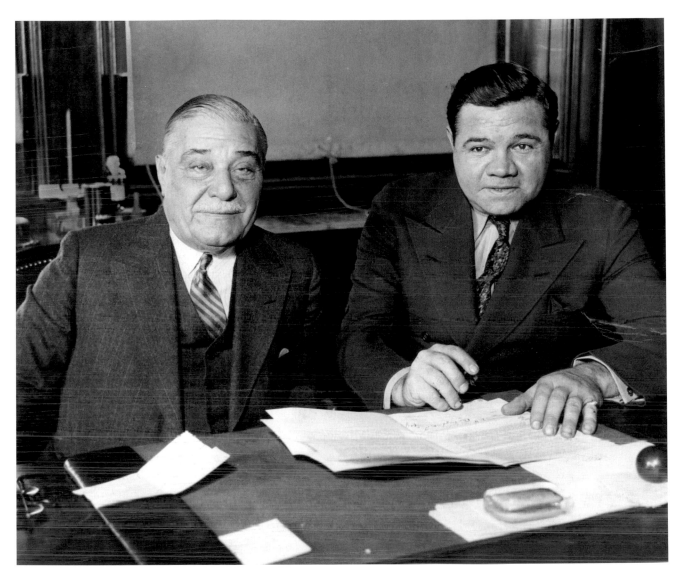

also returned the $5,000 the Babe had been fined in his 1925 dispute with Huggins.

When the Babe was asked if he deserved an $80,000 salary that was higher than President Herbert Hoover's $75,000, he said, "Why not? I had a better year than he did."

The Babe responded with 49 homers, but when the Yankees finished third, behind the Athletics and the Senators, Shawkey was out. Barrow hired Joe McCarthy, who had won the 1929 National League pennant with the Cubs, and the Babe demanded an explanation as to why he wasn't considered. When Ruppert mentioned that he didn't believe in player-managers, the Babe grumbled, "Speaker was, Cobb was." For the rest of his Yankee years,

the Babe would resent McCarthy, but in 1931 it didn't prevent his slugging 46 homers and batting .373 as the Yankees finished second to the Athletics—their third straight year without a pennant.

For the 1932 season, the Babe needed a new contract, but with the nation's economy struggling in the Depression, Col. Ruppert offered him $70,000, a $10,000 cut. After demanding another two-year deal at $80,000, the Babe agreed to $75,000 for one year. Jimmie Foxx hit 58 homers, the first threat to the Babe's record 60, but at 38 the Babe hit 41 and drove in 137 runs as the Yankees won 107 games and the pennant; the Red Sox finished last, 64 games behind. In the Yankees'

turnover, three new names would go to the Hall of Fame—pitchers Vernon (Lefty) Gomez and former Red Sox right-hander Charles (Red) Ruffing and catcher Bill Dickey.

In the Series sweep of the Cubs, the Babe relished one of his most memorable moments. Although shortstop Mark Koenig, acquired from the Yankees in midseason, had batted .353 in helping the Cubs win the pennant, his teammates had voted him only a one-half share of their Series money, prompting the Babe to yell into their dugout, "Hey, Mark, who are those cheapskates you're with?"

In the first inning of Game 3 at Wrigley Field, the Babe hit a three-run homer. In the fifth, with the score 4-4, he took right-hander Charlie Root's first pitch for a called strike. Here, in an era long before instant replay, the facts got fuzzy. After that pitch, the Babe supposedly held up the index finger on his right hand. When he took another strike for a 2-2 count, some say he held up two fingers, others insist he pointed his bat toward center field. Behind him, catcher Charles (Gabby) Hartnett heard him say, "It only takes one to hit it." In the batter's box, Gehrig, as he said later, heard him say, "I'm going to knock the next pitch down your goddamn throat."

On Root's change-up, low and away, the Babe smashed the longest homer ever hit in Wrigley Field at the time, a majestic shot deep into the center-field bleachers. He rounded the bases with his hands clasped above his head and as he turned toward home, he stared at the Cubs dugout and shouted, "Squeeze the Eagle club," a reference to short-changing Koenig.

Lou Gehrig, next up, also homered in the 7-5 victory but the question has raged ever since: Did the Babe "call" that home run?

Some witnesses swear he did, others swear he didn't. As for the Babe himself, he never really confirmed it. Then again, he never really denied it. He apparently was willing to let people think that yes, he had called it.

That home run was the Babe's last hurrah. In 1933, with America deeper into the Depression, he was offered only $50,000. To him, that $25,000 cut was "no cut, that's an amputation." He finally signed for $52,000, but with unemployed men selling apples on street corners and banks folding, America had no sympathy for a .301 hitter with 34 homers making that much money. In the first All-Star game, he hit the first homer, a two-run shot off Cardinals left-hander Bill Hallahan as the A.L. won, 4-3. On the final day of the season, with the Yankees entrenched in second place behind the Senators, he pitched against the Red Sox and went nine innings, winning, 6-5, and walking only three while giving up 12 hits, all singles.

In 1934, the Babe took another salary cut to $35,000, but he was still baseball's highest paid and most popular player; the Associated Press described him as "the most photographed person in the world," ahead of President Franklin Delano Roosevelt, the Prince of Wales, and two rising European dictators, Adolf Hitler and Benito Mussolini.

That season the Babe's average dropped to .288 with only 22 homers as the Detroit Tigers won the pennant. But he was still in Boston's blood. In his last appearance at Fenway Park as a Yankee, an Aug. 12 doubleheader, he was accorded several standing ovations by the record crowd of 47,766 that overflowed onto the field from the right-field foul line to the center-field flagpole. Outside, another 15,000 had gathered in the streets.

"Boston has always been kind to me," he said. "I was a bit disappointed that I couldn't have hit a home run for that big mob."

When the season ended, the Babe announced, "I'm through with the Yankees. I won't play with them again unless I can manage. But they're sticking with McCarthy and that lets me out." He was bitter. He had no respect for McCarthy and had quarreled with Gehrig. He wanted to manage, but had refused an offer to go to the Newark farm-team. Frank Navin, the Tigers' owner, wanted him as manager after the 1933 season but the Babe said he would discuss it after his trip to Honolulu for a series of exhibition games. Navin, annoyed, hired Mickey Cochrane. After his "called" homer in the 1932 Series, prospective purchasers of the Red Sox had talked to him but he felt he was still a productive Yankee—not that the Yankees would have let him leave then.

When Tom Yawkey purchased the Red Sox in 1933, he wanted the Babe as manager but Eddie Collins, the Hall of Fame second baseman who now was the Red Sox general manager, persuaded Yawkey to look elsewhere. Collins later obtained Senators shortstop Joe Cronin as player-manager. The Senators' owner, Clark Griffith, also wanted the Babe to manage, but offered a salary of only $15,000 with a share of the attendance. The Babe declined.

After an exhibition tour of several Japanese cities, Shanghai and Manila, the Babe continued on an around-the-world trip through Paris and London before arriving in New York on the S.S. *Manhattan* on Feb. 20, 1935. In the Yankee offices the next day, Col. Ruppert informed him that the Boston Braves' owner, Judge Emil Fuchs, although committed to Bill McKechnie as his manager, wanted the Babe as a player, an assistant manager and a vice-president who would share in the profits.

"You have been a great asset to all baseball, especially to the American League," Fuchs wrote in a letter, "but nowhere in the land are you more admired than in the territory of New England that has always claimed you as its own and where you started your career to fame."

Before granting the Babe his unconditional release, Ruppert asked Fuchs if the Babe would make at least as much as the $35,000 he had with the Yankees in 1934. "Yes, I hope he will, and more," Fuchs said vaguely. But the Babe soon told friends that in another year he would be the Braves manager. In his return to Boston in the season opener at Braves Field, his two-run homer off Carl Hubbell, the Giants ace left-hander, sparked a 4-2 victory but as he settled into a slump, the Braves settled into last place. In early May he and Fuchs argued. He even told Fuchs and McKechnie he was through as a regular player.

Fuchs, knowing the Babe would boost the Braves' share of the gate on a Western trip, persuaded him to keep playing. In a Saturday game at Pittsburgh on May 25, he hit three home runs, the last a towering moon shot over the roof of Forbes Field's double-deck in right field in an 11-7 loss—his 714th homer, 659 of them for the Yankees. When both Duffy Lewis, the Braves' traveling secretary, and his wife Claire told him that night he should retire then and there, he said, "I can't. I promised the son of a bitch I'd play in all the towns on this trip."

The following Thursday, in the first inning in Philadelphia, he struck out, then jammed a knee running in the outfield. He limped to the dugout and never played again. With the Braves back in Boston against the Giants, he gathered the New York writers and told them, "I'm quitting." In 28 games, he had batted .181 with six homers. The Braves were 10-27; overall they would be 38-115, the worst N.L. percentage in the 20th century. For all his fame, the Babe would never get the opportunity to manage a major-league team.

But the Yankees went on to win 22 more World Series through the year 2000 while the Red Sox won none. As if the Babe knew all along the Curse that Harry Frazee had put on the Red Sox.

"He has done more to hurt baseball in Boston," the Babe had said after his 1920 sale to the Yankees, "than anyone who was ever connected with the game in that city."

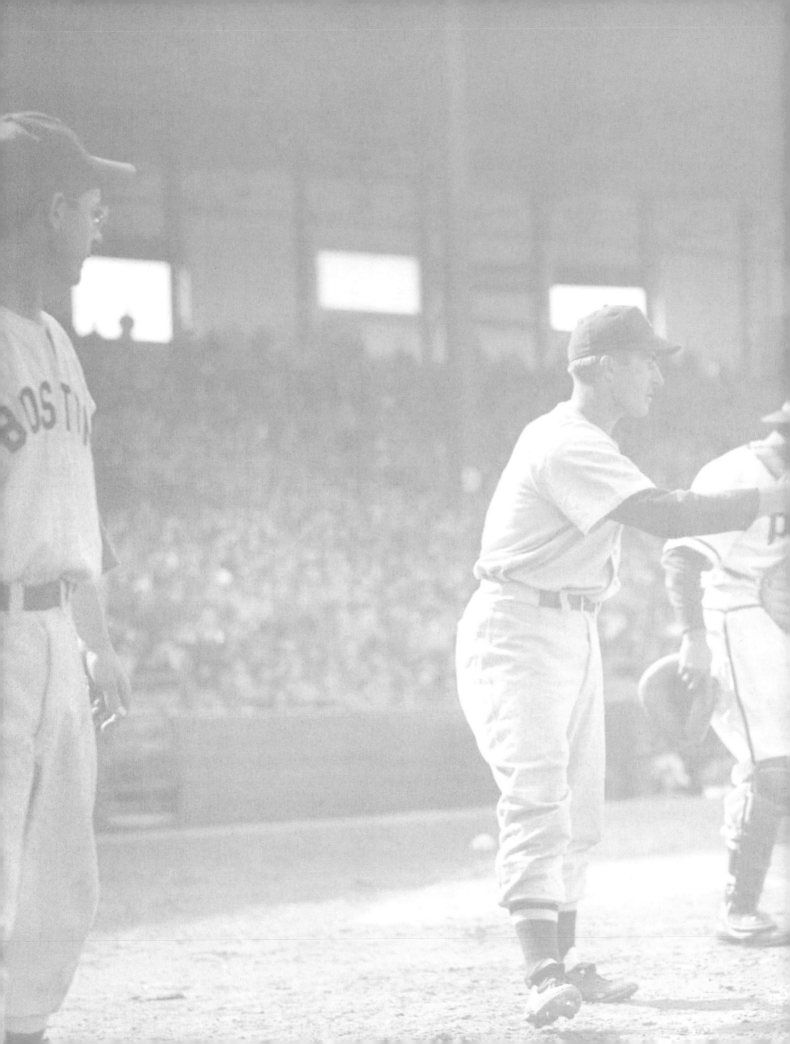

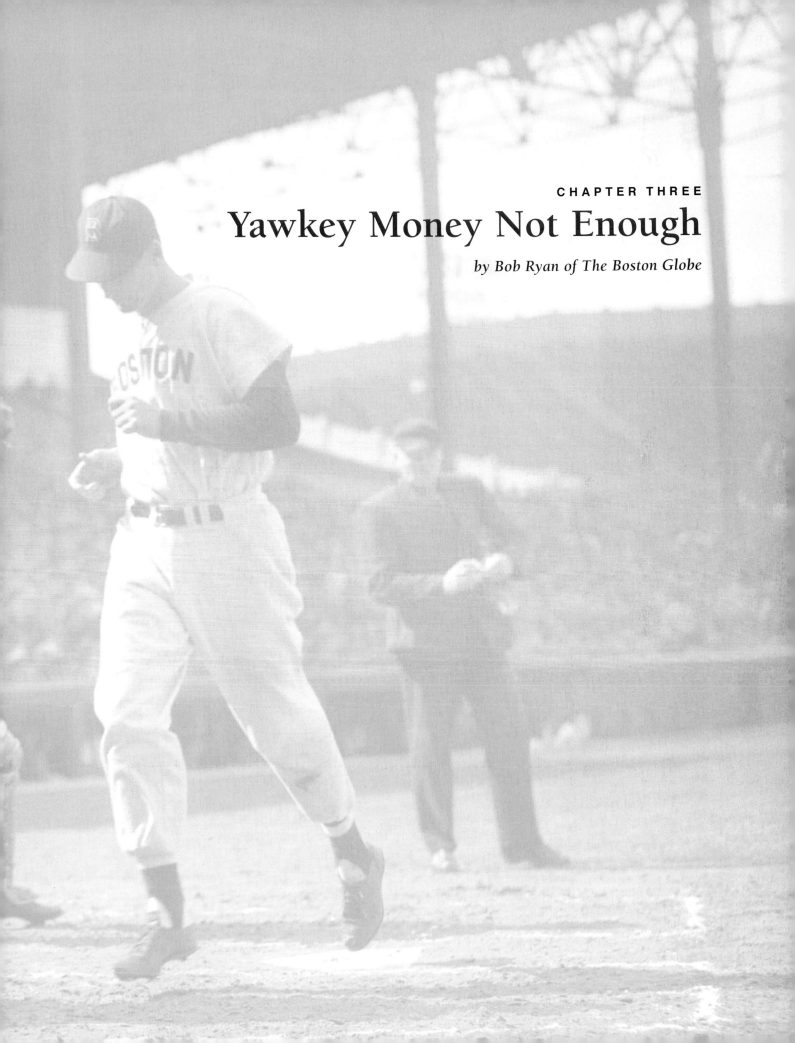

CHAPTER THREE

Yawkey Money Not Enough

by Bob Ryan of The Boston Globe

The year was 1923 when J.A. Robert Quinn, who had been the vice-president and business manager of the St. Louis Browns, decided that it would be in his best interests to get a group together to purchase the Boston Red Sox from the much-despised Harry Frazee.

As famed Boston columnist Bill Cunningham put it in a 1955 essay (for *Sport* Magazine's *Book of Major League Baseball Clubs*), "No committee of sportsmen ever meant better or did much worse." The Quinn era ran from 1923 through 1932, and it was astonishing its unrelentless futility. If only the Red Sox had just been bad . . .

The team finished eighth and last eight times, seventh once and a dizzying sixth once during those ten seasons, never finishing closer than 25 games out of first. The only time the National League Braves ever outdrew their American League counterpart in 52 years of head-to-head competition was during that dismal stretch.

Poor Mr. Quinn, a genial man of very good intentions, fell deeply in debt ($350,000) trying to keep the franchise afloat. It was Depression time, and things got so bad for Bob Quinn that he was forced to borrow on his life insurance in order to finance training camp in 1933.

What he needed was a miracle. Failing that, how about a 30-year-old heir to a fortune whose lifelong dream had been to own a baseball team? But this was real life, not Hollywood; no such man could possibly materialize at just the right time to solve all Bob Quinn's problems, could he?

Yes, he could.

The man was Thomas Austin Yawkey, the foster son and nephew of William Yawkey, who had owned the Detroit Tigers. The elder Yawkey had made a fortune in mining and timber, and when the young man turned 30 he inherited more than $7 million and he knew just where he wished to spend it. The Red Sox were more than available, and on

Feb. 25, 1933, Yawkey purchased the team from Quinn and his investors. Quinn took his share of the proceeds to pay off his debts. Financially speaking, he was right back where he had been a decade earlier, but he was out of debt and, "I actually breathed a sigh of relief when it was over," he recalled.

The New York Times — February 26, 1933

FAMOUS MEMBER OF "$100,000 INFIELD," NEW VICE PRESIDENT OF THE CLUB, WILL BE ACTIVE IN DIRECTION OF PLAYERS

Sale Announced at Club Luncheon

By James C. O'Leary

Thomas A. Yawkey, New York millionaire business man, with general investments in national resources, and Eddie Collins, connected with American League clubs as player, manager and assistant manager for the past 10 years, are the new owners of the Boston Red Sox. No others have been mentioned as stockholders.

The sale of the club was consummated shortly after 11 o'clock yesterday at Fenway Park offices of the Red Sox, but was not officially announced until about 3 o'clock, at the luncheon given by Bob Quinn at the Copley-Plaza Hotel to the new owners, President Harridge of the American League, some other guests, and Boston newspapermen.

Ask Quinn to Stay

Bob Quinn was asked to retain an interest in the club, but could not see his way clear to do so. He said he had had his chance; that he had

not been able to do what he had hoped to do when he came here, and that he thought it to the best interest of those associated with him and himself to step out and give others a chance to build up a winning club.

Neither Mr. Quinn nor the new owners of the club would say anything as to the price paid for the club.

Eddie Collins is to be vice president and general manager of the club. Marty McManus is to be retained as manager, with Collins in close touch at all times with the activities of the club.

The new owners propose to start at once in strengthening the club in every way possible, and hope eventually to build up a winner. They realize that this will take time and money, but they have plenty of both. ▪

Boston being Boston, people wanted to know about Yawkey's "connections." His ancestry? Well, he was descended from "the early settlers of America who came from England and Holland." In addition to his other biographical information (born Feb. 21, 1903, in Detroit; educated at the Irving School, Yale and the Sheffield Scientific School), the people were informed that he was a member of the New York Athletic Club, the Detroit Athletic Club, the Congressional Country Club in Washington, D.C., the Sleepy Hollow Country Club and, of course, the Yale Club. Mr. Yawkey indicated that he would maintain a primary residence in, ahem, New York City.

Tom Yawkey began spending on the Red Sox in the spring of 1933 and never really stopped until his death 43 years later. During his first year his general manager Eddie

Red Sox owner Tom Yawkey in his office, 1949. (NESM/*The Boston Globe*)

Collins, who was Yawkey's certified boyhood idol, traded for or purchased 12 players, including such notables as Lefty Grove, Rube Walberg, Billy Werber, George Pipgras and the Ferrell brothers: Wes, a fine right-handed-pitcher, and Rick, a catcher who would be elected to the Hall of Fame. What cheered Boston fans most of all was the fact that Yawkey was actually buying some Yankee players, not the other way around.

The results were only partially evident in the standings. The 1933 team finished seventh, but went from a record of 43-111 the year before to 63-86 and finished substantially closer to the pennant-winning Washington Senators (34 games out) than they had to the 1932 champion Yankees (64 games in arrears). Boston Red Sox baseball had a pulse.

Things got even rosier the following year. Yawkey spent $750,000 to redo Fenway Park, which had been built in 1912 and was in need of an overhaul. He got rid of an incline in left field (the famed "Duffy's Cliff"). He replaced wood with steel and concrete. He improved the dugouts and locker rooms, even installed carpeted bat racks. He also established the left-field wall as we know it today.

Opening Day was a huge coming out party for the Yawkey regime. The Red Sox lost an 11-inning game to the Senators, but the refurbished ballpark was the new star. Gushed *The Boston Globe*, "The early comers to the park marveled at the most modern of baseball structures."

The team finished a respectable fourth at 76-76. It was the first break-even season since 1918, and attendance more than doubled to 610,640, a very impressive total by Depression standards. In just two seasons, Yawkey's combination of personal passion and a seemingly limitless pot of money had made the Red Sox a team of stature.

Yawkey's other significant move in 1934 came at the conclusion of the season with the acquisition of star shortstop Joe Cronin, obtained from Washington for shortstop Lynn Lary and $250,000. Cronin was immediately installed as the team's player-manager. He would be a Fenway fixture for three decades before assuming the presidency of the American League.

The highlight of the season came on Aug. 12, 1934, when the Red Sox paid tribute to Babe Ruth. A then record 46,766 poured into Fenway for the doubleheader, with an estimated 15,000 turned away. The fans rooted for their Sox, but they also wanted to see a farewell wallop from the Babe.

The Boston Globe • August 13, 1934

WHAT ABOUT IT?

Babe Ruth's Farewell?

Taken on his own word (and who am I to doubt it), Babe Ruth yesterday appeared for the last time at Fenway Park in the role of a regular player. The man who made baseball a double-decker proposition yesterday appeared in his valedictory game on the field where he made his major league debut.

Baseball had its share of personalities and stars before Ruth. Baseball will have its share of personalities and stars after Ruth. But baseball may never have another individual with the crowd-appeal and all-around ability of the Babe.

During his active career Ruth has had his name inscribed in the record book more often than any other player. Some of the records he still possesses will remain for some time. Eventually, perhaps, all will have been broken. But one thing with the Babe did always stick.

Babe Made Tormentors Swallow Their Words

You, perhaps remember the circumstances. The Yankees and Cubs were playing in the World Series of '32. The Babe had been the subject of ridicule from the Chicago bench since the opening pitch of the series.

It was the third game and the Yanks had won the opening pair. The scene was Wrigley Field, Chicago, and the score was tied. The Babe came up and the Cub bench renewed its verbal attack on the Sultan of Swat. "You're all through, Babe; why don't you quit?" "There's better men than you sittin' on the bench," were some of the remarks by the Cubs "jockeys."

"I'm all through, huh," replied Ruth, and waving his bat in the general direction of the center-field stands. "You watch the next pitch. If it don't go out there, then perhaps I am through."

The rest of course is history. The Babe kept his word. The next pitch landed in the exact spot that Ruth had pointed out with his bat. It broke the Cubs' hearts and enabled the N'Yorkers to stride on in to the championship. No single deed ever stood out on a baseball field as did that and more than likely none ever will.

What was more fitting for the Ruthian farewell than a record turnout of New England fans? If those who were not able to get to the park were added to those who were in, the crowd would pass all previous marks by a good 10,000. New England in general and Boston in particular loves its baseball, and methinks it loves its Ruth, too.

Don't think for one moment the crowd wouldn't have stood up and cheered if the Babe had blasted a game-winning home run during the afternoon," wrote the *Globe*'s Hy Hurwitz. "They shouted for a circuit smash every time Ruth came to bat. Twice during the afternoon the Babe was given free transportation to first and on both occasions the crowd booed."

It would be a very long time before any member of the New York Yankees would hear another kind word in Fenway.

The birth of the Boston-New York rivalry we know today took place on May 30, 1938. The Yankees were the two-time defending champs; the Red Sox were a team on the make. They had never been true competitive rivals. When the Red Sox were winning their five World Series earlier in the century, the New York team was an irrelevancy. When the Yankees were making their reputation with six American League pennants and three World Championships in the 1920s, the Red Sox were a pitiful cellar dweller.

But now, for the first time since the Yankee dynasty had begun, the Red Sox were a threat. The 1938 Red Sox were good and they wanted the Yankees to know it. The fans in New York certainly sensed the shift, for on this Memorial Day afternoon a crowd of 82,990 came to Yankee Stadium for a showdown doubleheader with the revived Red Sox.

The Yankees were leading the first game by a 7-0 score in the fourth when Boston reliever Archie McKain nearly beaned Yankee left-fielder Jake Powell, who had been similarly dusted off by fallen starter Lefty Grove the previous inning. When McKain did succeed in hitting Powell on the thigh, the angered Yankee headed not to first base, but toward the mound, where he and McKain locked arms.

At this point manager Cronin came charging in from his shortstop position, pushing McKain out of the way, and, according to the *Globe*'s Gerry Moore, began "swinging on Powell, almost in one motion." The fight was broken up by a combination of players and umpires, and the combatants were ejected from the game. Unfortunately, no one thought it necessary to accompany Cronin and Powell to their respective locker rooms.

When Cronin entered the runway leading to the clubhouses, Powell was waiting. They exchanged words and then began throwing more punches. Before the umpires could make their way in from the field to break up Round 2, Cronin was bleeding from some facial wounds. Said Red Sox coach Herb Pennock, "Joe had several gouges on his face that didn't come from punches and the best information I could gather was that he had a headlock on Powell and was about to give him the business when a bunch of Yankees pulled Joe off and somebody grabbed his face in the process."

The modern Red Sox-Yankee era had begun.

Another way to look at it, of course, was that the era of the Great Tease for the Red Sox had also begun. That 1938 team did finish second to the Yankees. According to information furnished by the Elias Sports Bureau, they split the season's series at 11-11 (their record against the Yankees for the first five years of Yawkey's tenure was 41-78). But they still wound up nine games out. The following season was even more aggravating. This time the Red Sox actually won the season's series at 11-8, with one tie and two cancellations. But

the Yankees won the 1939 pennant by a discouraging 17 games. Historians now rank the '39 Yankees among the handful of greatest teams ever. No one cares that the Red Sox had actually improved by a game in the victory column from the year before (89-88).

But 1939 was a very significant year in Red Sox history, as well as Red Sox-Yankee history. For in that season Ted Williams became a member of the team.

Theodore Samuel Williams. Teddy Ballgame. The Splendid Splinter. The Kid. The Thumper. He would become more than just a great baseball player. He would become the walking, talking symbol of the perceived difference between the Red Sox and the Yankees. He would win his batting crowns and his Triple Crowns and his slugging percentage titles and his on-base percentage titles (not that anyone paid much attention to such a thing during his time), but he would only be on one pennant-winning team in 19 full seasons spanning 22 calendar years and he would never play on a World Series winner.

Of course, neither has any other Red Sox player in the last 86 years. Unless he did it with another ball club.

There must be some sort of irony involved in the fact that Ted Williams's first hit came in Yankee Stadium. An injury had delayed his major league debut. But he was ready to play by April 20, and on that afternoon in 1939 Cronin put him in the lineup. He struck out his first two times up against the crafty Red Ruffing, but on his third attempt he saw a pitch he liked and gave it a ride. According to the *Globe*, "Ted poled a slashing drive that caromed off the right center-field fence about 400 feet from where the drive originated. It was good for a double and Ted's initial big-

league wallop, and it would have given the Sox a run if [Joe] DiMaggio hadn't robbed [Jim] Tabor just one pitch previously."

It was the first of 2,654 hits, and the first of 1,117 extra-base hits. It was the beginning of a career that would end with Williams hitting a dramatic home run in his final at-bat 21 years later, and which would end with Williams (and many others) believing he had been the greatest hitter of all time. And for all those 22 seasons, even when Ted would be far away from Boston, he would be the town's living soap opera.

He had joined a good ball club. The first

baseman was future Hall of Famer Jimmie Foxx, one year removed from a 50-homer, 175-RBI season (both still Red Sox records). The second baseman was Hall of Famer Bobby Doerr, who, like Williams, had grown up in San Diego. The shortstop was Cronin, another Hall of Famer. The third baseman was Jim Tabor, who would hit 14 homers that year while driving in 95. The leftfielder was Joe Vosmik, a solid player. The center fielder was Doc Cramer, who compiled 2,705 lifetime hits. Williams was in right. The only undistinguished regulars were the catchers, Johnny Peacock and Gene Desautels.

The pitching was the problem. Lefty Grove, no longer a flamethrower, won 15, but no one else won more than 11. It would be, with few exceptions, the recurrent theme of the entire Ted Williams era.

As great a season as 1939 was for the Yankees, there was still a moment of satisfaction for the Red Sox. The Sox put it all together in July, smashing the A's in a July 4 doubleheader by scores of 17-7 and 18-12 before arriving in New York for a five-game series. To the astonishment of everyone in baseball, they won them all by scores of 4-3, 3-1, 3-2, 4-3 and 5-3. Joe Cronin went to his grave saying it was one of his proudest moments.

With any pitching at all, Williams might have had a shot at his elusive championship the following year. The Yankees, by their lofty standards, had an off year, winning 18 fewer games than in 1939 (106-88), but still finishing a solid third, two games out. But the Red Sox didn't have a pitcher with more than 12 victories, and it was Detroit that took advantage of New York's fall. The Red Sox scored a league-leading 872 runs, but their pitchers surrendered 825, a figure exceeded only by the bottom-feeding Browns and Athletics.

Yawkey himself had something to do with his team's powerful offense. After the 1939 season he ordered the construction of new bullpens in right field. They were nicknamed "Williamsburg," the idea being that the shorter distance to the fence would benefit his left-handed slugger, who had hit 31 homers as a rookie in 1939. But although his batting average went from .327 to .344, the Kid's home run production dropped to 22 and his runs batted in fell from 145 to 113. But his runs scored increased from 131 to 134, so someone had to be driving him in.

The Yankees returned to their normal state in 1941, and the Red Sox did, too, finishing second to the Bronx Bombers by 17 games. New York won again in '42, this time by nine games. The Red Sox never really threatened anyone for the remainder of the war.

Everything changed in 1946. Everyone in baseball was welcoming back their stars from service duty, but the Red Sox made it an even happier occasion for their fans by making a major deal, acquiring slugging first baseman Rudy York from the Tigers for wartime shortstop Eddie Lake, who was not going to be needed with Johnny Pesky ready to reclaim his job. Pesky had broken into baseball by knocking out more than 200 hits in 1942, and he was ready to resume his post as table-setter extraordinaire. York, a rather classic good-hit, no-field masher who was least harmful to the cause with a first baseman's mitt on his hand, would drive in 119 runs for the '46 Sox.

The Red Sox started fast, and by Memorial Day the only question was when the pennant clincher would be. The answer was: September 13. The Sox beat Cleveland, 1-0, when Ted Williams beat Lou Boudreau's "Williams Shift" with the only inside-the-park homer of his career, an opposite field poke to left.

The Yankees were never a factor. They finished third and went through three managers. Detroit was never a factor. Cleveland was never a factor. No one was a factor. The Red Sox won 105 games and would have won a lot more if they hadn't gone into cruise gear after clinching the pennant with two and a half weeks to go.

This was one Red Sox team that had some pitching. The starting rotation of Boo Ferris,

Tex Hughson, Mickey Harris and Joe Dobson were a combined 77-33. That'll get it done. And the Red Sox hitting was its usual robust stuff. Dominic DiMaggio and Pesky combined for 367 hits and 200 runs scored at the top of the order. Doerr drove in 116 runs. Ted checked in with .342, 38 and 123 numbers. He also had a dazzling All-Star game, going 4-for-4 with two home runs as the American League spanked the National League, 12-0, at Fenway Park.

The strangest occurrence was a decision by Cleveland player-manager Lou Boudreau to implement a radical shift on Williams for the second game of a doubleheader on July 14. By way of background, Williams had hit three home runs and driven in eight in the first game. When Ted came up with no one on in the second game, this is what he saw: the first baseman and rightfielder were standing on the right-field foul line; the second baseman was about 25 feet out on the grass and perhaps 15 feet from the foul line; the shortstop was where the second baseman would normally be; the centerfielder was essentially playing right field; and the leftfielder was in short left-center field, about 30 feet beyond the infield. Finally, the third baseman was playing shortstop.

Williams took the bait, refusing to try hitting to the opposite field. He grounded out to second. In his final two appearances that day, he walked.

This pretty much positions Ted Williams among all other hitters of his era. There were better fielders, throwers and runners in the game. But Ted Williams was the game's most feared and respected hitter. The only problem was that by the time the World Series began on October 6 he was not among the healthiest.

Much has been written and said about the fact that Ted Williams was 5-for-20 with no extra-base hits as the Red Sox lost the 1946 World Series to the St. Louis Cardinals in seven games, but for some reason most accounts ignore that fact that Ted Williams played the entire series with a badly swollen right elbow.

While the Red Sox had romped home in the American League, the National League had seen a right proper pennant race involving the Brooklyn Dodgers and St. Louis Cardinals. These two were tied after 154 games, necessitating a three-game playoff for the pennant. The Red Sox, who had played poorly after clinching so early, were in need of some competition and it was very much the custom of the day to think in terms of arranging a little series against some stray American League All-Stars (including Joe DiMaggio himself) in order to keep the team sharp.

So it was, that before 1,996 fans shivering in Fenway on a raw October day, Mickey Haeffner, a veteran left-hander, hit Ted Williams on the right elbow during his third at-bat of the game. It turned out to be more than a little owie.

The rest of the series was called off.

The Red Sox lost that World Series in seven games, and in 1947 the Yankees returned to show the Red Sox how to win. The Red Sox didn't know it, but the worst was yet to come. In Jolsonesque terms, they hadn't seen nuthin' yet.

New York didn't have much to do with Red Sox angst in 1948, unless you count a 17-inning tie game—in spring training. This time the party of the second part was Cleveland, which defeated the Red Sox by an 8-3 score in a one-game playoff for the American League

Ted Williams (right) and Red Sox general manager Joe Cronin after signing Williams's 1950 contract for more than $100,000. Williams, an avid fisherman, is dressed in the outfit he wore while giving fly casting demonstrations at a local sportsman's show. (Associated Press)

pennant. The great issue coming out of that game was the identity of Boston's starting pitcher. With several more viable options available, manager Joe McCarthy called upon journeyman Denny Galehouse. Boudreau went 4-for-4 with two homers, which he might have done against anyone. But probably not. The Yankees were a voyeuristic third.

The Red Sox-Yankee thing took on new overtones in 1949. First of all, DiMaggio missed the first 65 games of the season with a heel spur. So where did he make his return? Fenway Park. And what did he do? He hit four home runs in three days and led the Yankees to a three-game sweep.

It all came to a head on the final weekend of the season. The Red Sox led New York by one game entering a two-game series in New York. The Red Sox needed one victory. The Yankees needed two. Yankee manager Casey Stengel remained confident. Addressing his team prior to the game, Stengel said, "Boys, did you ever win a doubleheader? Did you

ever win two in a row? Well, now's the time to do it.—man to man. We've done it before. Let's do it again."

It was brave talk, but his team had lost six of its previous nine. Any momentum involved belonged to the Red Sox.

As if the Yankees needed any extra emotional edge, they had thoughtfully made the 153rd game of the season "Joe DiMaggio Day." The Yankee Clipper was hobbling with that bad heel, and his participation in the game was in some doubt, but that was all forgotten after the speeches were made and the gifts extended. Joe D was ready to play.

The Red Sox gave 25-game winner Mel Parnell a 4-0 lead, but he could not hold it. Stengel turned the game over to reliever Joe Page, who shut out the Red Sox for the last six-plus innings and when Johnny Lindell hit an eighth-inning homer off Joe Dobson New York had won, 5-4, and it was now a one-game season.

McCarthy had another 25-game winner to

Captain Ted Williams boards his plane in 1952, just when the World Series is opening in New York. Williams did not fight during World War II because he was considered too talented a flyer, so he taught others. But he was called up in 1952 for a tour of duty in Korea. (Associated Press)

pitch the final game. Ellis Kinder had not been beaten in 20 starts, and was 5-0 against the Yankees during his two seasons with the Red Sox. But Ellis Kinder had also pitched in four of the previous seven games, three times being used in relief. New York's Vic Raschi, himself a 20-game winner (21-10), was rested and ready for New York.

Two inches. Two teeny-weeny inches. That, according to the *Globe*'s Hy Hurwitz, is how far away Al Zarilla was from keeping the Yankees scoreless in the eighth inning of game number 154. Two inches more and the Boston rightfielder, who had been identified coming into the game as having played the last week with a very sore back, would have caught a little two-out blooper by Gerry Coleman. Two inches more and the blooper would have been an inning-ending fly to right—and not a game and pennant-winning three-run double. As

Sox, refused to tip his hat to the crowd throughout the game.

"An individual to the end," a fan said in admiration.

Williams made his last official appearance as the Sox stellar attraction in the top of the ninth inning. He had just slugged a homer in the top of the eighth. Even then, when the crowd of more than 10,000 gave him a lengthy standing ovation, Williams refused to tip his cap, a player's traditional acknowledgment to the public.

No one expected him on the field again, and when he did appear in the ninth, the fans jumped up and waited. "Mike Higgins must of put him in just to give him a last chance to tip his cap," a burly fan observed. "I sure would of liked to have seen him do it but, then, I didn't expect he would."

A lot of the fans said they'd like Williams to play a few more years.

"He's only 42, and if he stayed on another year, he would beat Foxx' record," said Lou Weinstein of Mattapan.

Miss Alice F. Soper, 85, of 109 Peterborough St., a baseball fan since 1906, said the Sox "won't be the same without Ted. If Babe Ruth played in the years Williams did, Ted would have beat him, too. They didn't have to work as hard, then."

"A couple of good Ted-Sox," showed up yesterday from Warwick, Rhode Island. They were Mrs. Alroy Cooper and Mrs. Albert Hayes. "We love Ted, and our husbands don't mind," one of them said.

Both have watched Ted and the Sox at Winter training days in Sarasota. "He's a great self-disciplinarian," Mrs. Hayes said. "When the other players would be loafing under trees, Williams was running himself ragged to keep in trim. He would be a great general manager."

Everyone hoped Williams would get a homer yesterday. Said Joseph Day of Waltham—a fan—"They ought to feed him one [a homer] today." Then, as an afterthought, loyally, "He'll get one anyway."

Mr. And Mrs. Dan O'Dea of Lowell said, "We came yesterday because of him. He's in a class by himself. A character like all great athletes are," O'Dea mused. "I saw him the first day he played here 21 years ago and I came today to see him play his last."

Another one who has stood by Ted from start to finish was Mrs. Eddie Collins of Brookline, who sat just behind the dugout. Mrs. Collins is the widow of baseball's Hall of Fame Collins, who as general manager of the Sox personally scouted Williams. "My husband brought him here, and I'm going to see him off."

And Judge Emil Fuchs of Boston, who was president of the Boston Braves when Babe Ruth ended his career, said: "Everything good that was said here today about Ted was true. He is sort of a supernatural power."

And a supreme compliment came from an unexpected source—the umpire. Said Cal Hubbard, head of the American League umpires, "We never had to call any on Williams. If they were good he hit them." ▪

A significant part of the Tom Yawkey legacy was his sorry attitude on the subject of race. It is the eternal shame of the Boston Red Sox that they were the last of the existing 16 major league teams to integrate their lineup, not doing so until 12 full years after Jackie Robinson broke in with the Brooklyn Dodgers.

Yawkey was not a Southerner by birth, but

Pumpsie Green *(right)* was the first African-American to play in the major leagues for the Red Sox, in 1959. Earl Wilson is on the left. (Leslie Jones Collection/Boston Public Library) he had adopted early a 1950s traditional Southern sensibility, shall we say, by virtue of a longtime residence on rural property he owned in South Carolina. His apparent attitude toward racial matters was one of benign neglect, at best. Meanwhile, he was open to the charge of guilt by association, since he insisted on employing as both manager and general manager Mike ("Pinky") Higgins, a former drinking buddy (Yawkey would even-

tually renounce alcohol) who made no secret of his contempt for blacks.

Amazingly, the Red Sox were the first major league team to take an official look at Jackie Robinson. On April 16, 1945, Red Sox coaches Hugh Duffy and Larry Woodall held a "tryout" at Fenway Park for Robinson, Sam Jethroe and Marvin Williams. This historic event merited a mere three paragraphs in the morning *Boston Globe*, which referred to them

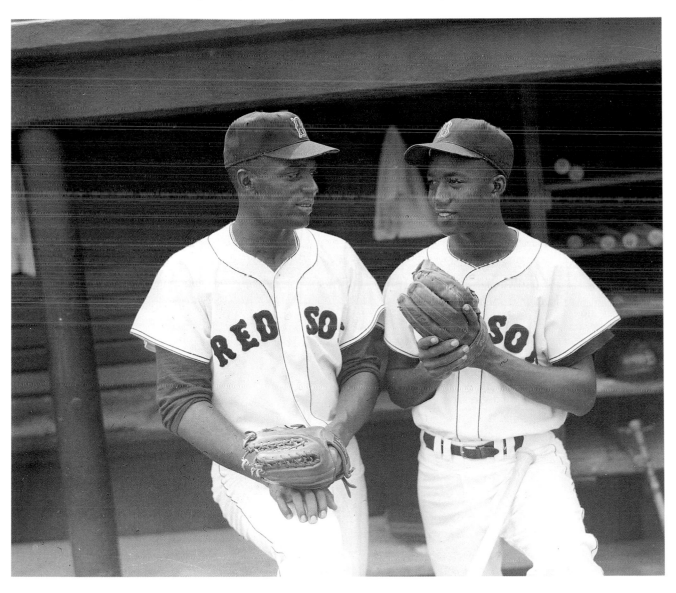

as "three hustling Negro players, all eager for a big league tryout."

"Pretty good ballplayers," declared Duffy. A long unsubstantiated story maintains that a voice was heard screaming, "Get those (N-words) off the field!" during the tryout.

The Boston Globe • April 17, 1945

THREE NEGROES GIVEN WORKOUT BY RED SOX

By the Associated Press

Something new was written in Boston baseball history today when the Red Sox gave workout to three Negro baseball players—aspirants to big league berths.

Jackie Robinson of Pasadena, California, former U.C.L.A. football and baseball star; Sam Jethroe of Erie, Pennsylvania, 1944 Negro American League batting champion, and Marvin Williams of Philadelphia Stars of the Negro National League, were watched by Red Sox Manager, Joe Cronin and his coaches.

Jethroe is an outfielder for the Cleveland Buckeyes.

Cronin exhibited interest in the work of Robinson, a former Army lieutenant who was 31 months in service, now a shortstop for the Kansas City Monarchs of the Negro-American League. Coach Hugh Duffy commented that Williams seemed to be a good ball player, that he was fast and had possibilities.

All three were given the customary forms in which to enter their athletic history and background.

They were brought to Fenway Park—where they worked out with other aspirants—by Boston City Councilman Isadore Muchnick and Wendell Smith, sports editor of the *Pittsburgh Courier*, which sponsored the players' trip to Boston.

They reported to General Manager Eddie Collins, who immediately sent them to the dressing rooms to be issued uniforms for their history-making tryout. Muchnick argued that the American game should conform with the tradition of democracy and that Negro baseball players should have equality of opportunity. His comments drew a response from the Red Sox that no Negro had ever sought a place on the team.

A few years later the team matched their judgment on Robinson's skills when a Red Sox scout dismissed a young Birmingham Black Barons player by the name of Willie Mays as incapable of playing major-league ball.

And so the Red Sox drifted through the rest of the 1940s and most of the 1950s as an all-white team until, on July 21, 1959, they recalled a 24-year-old Negro infielder Elijah (Pumpsie) Green from their Minneapolis affiliate, and he entered that night's game against the White Sox as a pinch runner in the eighth inning, remaining at shortstop in the ninth.

The Red Sox had finally broken the color barrier.

What they had not done, however, was eradicate the team culture. The perception that the Red Sox were a troublesome place for athletes of color lasted as long as Yawkey was alive (he died in 1976), and right into the mid-1990s. Not until Dan Duquette took over as the team's general manager in 1995 were the Red Sox able to convince anyone that they truly had a color-blind organization.

The Red Sox flopped around in the immediate post-Ted years. The new marquee player was future Hall of Famer Carl Yastrzemski, who just happened to be a leftfielder. But he was no Ted at the start, and the Red Sox were not much of a team, finishing no higher than sixth between 1961 and 1966 and seeing their attendance fall as low as 652,201 in 1965.

The Yankees, of course, just kept rolling on, the only difference being that they didn't happen to win every World Series they played in. But they did manage to win everything in 1956, 1958, 1961 and 1962. And don't think Red Sox fans didn't notice. As the Yawkey stewardship reached its 33rd anniversary in 1966, the attitude of the typical Red Sox fan was "My favorite team is the Red Sox, and my second favorite team is whoever's playing the Yankees."

CHAPTER FOUR

The Clipper and the Kid

by George Vecsey of The New York Times

Babe Ruth's gargantuan success in New York was not immediately codified into myth and legend and Curse, nor was it bandied about as an excuse for the Yankees' superiority.

In those ancient days, there was far less psychobabble and rehashed history and gaping space in the press and air waves to be filled by assorted yakkers and pundits than there is today.

Nevertheless, things were happening between these two old northeastern cities. In the years when Joe DiMaggio's Yankees were generally beating up on Ted Williams's Red Sox, fans in New England were not exactly going, "Oh, boo-hoo, those dastardly Yankees have our number because the Sox sold Babe Ruth."

It takes time to create a rivalry—years, even decades. And New England fans were storing up enough resentments to set up the true hostilities that would emerge later in the century.

Back then, there was a soft underbelly of the American League, consisting of all seven existing teams. The Yankees were equal-opportunity tormentors, and Sawx fans were only beginning to enter the solipsistic stage of taking it personally when the Yankees belted the whey out of the American League.

The rivalry soon became centered not on the transfer of Babe Ruth but on the presence of two superb sluggers, Joe DiMaggio and Ted Williams. For nine unforgettable seasons, they staged a head-to-head competition that still smolders and sizzles.

The two stars even came to personify their respective teams. DiMaggio was icy near-perfection and Williams was flaming imperfection. At least that was the perception, hardened now into stereotype.

The Yankees were star-driven but always an organization, intent on winning. The Red Sox were dominated by their stars, who remained close into old age, yet the team itself was characterized as "25 players, 25 cabs," rushing off individually toward second place.

The DiMaggio-Williams years arrived only a few ticks of the clock after Babe Ruth was pushed out after 1934. This meant that Lou Gehrig, the underpaid and overly loyal captain, was the resident superstar for exactly one year.

In 1935, the Yankees finished second to Detroit, as Gehrig had a perfectly normal season, for him, of a .329 batting average and 30 homers and 119 runs batted in. The Red Sox finished, as they almost always did, well behind the Yankees, in fourth place.

There was never a Lou Gehrig Era. The next year the Yankees had a brand-new toy, a sleek, quiet, outfielder from San Francisco, who excited fans' passions just by arriving.

Joseph Paul DiMaggio was a mixture of grace and mystery, recognized, almost immediately, as the complete player, with all the tools on offense and defense. He took over center field in short time and roamed the vast reaches of Yankee Stadium.

It was too soon in history for everybody to say, "Ugh, the Yankees have done it again," as people eventually would say as the Yankees produced or acquired Berra, Ford, Mantle, Maris, Guidry, Jackson, Mattingly, Jeter and Rivera in decades to come.

Back then, the concept of Yankee Luck, or Yankee Diligence, was only just materializing in front of everybody's eyes.

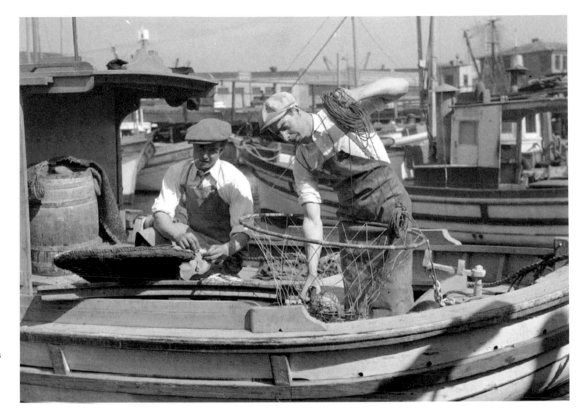

Joe DiMaggio visits his brother Mike *(left)*, on the family fishing boat in San Francisco after his rookie season with the Yankees in 1936. (Associated Press)

DiMaggio caught everybody's attention in 1936 by batting .323 with 29 homers and 125 runs batted in, one of the great rookie seasons in baseball history.

Baseball fans fell in love with him. He was long and graceful, like an El Greco painting, with elongated lines and an inchoate sense of spirituality that existed in people's minds, at least as long as he kept his thoughts to himself.

The child of Sicilian immigrants in the fishing community of San Francisco, DiMaggio dropped out of high school after one year and retained an outsider's suspicion of the world in general. He understood the rapacity of Yankee management better than Ruth and Gehrig had, and was prepared to combat it with stubbornness and cunning.

In that far-ago time, before free agency and agent negotiators, DiMaggio caused himself public grief by demanding more money. His demands were construed as acts of blatant disloyalty by the ruthless Yankee front office and the pliant press.

Quickly, however, DiMaggio made people forget his salary squabbles as he ran down 450-foot drives in Death Valley of left-center field in Yankee Stadium, and whacked extra-base hits to all corners.

The Yankees promptly ran the table with four straight pennants and four straight World Series, the first time that had ever been done. The stolid Gehrig produced another monster season of .351 with 37 homers and 159 RBI in 1937, but DiMaggio was the hot ticket now.

This was eons before DiMaggio became famous as the man who sent roses to Marilyn Monroe's grave. But somehow it was all of a continuum. Even before DiMaggio was fabled for being the wounded lover of an imperfect goddess, he had that aura to him.

DiMaggio accepted all forms of adulation. Women had a defined place in his life—in his hotel suite. And his coterie of male devotees—somewhere between valets and friends—were good for praising him as well as drinking, eating, smoking, chatting, performing errands and services, watching boxing matches and generally passing the hours.

He was Joe DiMaggio, aka the Yankee Clipper, and this was how, in the late 1930s, he was supposed to live his life, halfway between the publicly crude Ruth and the privately abstemious Gehrig. He commanded the awe of that allegedly sophisticated and complex city: New York. He was blending the personas of the first two great Yankees, creating the enduring aura of the Yankees—haughty, successful, entitled.

The Red Sox, meanwhile, finished sixth in 1936, fifth in 1937 and a distant second in 1938. But in 1939, they brought up their own Californian, Theodore Samuel Williams. This guy was even more lean than DiMaggio—the alliteration-minded sportswriters called him the Splendid Splinter—and he was left-handed, whereas DiMaggio was right-handed, and he was tempestuous whereas DiMaggio was shy, and he came from sunny San Diego rather than nippy San Francisco.

The DiMaggio-Williams rivalry was not Boston against New York, or Athens against Sparta. It was a personal duel that would endure for nine full seasons—and persist to the painful ends of both lives.

They were well-matched from the moment Williams arrived, skinny and raw, but with a marvelous swing that made some of the older Red Sox outfielders brood where they might be playing next.

Williams came along a few months before Gehrig retired in June, stricken with the fatal illness that would soon bear his name. DiMaggio led the league in hitting with .381 while the new kid up in Boston led the league in RBI with 145. The game was on.

Their temperaments were their own, shaped by their personal histories and the regions where they played.

When DiMaggio sulked or became haughty—and he did, early and often—New York fans and writers took this as a sign of majesty, befitting the greatest city in the history of humankind.

When Williams brooded or blew his top—which was known to happen—this was taken as bad manners in Boston, and he was publicly spanked for violating the city's prickly high standards.

There was no great baseball antipathy between the two cities since Detroit and Cleveland had better and more consistent teams than Boston did. And the two cities had no reason to be jealous or scornful of each other.

Many New Yorkers who have sampled the best of Boston (Harvard, a weekend in the fall, jogging along the Charles River, the Boston Symphony, zabaglione in the North End) suspect they could be quite happy as Bostonians. And many Bostonians who come to New York suspect they have the wits to survive quite nicely in that vertical jungle—that is, if they wanted to leave their quaint city of hills and water and history. There are no Woody Allen-style jibes at Beantown as there are at L.A.

No, it was more a rivalry between the Yankee Clipper (stately sailing vessel) and the Kid (terrible-tempered juvenile). And what a time it was.

Fans debated their relative merits in 1940 as Williams followed with a second season of .344 while DiMaggio once again led the league, this time at .352. The impending war cast a pall on this potential golden age between two great young players, as Detroit won the pennant and the Yankees finished third, once again ahead of the Red Sox, who finished fourth.

Then came the landmark season of 1941, during which poor Gehrig died and DiMaggio hit in 56 consecutive games, one of the great feats in baseball history. Reams have been written about the streak itself, the pressures and the late-inning hits, the scrambling defense by Ken Keltner, the Cleveland third baseman, who finally stopped DiMaggio, the awed tribute by the Yankee teammates when it was finally over. Everybody knew they were witnessing one of the great runs ever by a man in baseball flannels.

The New York Times — July 18, 1941

DIMAGGIO'S STREAK ENDED AT 56 GAMES, BUT YANKS DOWN INDIANS BEFORE 67,468

Smith and Bagby Stop Yankee Star

DiMaggio, Up for Last Time in Eighth, Hits Into a Double Play With Bases Full

By John Drebinger
Special to The New York Times

Cleveland, July 17—In a brilliant setting of lights and before 67,468 fans, the largest crowd ever to see a game of night baseball in the major leagues, the Yankees tonight vanquished the Indians, 4 to 3, but the famous hitting streak of Joe DiMaggio finally came to an end.

Officially it will go into the records as fifty-six consecutive games, the total he reached yesterday. Tonight in Cleveland's municipal stadium the great DiMag was held hitless for the first time in more than two months.

Al Smith, veteran Cleveland left-hander and a Giant cast-off, and Jim Bagby, a young right-hander, collaborated in bringing the DiMaggio string to a close.

Jolting Joe faced Smith three times. Twice he smashed the ball down the third-base line, but each time Ken Keltner, Tribe third sacker, collared the ball and hurled it across the diamond for a put-out at first. In between these two tries, DiMaggio drew a pass from Smith.

Then, in the eighth, amid a deafening uproar, the streak dramatically ended, though the Yanks routed Smith with a flurry of four hits and two runs that eventually won the game.

Double Play Seals Record

With the bases full and only one out Bagby faced DiMaggio and, with the count of one ball and one strike, induced the renowned slugger to crash into a double play. It was a grounder to the shortstop, and as the ball flitted from Lou Boudreau to Ray Mack to Oscar Grimes, who played first base for the Tribe, the crowd knew the streak was over.

However, there were still a few thrills to come, for in the ninth, with the Yanks leading 4 to 1, the Indians suddenly broke loose with an attack that for a few moments threatened to send the game into extra innings and thus give DiMaggio another chance.

Gerald Walker and Grimes singled, and, though Johnny Murphy here replaced Gomez, Larry Rosenthal tripled to score his two colleagues. But with the tying run on third and nobody out the Cleveland attack bogged down in a mess of bad base-running and the Yanks' remaining one-run lead held, though it meant the end of the streak for DiMaggio, who might have come up fourth had there been a tenth inning.

Started May 15

It was on May 15 against the White Sox at the Yankee Stadium that DiMaggio began his string, which in time was to gain nationwide attention. As the great DiMag kept clicking in game after game, going into the twenties, then the thirties, he became the central figure of the baseball world.

On June 29, in a double-header with the Senators in Washington, he tied, then surpassed the American League and modern record of forty-one games set by George Sisler of the Browns in 1922. The next target was the all-time major league high of forty-four contests set by Willie Keeler, famous Oriole star, forty-four years ago under conditions much easier then for a batsman than they are today. Then there was no foul-strike rule hampering the batter.

But nothing hampered DiMaggio as he kept getting his daily hits, and on July 1 he tied the Keeler mark. The following day he soared past it for game No. 45, and he kept on soaring until tonight. In seeking his fifty-seventh game, he finally was brought to a halt.

Actually, DiMaggio hit in fifty-seven consecutive games for on July 8 he connected safely in the All-Star game in Detroit. But that contest did not count in the official league records.

. . .

In that very same season, Williams went into a doubleheader on the final Sunday with an average of .39955, which would have been rounded out to .400 but did not have the ring of .400 to it, and Williams knew it. To his everlasting credit, Williams refused to sit it out, but instead blasted six hits in eight at-bats (all right, it was against the depleted Philadelphia Athletics) to finish with a .406 average.

For both young men—DiMaggio was 26 that summer, Williams would turn 23—this would be their signature season, simultaneously.

There was a complication in the contrast between the two sluggers. In 1940, Joe's youngest brother, Dominic, small and bespectacled and dubbed the Little Professor, became ensconced as the Sox' center fielder. Loyalists in Fenway Park would sing a ditty to the tune of "O Tannenbaum":

"He's better than his brother Joe,
Dominic DiMaggio."

Apparently, the ever-sensitive Joe DiMaggio took offense to the Red Sox fans' chant. The DiMaggio boys had their own familial dysfunction, which only emerged publicly in Joe's later years. During their careers, whenever photographers could arrange a photograph with Williams and Joe D and Dominic, the odd trio, there were often interesting studies in body language: Joe D would be staring obliquely into space in one plane, while Williams would be looking off into another sector of the wild blue yonder, and Dominic would be smiling opaquely, often in the middle. There were plenty of stories of the two brothers fraternally going off for dinner when the two teams met, but their true feelings were somewhat more murky.

According to legend, during the crucial

The trio of American sluggers: Joe DiMaggio, Ted Williams and Dom DiMaggio in 1942. (*The New York Times*)

stages of Joe D's streak in 1941, Williams would get an update from the keeper of the scoreboard in left field and would shout the news to "Dommy" in center field.

Years later, the hypersensitive Joe suggested that something in Dominic's voice had convinced him his kid brother wished the whole streak would come to an end quickly. But nothing like that ever came out in their playing days.

The two sluggers would always be judged on the basis of this prewar flash. Their stereotypes and their rivalry were set in motion.

In the old western movies, you never had to guess which cowboy was going to ride off into the sunset—or stick around and marry the leading lady. It was the cowboy in the white hat.

DiMaggio played that role in this melodrama because, despite his many injuries (Yankee history is chockfull of gloom and doom and sore heels), DiMaggio came off as the strong, silent type. Gary Cooper, a "yup" and "nope" type, played the doomed Lou Gehrig in the movie *The Pride of the Yankees*, but he also could have portrayed Joe DiMaggio if that film had ever been made. (Who would have played Marilyn Monroe is another question.)

Williams was a more cantankerous, flawed type, who, in the cowboy vernacular, shot himself in the foot with his feuds with the fans and his frequent tirades. In later life he would be compared, usually favorably, to the cinematic hero John Wayne—the difference being that Williams had actually performed war heroics.

However, in the baseball business, Williams was sometimes cast as second banana to Joe D, which steamed him no end.

Williams, who would rarely swing at a pitch off the plate, even if the Sox needed a runner driven home, saw himself the protector of a pure art, hitting only strikes and only to right field. He wanted to be judged as the greatest hitter of all time. Why bring up all this business of fielding and baserunning and pennants?

The two stars were different enough that many fans could appreciate the existence of both. But you know how that works. Each man felt there was room for only one at the top of the mountain.

There were grievances on both sides. In 1940, DiMaggio had been hitting .408 with a month to go, but came down with an infection in his left eye, the forward eye in his batting stance. The Yankees were way ahead in the pennant race, but Manager Joe McCarthy did not rest him, and DiMaggio's average fell all the way to .381, still enough to lead the league.

Decades later, when people gave Williams respect for hitting .406, DiMaggio would mutter that he could have done it if McCarthy had rested him.

The fading clips in the Baseball Hall of Fame in Cooperstown, New York, contain evidence of the sly little digs between DiMaggio and Williams.

"He throws like a broad, and he runs like a ruptured duck," DiMaggio was quoted as saying to one of his supportive writers in New York.

DiMaggio also once said, "Sure, he can hit. But he never won a thing."

In his book, *Joe DiMaggio: The Hero's Life*, Richard Ben Cramer quotes DiMaggio as telling Lou Effrat, a friendly reporter from *The New York Times*: "He may out-homer me, but I will out-percentage him, I can out-throw him, and out-think him."

Williams was publicly gracious when DiMaggio got the MVP in 1941, saying, "It took the Big Guy to beat me."

In later years, Williams often said, "I believe there isn't a record in the books that will be harder to break than Joe's 56 games. It may be the greatest batting achievement of all." How gracious—from a man who batted .406.

However, the Yankees won the 1941 pennant and beat the Brooklyn Dodgers in the World Series while the Red Sox finished another of their distant seconds, 17 full games behind the Yankees.

DiMaggio was voted the Most Valuable Player, which he accepted with the same diffidence that he would accept being led to the best table in a crowded restaurant or having somebody introduce him to a beautiful woman. It was his right.

The following year, with war already blazing in Europe and Asia, Williams hit for the Triple Crown—leading the league in the three prominent categories, something DiMaggio never did. But the Yankees won the pennant again, and DiMaggio was MVP again.

From 1943 through 1945, the rivalry was suspended as both men enlisted into the service. DiMaggio's admirers made sure there was a baseball uniform waiting for him in secure Army bases. He was hardly the only ballplayer who spent the war chasing the white ball; the spectacle was thought to be good for morale.

Williams was goaded by the press until he signed up for the Naval Air Corps Reserves. His eyesight had been graded at 20/10 by civilian doctors, but, by the more demanding military standards, he tested higher than any potential pilot who had ever come along. Any baseball umpire could have told you that. Williams was deemed too great a flyer to be sent into combat, and became a teacher of other lesser flyers.

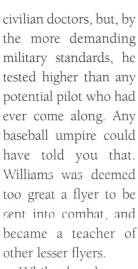

Staff Sergeant Joe DiMaggio visits New York in 1944. During the war he joined the Army Air Force. (Associated Press)

While the sluggers were away, the Yankees finished first, third and fourth, while the Red Sox finished seventh, fourth and seventh.

Then came the season of 1946, when all the survivors were home from the war. DiMaggio had a lackluster season whereas Williams responded with a superlative .342-38-123 season. Not only that, but the Red Sox won the pennant, finishing 17 games ahead of the third-place Yankees, who went through three managers.

In 1946, it was time for Williams and Dominic DiMaggio to have their first crack at a World Series. Was there any vindication? No way. Williams was clipped on the right elbow in a tune-up game before the World Series, and had a highly unproductive batting average of .200 as the Red Sox lost to the Cardinals in seven games.

Years later, Ed Linn, in his biography, *Hitter: The Life and Turmoils of Ted Williams,* described the chest cold or flu that seemed to strike Williams every fall, and how Williams had been taking antibiotics during that World Series. Williams never mentioned the illness at the time, but for the rest of his life his weak performance in 1946 would be held against him.

In 1946, the Red Sox had reason to feel they were on their way to some kind of post-war dynasty, but always there are the Yankees.

The Yankees did not have rivalries, did not need them. It was up to the common people to have such earthy ways. Yankee fans tended to respect Williams when he came to Yankee Stadium. In fact, he was booed far more in Fenway than in the Bronx.

Even though the two stars came to represent their franchises, there was often baseball scuttlebutt about trading the two of them.

It was almost a laboratory exercise. How would DiMaggio do taking dead aim at the Green Monster in left field of Fenway Park? And how would Williams do with the short porch in right field at Yankee Stadium? In reality, the two men never showed much power in their rival's home park—but what would happen if they had an entire 77-game home schedule to refine their strokes?

Apparently, the subject intrigued the two owners of the clubs, Tom Yawkey of the Red Sox and Dan Topping of the Yankees, as they drank together at Toots Shor's late on an April night in 1947. They may even have agreed on a trade. Things that happened late at night at Shor's tended to be blurry.

The next morning, Yawkey called Topping, who asked, "Do we have a deal?" Yawkey said

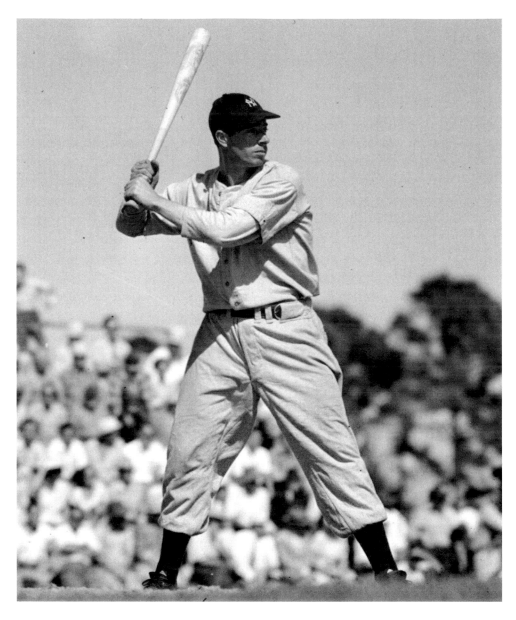

Joe DiMaggio stands at bat in an exhibition game with the Boston Red Sox at Sarasota, Florida, in 1946. For more than six decades he flourished as an icon for baseball. (Associated Press)

he was afraid of the reaction of the Boston fans, and he added, "I'll tell you what. It is a deal if you throw in your little left fielder."

Topping said he did not think he could do that. The "little left fielder" was also a part-time catcher by the name of Yogi Berra.

In the spirit of the times, it was good that both men stayed home. Fans got used to the continuity of homegrown players, who had not yet become millionaire free agents, rock-star types who come and go.

For example: The laughing cavalier, Stanley Frank Musial of the St. Louis Cardinals, could come to Ebbets Field in Brooklyn and wallop

doubles all over that quaint little ball yard, yet loyal Dodgers fans would applaud Musial as he stood atop second base. Stan the Man, they called him.

Imagine that today. Imagine Pedro Martinez being applauded in Yankee Stadium. Yes, the Boston fans did stand up and cheer Roger Clemens's last appearance in a regular-season game in Fenway Park in 2003, and it was a lovely touch, but times are meaner now.

Personally, I blame George Steinbrenner and Rupert Murdoch for the cruel and sniggering air in baseball and the media. But maybe it's more complicated than that.

It's not that fans did not have their vendettas back in the old days. The best rivalry in all of baseball was a nasty intramural battle between the New York Giants of uptown Manhattan and the Brooklyn Dodgers of the Flatbush section of the Borough of Churches. Those two teams met 22 times a season, which often induced hard feelings, up close and personal, a forerunner to the banners in the age of "Steinbrenner Sucks!" "Red Sox Suck!"

Back then, there were no banners, but Dodger fans and Giant fans got in each others' faces, while Yankee fans hung back, bemused, at the low-life behavior and vulgar passions of those two segments of humanity.

This is not to suggest that Yankee fans all came from the upper crust. Hardly. Yankee fans came from the same economic levels as the other two New York teams, but they had a different view of the world. They were attracted to winning and excellence. Why not root for a winner?

For a long time, the Yankees and Red Sox ignored the African-American players who became available once the Dodgers and Giants signed Jackie Robinson and Willie Mays and a dozen other stalwarts of the Negro Leagues.

Talk about rivalries. The two American League teams seemed to be trying to out-Jim Crow each other. The Yankees, owned by Dan Topping and Del Webb, finally brought up— in 1955!—Elston Howard, while the Red Sox, owned by Tom Yawkey, ignored the entire subject until, virtually forced, they brought up a marginal player named Pumpsie Green in 1959.

Ultimately, the Yankees found stars of color like Reggie Jackson, Dave Winfield, Bernie Williams and Derek Jeter while the Red Sox, despite Jim Rice and Mo Vaughn, came into

the next century known as a white fan's team. This legacy of division in the stands and the clubhouse may indeed haunt the Sox more than the cuddly myth of the Curse of Babe Ruth.

None of that was the fault of Ted Williams. Only very late in his life did the general public come to know that Williams's mother was half Mexican, which may have explained his well-known antipathy to prejudice.

The real juice in postwar rivalries came from the National League. The Dodgers captured six pennants in ten seasons, from 1947 through 1956, while the Giants won two pennants in 1951 and 1954. During the same period, the Yankees won eight pennants, meeting a team from their own city in seven of those World Series. From a New York perspective, the Red Sox were just that team with a lot of sluggers in a city that was fun to visit if you could understand the local patois.

Williams produced another Triple Crown in 1947—and the Red Sox finished third, 14 games behind the Yankees, who promptly won one of the epic World Series in seven games from the Dodgers. That Series is famous for the shot that DiMaggio hit into the left-field corner that was plucked by a tiny substitute outfielder named Al Gionfriddo.

For one of the rare times in his career, DiMaggio showed emotion, scuffing at the dirt as he approached second base. Joe D almost could not stop himself from showing dismay that a marginal player had robbed him with a lurching catch, after starting out of position. In his mind, DiMaggio's real rival was, of course, himself.

In 1948, basically for the first time while DiMaggio and Williams were in uniform, the two teams tangled in a tight pennant race. The

Ted Williams *(left)* and Jackie Robinson at a Boston Baseball Writers dinner. (Dick Thomas Collection/Boston Sports Museum)

Yankees had been tied with Cleveland and Boston with a week to go, but were trailing by a game with two games left at Fenway. Williams hit a two-run homer in the first inning to put the Sox ahead (this game is never mentioned when people talk about Williams's failure in big games) and they clinched with a 6-1 victory. DiMaggio, playing with a number of injuries, had four hits on Sunday but the Sox won to force a playoff with Cleveland. (It is worth noting that Boston fans cheered the weary DiMaggio when he came off for a pinch runner in the ninth inning. Different times.)

The Sox promptly lost to Cleveland in a special playoff for the pennant. In 1949, the Yankees had a new manager. Bucky Harris was gone, replaced by the garrulous Casey Stengel, who had failed in previous managing hitches with the Dodgers and Boston Braves. (While managing the hapless Braves in 1943, Stengel had been hit by a taxi and missed two months of the season. The caustic Dave Egan of the *Boston Record*, also Ted Williams's nasti-

est tormentor, nominated the cabby as the man who had done the most for Boston baseball that season.)

Stengel rebounded with the Oakland Oaks of the Pacific Coast League. DiMaggio, with his roots in the Bay Area, surely regarded Stengel as somewhat of a failure and a clown—not a Yankee type. Now Stengel was his manager.

It was a mistake to underrate Stengel, who had married into an affluent banking family in Glendale, California, and was formed by everything he had observed on travels in the United States and barnstorming trips to Japan and Europe. The very secure Stengel drank a bit and babbled to keep the writers amused, but he was not afraid to alternate Yankees who believed they should play every day.

In his very first season, Stengel had to "commence" (a verb he used rather than the prosaic "start") the season without DiMaggio, who had a heel injury. DiMaggio was rounding into shape in June but did not travel with the team as it left for a three-game series in

Boston. That morning, he visited the restaurant of his pal, Toots Shor, who bluntly told him to get on a plane and go play some ball.

The first time up, DiMaggio hit a single and scored on a three-run homer by Hank Bauer. Next time up, he lashed a two-run homer into the screen over the scoreboard. Later, he slid hard to break up a double play. And in the ninth, with the tying run on third base, Williams hit a 400 foot drive to deep right center, where DiMaggio ran it down for the final out.

DiMaggio hit two homers in the second game as the Yankees won. And in the third game, he was silent until the seventh inning, when he came to bat with two men on. After Billy Goodman dropped DiMaggio's foul popup behind first base, DiMaggio belted a three-run homer off the light stanchion high above left field.

The Yankees won all three games and DiMaggio hit four homers—not a bad weekend for a man who at noon on Friday had been freeloading lunch at Toots Shor's.

In August of 1949, the two sluggers had their most public spat, after Williams was criticized in print for not running hard on a ball to center field that could have been a triple.

"When I picked up that ball and then looked up and saw Williams standing on second I was stunned. I thought sure he'd be resting on third," DiMaggio was quoted as saying.

When that quote was relayed—as quotes always are—to Williams, he snapped, "Nobody said anything when DiMaggio failed to reach second on Tuesday night, when he hit the top of the left-field wall."

Told of Williams's remark, DiMaggio called Williams "a cry baby." Quickly, DiMaggio said he meant nothing by it, calling it "an offhand remark." The flap died down, but there was no missing the tension between the two sluggers.

In mid-September, DiMaggio came down with a nasty virus that needed penicillin and was being nursed at home by a couple of friends.

This year, the two northeast rivals would play head-to-head for a pennant, as the Sox came to town with a one-game lead over the Yankees with two to play. This was the best yet.

On Saturday, October 1, DiMaggio, still weakened by the virus, was in uniform on what had long since been scheduled as "Joe DiMaggio Day." After being given an estimated $50,000 worth of gifts and a huge dose of adulation, Joe D decided he could play.

With 69,551 fans watching, the Sox took a 4-0 lead after three innings. If that sounds familiar in light of latter-day Boston collapses, keep reading.

The Yankees came back for two in the fourth, started by DiMaggio's ground-rule double. He also whacked a single off the pitcher's glove in the two-run fifth inning.

Then in the eighth inning, the game was decided not by Williams and not by DiMaggio. Just as Bucky Dent's home run would decide the historic 1978 playoff and Aaron Boone's home run would end the epic 2003 American League series, in 1949 it was Johnny Lindell, a spare outfielder, who would make the difference.

Stengel gave the right-handed Lindell a start because the Red Sox were going with their ace lefty, Mel Parnell, but the Old Man was never locked into any pattern.

"But Stengel, riding perhaps a hunch, allowed him to remain when Dobson replaced Parnell," noted John Drebinger in the *The New York Times* the next day.

Lindell hit a home run off the right-handed Joe Dobson in the bottom of the eighth. Joe Page, the boisterous relief pitcher, finished off the Sox in the ninth. Now the teams were tied going into the final game on Sunday.

This time the Yankees scored four times in the eighth, three of them on a bases-loaded bloop double to right that Al Zarilla could not contain. The clutch hit by Coleman is still recognized as one in a long series of timely plays in vital autumnal games by light-hitting Yankee second basemen, including Billy Martin, Brian Doyle and Luis Sojo.

Coleman's freak double gave the Yanks a 5–0 lead behind Vic Raschi, their burly right-hander. But in the ninth, with one out, Williams walked, went to second on a wild pitch and moved to third on a single by Vern Stephens. Then Bobby Doerr hit a shot to center field.

"A well-conditioned Joe DiMaggio doubtless would have caught it," Drebinger wrote the next day. "But the ailing Clipper couldn't, and the hit went for a triple, two scoring. It was here DiMaggio withdrew."

Embarrassed at not being able to catch up with Doerr's drive, DiMaggio walked off the field, letting a healthier Yankee finish up on defense. The Yankees shut down the Red Sox for two more outs and the pennant.

Stengel and his veteran pitchers knew the value of giving Williams nothing he could drive. In two of the key games of his career, Williams had one hit in five official at-bats

that weekend, although he did score twice.

These games would forever be cited by Dave Egan and others as part of the .208 batting average by Williams in the alleged ten biggest games of his career: the seven World Series game of 1946, the playoff game against Cleveland in 1948 and the two last games of the 1949 season. That charge would infuriate Williams and his supporters, who insisted he had carried the Sox that far with his lusty hitting.

While Williams nursed psychic pain, DiMaggio wobbled into the World Series as the Yankees demolished the Dodgers in five games.

For all the championships, DiMaggio's career was heading in a direction of exhaustion, injuries and perceived insults.

One day in 1950, Stengel sent DiMaggio out to play first base, just to see what would happen. DiMaggio sweated through his uniform, and, most likely, went behind Stengel's back to make sure he never had to play first base again. It was his only appearance at a position other than outfielder. (Williams pitched two innings once in 1940 as a lark, but otherwise never ventured off the outfield grass.)

Running down, physically and psychically, his body in pain, long divorced from his first wife and mostly estranged from his only child, DiMaggio lived in hotel rooms, with his pals taking care of his laundry, his meals, and his social connections. Saved from expending much energy off the field, DiMaggio batted .301 in 1950, but retirement was on his mind.

In spring of 1951, the landscape had changed. DiMaggio, who had always been revered from a distance by his Yankee teammates, now had to confront the first real new

prospect for the role of Yankee superstar.

Mickey Charles Mantle, raw, blond and talented, was theoretically a shortstop, as DiMaggio once had been. But Mantle was far too unpolished to take on-the-job training in the infield, and was turned into a rightfielder. The shy country boy could barely glance at the aloof idol, much less talk to him.

Mantle had never seen a major-league stadium when the Yankees arrived in Brooklyn for a preseason exhibition. Stengel promptly marched him out to right field to show him the eccentric bounces that could come from the wall, but Mantle had trouble conceiving that the grizzled old man had once patrolled that very same right field for the Dodgers.

"He thought I was born old," Casey would tell reporters years later.

Mantle had a rocky first season, needing a trip to the minors to regain his swing. DiMaggio could have helped indoctrinate Mantle, but for reasons of his own he did not. Undoubtedly, he felt his own mortality. Ted Williams was not going to take anything away from DiMaggio—but this swift, powerful kid could.

The Yankees won the pennant, but the World Series was delayed as the Giants and Dodgers played a best-of-three playoff for the National League pennant. For all the great games the Yankees would play against the Red Sox and other pretenders over the first century, the Brooklyn-Harlem game on October 3, 1951, would become the greatest game in baseball history, as the Giants came from behind on Bobby Thomson's ninth-inning home run.

The Yankees caught the Giants on the rebound, their pitching somewhat depleted, and won the World Series in six games.

Mickey Mantle of the Yankees, and Ted Williams of the Red Sox, carry weapons that made them famous during a conversation before a doubleheader, July 4, 1956 at Boston's Fenway Park. (Associated Press)

DiMaggio's last hit was a double, and he retired a few weeks afterward with a glorious career record of .325 with 361 homers and 1,537 RBI.

Besides his 56-game hitting streak in 1941, DiMaggio also left behind the amazing ratio of only 369 strikeouts compared to his 790 walks and 361 homers. Every other slugger in history had a higher ratio of strikeouts to homers, including Williams, with that great eyesight, who would finish with 521 homers and 2,019 walks but also 709 strikeouts.

If only life were as controllable for DiMaggio off the field.

Soon after his retirement, DiMaggio added to his reputation by marrying Marilyn Monroe, the beautiful and tormented Hollywood actress. They were divorced after a few turbulent months that ranged from romantic to combative, but he remained the most constant and stable man in her life until her mysterious death in 1962.

The romance with Monroe only added to DiMaggio's mystique. So did his obvious

Marilyn Monroe and Joe DiMaggio kiss while they wait in a San Francisco judge's chambers to marry in 1954. (Associated Press)

hatred of men he felt had used her, including John F. Kennedy, Robert F. Kennedy and Frank Sinatra. If you factored out the public vendetta—which is, when you come to think of it, the most appealing thing about him—DiMaggio's post baseball life seemed vapid. He moved around like the Duke of Windsor, a royal figure of sorts, but without much purpose, dedicated mostly to being himself.

Williams kept going, through injuries of his own, various marriages and divorces and the disappointment of losing all those key games. He was also called up for a second tour of duty, this time as a Marine pilot in Korea, where he landed a flaming jet on an aircraft carrier as a better alternative to bailing out over water.

That hitch cost Williams almost all of the 1952 and 1953 seasons, but he kept swinging away, feuding with many writers, scorning the fans. He grumped and scowled and cursed

and spat, but he enjoyed his later years—.345, .356, .345, .388, .328, .254, and in 1960 he hit .316 with 29 homers and 72 RBI, including his final swing, a home run into the damp breeze at Fenway, captured for perpetuity by the writer John Updike, and then he ducked into the dugout, cap still on his head, and disappeared.

He never got back to a World Series. In Williams's 17 full seasons (factoring out five in the military), he finished ahead of the Yankees twice—1946 and 1948. He would bat .344 with 521 homers and 1,839 RBI. He would be quite satisfied to think of himself as "the greatest hitter that ever lived" (you can place his Rabelaisian modifiers wherever you want) whereas DiMaggio evolved into "the greatest living baseball player"—after the death of Babe Ruth in 1948, that is.

With Williams gone, there was absolutely no sizzle to games between the Red Sox and

Yankees. In the first half of the 1960s the Sox would come to New York like a reconstituted rock band—the Rolling Stones without Mick Jagger. The Yankees, with an aching Mantle and an imported Roger Maris, would go to Fenway and seem like the home team, as people from all over New England showed up to take a gander at them.

Rivalry? What rivalry? The Yankees, with Stengel gone, finished first four more times from 1961 through 1964, a total of five straight pennants. The Red Sox, handicapped by Yawkey's failure to pursue black players, finished sixth, eighth, seventh and eighth in a league now swollen to ten teams.

Even when the Yankees fell to sixth in 1965, the Red Sox finished ninth. The Sox did catch them in 1966. They finished ninth as the Yanks finished tenth.

Then in 1967, with Carl Yastrzemski and a good supporting cast and a new manager in Dick Williams, the Red Sox won the pennant, losing to the Cardinals in the World Series, whereas the Yankees inched up to ninth with a 72-90 record.

Mantle retired after 1968, with the real New York-Boston rivalry still in the future.

Once DiMaggio and Williams were both retired, they rarely encountered each other. In 1961, the first year of Williams's retirement, the American League expanded from eight to ten teams and the schedule was lengthened from 154 to 162 games.

With Maris on his way to hitting 61 homers in his so-called asterisk season, Williams was quoted as blaming the glut of home runs on "Eastern League pitching"— meaning 20 extra pitchers would otherwise have been in the minors.

"I am very sorry Ted had to make that crack about the pitchers and sneer at the Mantle and Maris competition," DiMaggio said, in a column by his supporter, Dan Daniel of the *World Telegram and Sun*.

The rivalry went on for the rest of their lives.

DiMaggio seemed to live in mourning for his own youth, as well as for Marilyn Monroe. He showed up as a coach in 1967 and 1968 with Oakland—he needed two years in the pension plan to reach maximum payments— but he seemed a trifle abashed at wearing the garish green and yellow uniforms and working with young players.

He could be charming, one of the boys, if he was in the mood. If not, he could point that long mainsail nose and stare right through you.

When he came around to Yankee Stadium, he basked in the glory, but he commanded an appearance fee, and the ground rule was that he had to be introduced last, after Mantle. Later, while the old players were trading stories, DiMaggio would sip a drink in a corner of the pressroom, surrounded by familiar reporters, photographers, officials, old teammates.

Williams was far more involved in baseball and life. He frequently disappeared on fishing expeditions but then surfaced, full of high-decibel opinions. After an eight-year sabbatical, his private life predictably chaotic, Williams managed Washington and Texas. He wasn't a bad manager, but he had to get over his deep-rooted belief that all pitchers were essentially goony birds.

After he gave up that gig, he became a profound and profane icon, who could boom his hitting theories at contemporary stars like Wade Boggs and Don Mattingly. The old boy

Ted Williams bats at the 1987 Fenway Old-Timers' Game. (Paul Benoit)

could light up a stadium—or a clubhouse.

I will never forget the day in 1982, when Williams agreed to appear at the first Old-Timers' Game in Boston only because it was for a charity. At the age of 63, he made a running shin-high catch in left field, and later he roared with delight when his aging colleagues called him "Leather."

After that exhibition, Williams sat at the desk of the Red Sox' manager, Ralph Houk, a crusty old foe from the Yankees. Houk, a World War II survivor in his own right, delightedly sat in the corner while Williams dominated the room, blasting reporters for old times' sake, expounding his theories on

hitting, teasing his old teammates, and telling salty tales. He was wonderful. He made you want the afternoon to go on forever. Stay and tell us some more stories, Uncle Ted.

One thing Williams and DiMaggio had in common was awe at contemporary salaries. DiMaggio tried to compensate with commercials for a coffeemaker and Williams promoted a sporting-goods chain. Both had people orchestrating the sale of their autographs—at high prices.

When the aging DiMaggio heard that the aging Williams was charging $350 an autograph—almost in defense, so he wouldn't have to sign too many—DiMaggio came up with a price of $375 for any photo with Williams in it. It sounds juvenile, but it was dead serious. The rivalry never ended.

When DiMaggio died of cancer early in 1999, his only surviving brother, Dominic, and his lawyer, Morris Engelberg, were at odds over the details. After a private funeral service in the church a few blocks from the old family home in San Francisco, the tiny group emerged into the street. There were more television crews than mourners on the street. In the park across the way, Chinese people were performing their daily Tai Chi exercises.

The New York Times — March 9, 1999

JOE DIMAGGIO, YANKEE CLIPPER, DIES AT 84

By Joseph Durso

Hollywood, Fla., March 8—Joe DiMaggio, the flawless center fielder for the New York Yankees who, along with Babe Ruth and Mickey Mantle, symbolized the team's dynastic success across the 20th century and whose 56-game hitting streak in 1941 made him an instant and indelible American folk hero, died early today at his home here. He was 84 years old.

DiMaggio died shortly after midnight, nearly five months after undergoing surgery for cancer of the lungs. He had spent 99 days in the hospital while battling lung infections and pneumonia, and his illness generated a national vigil as he was reported near death several times. He went home on Jan. 19, alert but weak and with little hope of surviving. Several family members and close friends were at his bedside this morning. DiMaggio's body was flown to Northern California for a funeral Thursday and for burial in San Francisco, his hometown.

In a country that has idolized and even immortalized its 20th-century heroes, from Charles A. Lindbergh to Elvis Presley, no one more embodied the American dream of fame and fortune or created a more enduring legend than Joe DiMaggio. He became a figure of unequaled romance and integrity in the national mind because of his consistent professionalism on the baseball field, his marriage to Hollywood star Marilyn Monroe, his devotion to her after her death, and the pride and courtliness with which he carried himself throughout his life.

DiMaggio burst onto the baseball scene from San Francisco in the 1930's and grew into the game's most gallant and graceful center fielder. He wore No. 5 and became the successor to Babe Ruth (No. 3) and Lou Gehrig (No. 4) in the Yankees' pantheon. DiMaggio was the team's superstar for 13 season, beginning in 1936 and ending in 1951, and appeared in 11 All-Star Games and 10 World Series. He was, as the writer Roy Blount, Jr., once observed, "the class of the Yankees in times when the Yankees outclassed everybody else."

He was called the Yankee Clipper and was acclaimed at baseball's centennial in 1969 as "the greatest living ballplayer," the man who in 1,736 games with the Yankees had a career batting average of .325 and hit 361 home runs while striking out only 369 times, one of baseball's most amazing statistics. (By way of comparison, Mickey Mantle had 536 homers and struck out 1,710 times; Reggie Jackson slugged 563 homers and struck out 2,597 times).

But DiMaggio's game was so complete and elegant that it transcended statistics; as *The New York Times* said in an editorial when he retired, "The combination of proficiency and exquisite grace which Joe DiMaggio brought to the art of playing center field was something no baseball averages can measure and that must be seen to be believed and appreciated."

DiMaggio glided across the vast expanse of center field at Yankee Stadium with such incomparable grace that long after he stopped playing, the memory of him in full stride remains evergreen. He disdained theatrical flourishes and exaggerated moves, never climbing walls to make catches and rarely diving headlong. He would go to the ball just as it fell into his glove, making the catch seem inevitable, almost preordained. The writer Wilfred Sheed wrote, "In dreams I can still see him gliding after fly balls as if he were skimming the surface of the moon."

Williams died publicly, by inches. David Halberstam's charming book, *The Teammates*, is based on an automobile pilgrimage by John Pesky and Dominic DiMaggio (Bobby Doerr couldn't make it) to visit their ailing friend and hero one more time.

I was privileged to get one of the last interviews with Williams, when he came to New York to promote a documentary about another old rival, Hank Greenberg. Williams promised maybe 15 minutes. With a charming apology in advance to the female publicist, Williams told some gloriously bawdy stories about his youth. The woman roared as loudly as the rest of us.

He talked about Dommy and Greenberg—not much about Joe D—and he roared that the Red Sox would have won more pennants if they had had Phil Rizzuto at shortstop—never mind that the Sox' shortstop was one of his best friends, Pesky.

Just as I had felt in the manager's office in 1982, I wanted this interview to go on forever. After an hour, one of his helpers said Ted needed some lunch and rest before his next appointment. As the few of us left, Williams turned to me. We had met over the years, but I was hardly one of his insiders.

"You sound like a nice guy," he roared, which told me that those marvelous eyes, which had helped him survive aerial combat, could not see a face at three paces.

When the old warhorse passed in 2002, people lined up around Fenway Park, pausing in front of mementoes of Williams's life. I talked with a young Marine honor guard who was proud to stand tall for his comrade. That night in a ceremony in the old ballpark, the old Red Sox trotted out to their positions, leaving left field empty.

The next step of the grisly story is well known, how two of Williams's children put his body in a chemical holding tank, preserving the chromosomes for who-knows-what. Almost everybody who ever saw him hit a ball—or met the handsome old slugger—recoiled in horror.

I would prefer to remember that memorial evening in Boston, how it was far more intimate and warm than all the tributes in the Bronx had ever been for DiMaggio. Perhaps this reflected Boston as a smaller, more insular city that guards its traditions well.

Maybe the nostalgia for Williams did not make up for the pennants and the Most Valuable Player awards that had migrated toward New York. But now, with the Yankee-Red Sox rivalry hotter than ever, Ted Williams had achieved parity with his grand old rival.

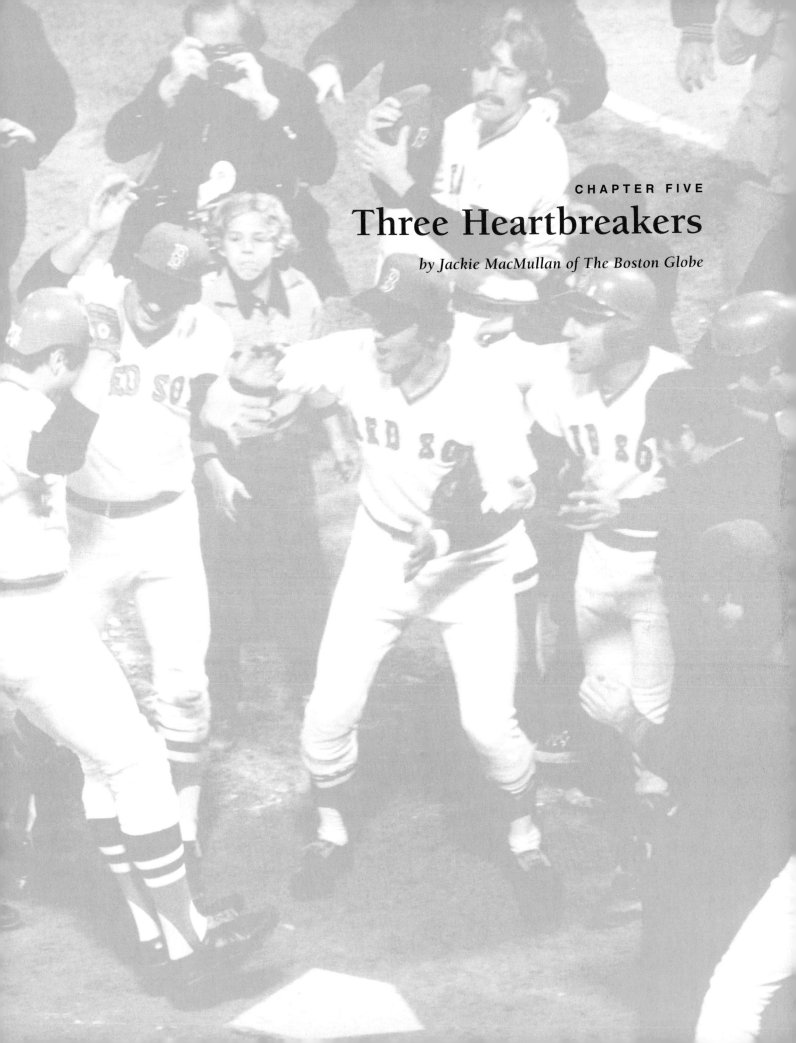

CHAPTER FIVE

Three Heartbreakers

by Jackie MacMullan of The Boston Globe

It would be futile to attempt to identify the single defining moment of 1967, when baseball suddenly mattered again in Boston. It was more of a subtle awakening for Red Sox fans, like reacquainting yourself with an old friend who had drifted away, then meandered back more vibrant and interesting and compelling than ever. The Red Sox had provided New England with a steady diet of sports drama for decades, yet in the early '60s, a malaise settled in at Fenway, and the quaint little park with the emerald lawn that had once been so alluring was dulled by the drabness of its product. Boston's roster was waterlogged with overpriced, underachieving players who lacked verve and accountability, who seemed either unwilling or unable to extricate themselves from the doldrums of their mediocrity.

The lone highlight of an otherwise unremarkable 1966 season was, for the first time in eighteen years, Boston finished ahead of the New York Yankees in the standings. Under normal circumstances, considering the depth of the hatred the Red Sox harbored for their more glamorous, more celebrated, more successful nemesis in pinstripes, this would be cause for great celebration. Yet the Yankees finished last in 1966, and the fact the Red Sox eked past them into ninth place was hardly something to crow about. Perhaps that's why owner Tom Yawkey had increasingly resembled an absentee landlord with only a passing interest in the fortunes of his investment.

As the 1967 season approached, prognosticators selected Boston as a 100 to 1 longshot to win the American League pennant. Even the blossoming of young Carl Yastrzemski was not enough to stir the masses.

Yaz, as he quickly became known throughout baseball, was an outfielder who batted left, threw right, and hit for power. He was a serious, driven player, one of the first of his era to engage in an offseason conditioning program. Manager Pete Runnels had bestowed the honor of the captaincy on Yaz in 1966, but he accepted the mantle reluctantly. The truth was, Yaz was uncomfortable in large groups and was a leader by example, not an inspiring orator who could rally his teammates with impassioned clubhouse speeches.

Yaz liked his game to do the talking, and what it had to say in '67 resonated throughout New England. The same held true for the offerings of pitcher Jim Lonborg, a lanky right-hander who would enjoy a career year, tying for the league lead in wins (22), and capturing the Cy Young award. They were aided by slugging first baseman George "Boomer" Scott, affable shortstop Rico Petrocelli, the young, dashing Tony Conigliaro, and a superb rookie outfielder named Reggie Smith. Collectively, they created a magical season marked by good fortune and indominitable spirit. Together, they were the embodiment of the Impossible Dream, and stirred fans from their apathetic baseball slumber.

By the time the leaves had turned and the cool October air breezed through Boston school children who were normally allowed to frolic on the bus ride home from school were suddenly instructed to sit quietly, with their hands folded, while bus drivers from Andover to Yarmouthport listened to the game on the radio. Even faithful churchgoers, to the horror of their clergy, would occasionally be nabbed in their pews, wearing an earpiece connected to their transistor.

The catalyst of the turnaround was general

manager Dick O'Connell, who loved baseball and the Red Sox, and understood the franchise was in need of a serious shake-up. He fired Runnels and hired manager Dick Williams, a gruff, curt authoritative man who thought nothing of telling his players the unvarnished truth about their deficiencies. He accepted no excuses, refused to tolerate a lack of hustle or effort, and immediately abandoned the star system that had become synonymous with the Yawkey reign.

Spring training was no longer a relaxing tune-up for another season. Williams ran his sessions like a boot camp, insisting baseball players should be in top physical condition. He erected a volleyball net in the left-field corner of Winter Haven, and instructed his pitchers to play games between their throwing sessions. "He thought the pitchers stood around too much," Lonborg recalled. "He wanted us to be more intense. Some of the guys thought it was a little odd, but I didn't mind. I had come from the California beaches. I loved volleyball. I had an edge."

Yaz, who had long been preaching fitness with his teammates, gladly went along with Williams's program, even after the new manager stripped him of his captaincy. He knew such discipline was necessary, particularly since the Red Sox would be fielding the youngest team in baseball on Opening Day.

Williams's debut as Sox manager was an underwhelming event in a sports town that was preoccupied with the Boston Celtics, who were coming off their eighth consecutive championship (and would go on to win their ninth) and a dazzling rookie defenseman for the Bruins named Robert Gordon Orr.

Less than 9,000 people trickled in to see Petrocelli's three-run homer clinch an Opening Day 8-5 victory over the Chicago White Sox. It was unfathomable on that dank afternoon to predict this very same baseball team would go on to lead the league in attendance with 1,727,832 fans before their remarkable run was over.

The Red Sox began to grab the attention of their fans on April 14, when they ventured into the Bronx for New York's Opening Day with lefthanded rookie Billy Rohr on the mound. Rohr was nearly perfect and, buoyed by an early home run by Smith, took a no-hitter into the ninth inning. Yastrzemski did his part by leaping up and robbing Tom Tresh of a sure-fire extra-base hit to lead off the ninth, but with Rohr one strike away from history, Yankees catcher Elston Howard slapped a single into right field. The no-hitter was gone, but the victory was preserved. The fact that it was over the Yankees made it feel like two wins. "This was a special day," Petrocelli remarked afterward. "I've got a good feeling about this team."

He wasn't the only one. Scott, the lumbering first baseman who was often the target of Williams's ire, batted .303 and delivered clutch hit after clutch hit. Lonborg, who was alternately insulted and inspired by the proddings of his manager, shed his Gentleman Jim moniker and became a feared pitcher who would not hesitate to brush back players. The Red Sox were developing an edge and an attitude, and nobody personified it better than Conigliaro, a local kid from St. Mary's High School in Lynn, Massachusetts who possessed a flair for the dramatic. Tony C hit a home run in his first at bat in the majors, and became the youngest player in major league history to lead the league in home runs when he belted 32 of them in 1965.

Conigliaro was forced to leave the team early in the '67 season to spend two weeks in the Army reserves. He was back by June 16, when the Red Sox found themselves locked into a pitcher's duel with the White Sox at Fenway. Chicago was clinging to a 1-0 lead in the tenth when infielder Joe Foy singled, and Conigliaro deposited a John Buzhardt fastball over the wall and into the net in left field to win it. The next morning, the *Boston Globe*, borrowing from the popular musical *Camelot*, coined the term "The Impossible Dream" to describe the surging baseball team.

Resident cynics awaited the inevitable col-

lapse, but it never happened. O'Connell made a series of key acquisitions, adding the versatile Jerry Adair and pitcher Gary Bell to the mix. The Sox went on the road in July and won 10 in a row. When they returned, they were greeted at Logan Airport by a mob of adoring fans. Airport personnel were so concerned for the safety of the players, they backed the plane up and taxied them to a different terminal.

Pennant fever was in full throttle. The Red Sox had suffered through a long and star-crossed history, but the vibes during the Impossible Dream season were all good. In preparation for the stretch run, the Red Sox had traded for Yankees catcher Elston Howard, who was so distraught at the thought of the uniform switch, he contemplated retirement. After speaking with the fired-up Williams, Howard changed his mind and reported for duty.

Howard was on hand on August 18, 1967, the night Tony C stepped into the batter's box against California pitcher Jack Hamilton. Hamilton unleashed a fastball that tailed away high and inside, and slammed into Conigliaro's cheekbone. The thud on impact was sickening, and the swelling started almost immediately. As the young slugger's face turned a nauseating shade of red and purple, teammates surrounded him protectively. Fenway was reduced to a whisper as Conigliaro was carried off the field.

Conigliaro's season was done, and, although he did not realize it, his career was all but over, too. Tony C did make a dramatic comeback in 1969, but he never completely regained enough of his vision to remain in the majors. In 1982, he suffered a devastating heart attack that left him inca-

pacitated until his death in 1990.

The sudden loss of Tony C led to the pursuit of the flamboyant Ken "Hawk" Harrelson, who had been released from the Oakland A's after engaging in a verbal sparring match with owner Charles O. Finley. Harrelson asked for 10 times his salary, got it from a rejuvenated Yawkey, and hit a home run in his first at bat in a Boston uniform. He became a valuable new weapon in a heated pennant race that included Boston, Minnesota, Chicago and Detroit. Sox fans were hard-pressed to choose what was more gratifying—having Boston in the thick of it, or knowing New York was a bunch of also-rans.

By September, the four teams were in a dead heat. Lonborg had established himself as the best pitcher in the American League, and Yaz was en route to winning the coveted Triple Crown with a .326 batting average, 44 homers and 121 RBI's. It came down to the final day of the season, with the Red Sox and the Twins sporting identical 91-70 records, and set to play one another. Detroit, meanwhile, was a half game back with a double-header against California.

Naturally, Williams called upon Lonborg to pitch the clincher at Fenway. Lonborg had discovered he pitched better on the road than at home, so he borrowed the keys to Harrelson's hotel room at the Sheraton and stayed there the night before the deciding game. After Lonborg fell behind 2-0, he started his own rally in the sixth with a bunt down the thirdbase line. Jerry Adair and Dalton Jones hit back-to-back singles to load the bases, and then Yaz came through again, this time with a sharp hit to center field that scored two runs and tied the game. From there, the Sox chased pitcher Dean Chance on

Red Sox player Tony Conigliaro is surrounded by teammates after being hit on the head by a fourth-inning fastball from Jack Hamilton of the California Angels. (Charles Carey/*The Boston Globe*)

a Ken Harrelson bouncer that scored another run. Reliever Al Worthington threw two wild pitches, Boston scored two more runs, and when Gentleman Jim coaxed Rod Carew (who would later become one of baseball's most reliable hitters) into a game-ending double play, the Red Sox had won, 5-3.

An elated Lonborg ran about Fenway Park in circles, and found himself cornered in right field by a throng of souvenir hunters. Eventually, he was escorted into the clubhouse tunnel by security. Lonborg was unharmed, but his jersey—and large chunks of that sparkling emerald Fenway lawn—were not so fortunate. Lonborg joined his teammates in the clubhouse to watch Detroit lose the second game of its doubleheader on

national TV, and the Red Sox were American League champions.

Their opponent in the World Series would be the heavily favored St. Louis Cardinals, featurin Bob Gibson, one of the best pitchers of all time, Roger Maris, a feared hitter with power, and the amazing Lou Brock, who stole bases, made sparkling defensive plays and specialized in clutch hits.

Yaz signed on with the *Boston Globe* to do a first-person column on the Series, and although the Red Sox were decided underdogs, he immediately provided St. Louis with bulletin board material when he predicted his team would win the championship in 6 games.

Gibson dampened Yaz's enthusiasm in

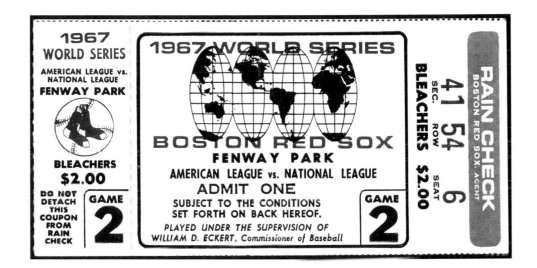

(Left) Red Sox manager Dick Williams gets a shower after his team clinches the pennant. (Frank O'Brien/*The Boston Globe*)

(Top) 1967 World Series ticket. (The Bostonian Society)

Game 1 by striking out 10 and giving up just one run—a solo home run to Boston pitcher Jose Santiago, no less—in a 2-1 Cardinals victory. Boston rebounded with its own ace, Lonborg, in Game 2. He retired 19 St. Louis players in a row, threw a brushback pitch at Brock, and had a no-hitter until the 8th. Boston 5, St. Louis 0.

In Game 3, Cardinals pitcher Nelson Briles, who complained the Red Sox were showing only Gibson the proper respect, drilled Yaz in the leg, and went on to win 5-2 behind 10 hits from his teammates. And, when Santiago got roughed up in Game 4, giving up four runs in the first inning, it looked bleak for Williams's proud band of scrappers, who were suddenly down 3-1 in games, and on the brink of elimination.

Howard delivered an impassioned speech to his teammates about how he and his 1958 Yankees team were down 3-1, but came back to win it it all. Lonborg listened well. He spun a three-hitter for a 3-1 victory. Sox pitcher Gary Waslewski, who had retired nine in a row in a relief appearance in Game 3, was the surprise starter for Game 6. Smith, Petrocelli and Yaz all hit homers in an 8-4 Boston win. The series was tied 3-3.

Asked who he'd go with for Game 7, Williams answered, "Lonborg and champagne." The answer infuriated the Cardinals. It didn't make Lonborg all that happy, either. He would be pitching on two days rest, had already dropped 25 pounds during his epic,

Reggie Smith rounds third base after hitting a home run in the '67 World Series. (Paul Maguire/*The Boston Globe*)

yet grueling season, and was unsure whether he had enough left to pull off the Dream.

His trepidation proved to be prophetic. The Cardinals chipped away at Boston's ace—with their own number one pitcher, Gibson, helping his own cause with a home run in the 5th—and St. Louis won easily, 7-2. Disappointed fans groused that Williams had left Lonborg in too long. The St. Louis players celebrated by chanting, "Lonborg and champagne."

In his final *Globe* column, Yastrzemski applauded the effort of his teammates and vowed, "We'll be back."

He was right—but only partly. It took the Red Sox another eight years to return to the World Series, and by then Lonborg, Smith, Harrelson, and Scott were gone. The only significant holdover from '67 besides Yaz was Petrocelli, who by then had moved over to third to make way for the young Rick "Rooster" Burleson at shortstop.

Rooting for the '67 Sox

By Bob Ryan of The Boston Globe

In more than 50 years of rooting for grade school teams, high school teams, prep school teams, college teams and professional teams, one rooting experience stands out above all others.

The epitome of fan passion for me was rooting for the 1967 Boston Red Sox.

It was special because it was baseball, the only legitimate everyday rooting experience, and because it was so utterly unexpected. No one living in Greater Boston believed at the beginning of the 1967 season that he or she would wind up living and dying with the Boston Red Sox, who had not contended for anything since 1949 nor won anything since 1946, and who had finished in ninth place the year before.

Nor, when the season began, did anyone foresee the ascension of Carl Yastrzemski to idol status or the rise of Jim Lonborg to Cy Young material. Yaz was a singles and doubles hitter who many thought was insufficiently motivated, while Lonborg was a marginally talented right-handed pitcher with a 19-27 career record when the 1967 season began.

I was a 21-year-old college student who had paid scant attention to the Red Sox during my first three years in Boston. On Memorial Day I took my girlfriend to a doubleheader with the Cleveland Indians. I still have one of the ticket stubs. It was a $1.00 bleacher seat, and on the back I wrote down the scores: Boston 4 Cleveland 3 and Boston 6 Cleveland 2. I also noted that "Scott HR wins 1st." That would be George Scott, the massive but graceful first baseman who hit .303 that year and drove in 82 runs while playing a superb first base.

Those were the first two of 27 games I would attend that year. And when I wasn't attending I was listening to Ken Coleman and Ned Martin on radio or watching on TV. In those days radio was the primary broadcast medium, and I can honestly say that as the season unfolded you really could follow the progress of most any game by walking or driving around town. At each stoplight you could hear the game on the radio of the car near you. If you were walking anywhere in Greater Boston, you could follow the game by the portable radios perched on every porch.

The Red Sox got themselves into the race with a 10-game winning streak just before the All-Star Game, and from then on the town was in a frenzy. People who had become disillusioned with the franchise and the sport had been reborn as baseball fans. The only watercooler talk allowable was of Yaz (by mid-July a hero of the highest order), Lonnie, Scott, Reggie Smith, Jose Santiago, Joe Foy, Rico Petrocelli and, of course, Tony Conigliaro, the ultimate hometown hero.

What made this race even more special was that it was a four-team race featuring the Twins, Tigers, White Sox, as well as the Red Sox. Night after night, there were three other games that mattered to us.

I was there on August 18, 1967, when

Jim Lonborg's bunt started the winning rally.... (Frank O'Brien/*The Boston Globe*)

Tony C's season was ended when he was hit in the face by a Jack Hamilton fastball. I even got a foul ball in the first inning. I was there when Lonborg won his 20th. I was there when Norm Siebern hit a bases-clearing pinch triple to beat the Angels and Petrocelli made a sensational play to preserve that 12-11 victory with the bases loaded and two outs in the ninth. I was there to see a game end with a rare 4-2-3 double play. And I was there for the last game of the season.

Here's how different it was in 1967. One day late in July I took a paycheck from my summer job and went down to Fenway to buy some tickets for me and my girlfriend, Elaine Murray. I saw that Minnesota would be the opponent for that final game, and I said "That might be fun." So for $3.00, times two, I wound up behind the screen at home plate in section 22, box 133 E, seats 9 and 10. Do I still have *those* tickets? Are you kidding? They are mounted right next to my framed score-card of that 5-3 Red Sox victory that gave them their first American League pennant in

21 years. (In those days you didn't need no stinkin' playoffs to determine a winner. 154 games sufficed.)

October 1, 1967 was one of the great days of my fan life, perhaps the best. Lonborg went into the sixth inning trailing Minnesota 20-game winner Dean Chance, 2-0. But Lonborg got things started by beating out a bunt. Before that inning was over the Red Sox had scored five runs, the highlight being Yastrzemski's bases-loaded single to center that tied the game at 2-2. I remember never being so sure of anything as I was that Yaz would get a hit in that particular at-bat. And Yaz ripped that ball on a line to center.

The climax came in the eighth, when Bob Allison ended a Twins rally by getting himself thrown out at third by Yaz to end the inning. I can still see a disgusted Tony Oliva, standing at second, glaring at Allison.

I can still see a lot of things. It was the greatest summer of my life. And, by the way, I've been married to Elaine Murray for 35 years.

All the euphoria that had built up from the '67 season imploded almost immediately. Lonborg injured his knee in a skiing accident during the off-season and was never the same pitcher. Santiago succumbed to arm trouble. Harrelson led the league in RBI's in 1968 with 102, but was distracted by a number of outside ventures. Smith grew unhappy, and demanded a trade. The hard-line approach Williams adopted was a major plus during the Imposible Dream, but by the time he was fired in the final days of 1969, his rants had been reduced to the Impossible Scream.

Over the next seven years, the Red Sox shuffled managers and players.

The Yankees similiarly changed their personnel, including fleecing the Red Sox by sending first baseman Danny Cater to Boston for Reliever Sparky Lyle. Cater toiled for three forgettable seasons in Boston, while Lyle saved 35 games for New York in 1972. No wonder the Sox would not engage in a transaction with the Yankees for another 24 years. The bad feelings between the two teams continued to percolate, and it was almost a given there would be some kind of melee during the course of the season. Few were quite as memorable as the free-for-all that erupted during the 1973 season, when the two teams engaged in a bench-clearing brawl with the two catchers, New York's Thurman Munson and Boston's Carlton Fisk, as the catalysts.

Fisk, a burly New Englander who stood taller than most catchers, quickly established

himself as a brash young leader in the Sox clubhouse. He batted .293 with 22 home runs and a league-leading nine triples in 1972, easily winning Rookie of the Year honors. Boston appeared to be on course to win the division in 1974 when Fisk tore ligaments in his knee, and was lost for the season. Without him, the Red Sox blew an eight-game lead in August, and watched helplessly as the Baltimore Orioles and—even worse—the dreaded Yankees overtook them in the final weeks.

The disappointment did not linger. Fisk came back (but not before he also broke his arm in June of '75), and rookies Fred Lynn and Jim Rice, who had cameo roles the previous September, appeared ready to take a regular turn in the big leagues. Yaz, who was now in his thirties and playing first base instead of left field, was still a dangerous hitter. There was optimism regarding young left-handed pitcher Bill Lee, nicknamed the Spaceman for his particularly unorthodox views on baseball and the world in general. Luis Tiant, a rotund Cuban with a flummoxing spinning curve ball, was more of a question mark (Sox officials weren't even sure how old he was), so Boston made a strong pitch for free agent Catfish Hunter. In what would become a maddening trend that continues into the 21st century, the free-spending Yankees outbid their rivals for the pitcher's services.

Boston manager Darrell Johnson, a former minor-league pitching coach, quickly realized he would count on his young hitters to return his team to the World Series stage. Lynn was a congenial Californian whose boyish good looks and total disregard for the rigors of throwing his body into the center field wall immediately endeared him to the throngs of New England fans. His performance in 1975 was staggering, earning him both Rookie of the Year and league MVP honors. Lynn was originally a high school draft pick of the Yankees, but he chose instead to go to USC where he played baseball and football. Sox fans loved him all the more.

On June 18, Lynn put on a batting show for the ages. He hit three home runs, knocked in 10 runs and accounted for 16 total bases, tying the American League record. The Red Sox were certain they were witnessing a Hall of Famer in the making. His fellow rookie outfielder, Rice, wasn't half bad either. During any other season, he would have been Rookie of the Year, but he wasn't even the best newcomer on his team. Rice was the antithesis of Lynn; quiet, reserved, unapproachable. Rice, who is African American, had reason to wonder if Lynn was better received in Boston because he was white. The scars of a racist Yawkey past never quite seemed to completely heal at Fenway.

And, yet, the darling of the fans and the media in 1975 was the Cuban Tiant, who, together with Lee and Rick Wise, had become the nucleus of a formidable rotation. Behind their efforts, Boston led by four games at the All-Star break, and six games by September. On September 21, Rice was hit by a pitch and broke his left hand. Six days later, the Red Sox clinched the division. Rice, who at the time was batting .309 with 22 home runs and 102 RBI's, was ruled out for the entire postseason. He was crushed.

According to a new playoff format, Boston played a best-of-five series with the Oakland A's for the American League pennant. The A's were loaded with stars: Reggie Jackson, who would be later known as Mr. October for his postseason heroics with the Yankees, pitchers Vida Blue and Ken Holtzman, and infielder Sal Bando.

Although Wise had led the team with 19 wins, it was Tiant who had become the money pitcher down the stretch for the Red Sox. Just as they turned to Lonborg to carry the pitching load in '67, the '75 Red Sox would turn to El Tiante, with his unusual hitch and unpredictable delivery to set the tone.

Tiant was masterful in Game 1, a breezy 7-1 Sox win. In game 2, starter Reggie Cleveland and relievers Roger Moret and Dick Drago combined for the 6-2 win, and in Game 3 Wise did his part to complete the sweep. For all the accolades Boston's killer offensive lineup received, it was pitching that carried the day.

Just as they were in 1967, the Red Sox were the underdogs in a World Series that was expected to be dominated by the Cincinnati Reds, a team that had rolled to 108 regular season wins. Their nickname, the Big Red Machine, indicated their ability to dominate games with a lethal lineup that included Johnny Bench, Pete Rose, Ken Griffey and Joe Morgan. It's been said that pitching and defense wins championships, and the Reds had plenty of that, too.

In Game 1, both Tiant and Cincinnati pitcher Don Gullett had pitched shutouts through seven innings before Tiant took matters into his own hands and started a Red Sox rally with a single. Dwight Evans followed with a textbook bunt, and Gullett, hurrying the throw to first, threw the ball away. Denny Doyle and Yastrzemski followed with hits, and the game broke open. When it was over, Tiant

had mesmerized Cincy with his dancing, spinning curve and the Sox had won, 6-0.

In Game 2, Johnson handed the ball to lefty Bill Lee, who, due to arm trouble and control problems, hadn't started a game in 21 days. Lee was sitting on a 2-1 lead in the seventh when the raindrops fell. After a 27-minute rain delay, Bench doubled, Dave Concepcion beat out an infield hit, and Ken Griffey doubled off reliever Dick Drago for a 3-2 Reds win.

The Reds jumped on Wise early in Game 3, and appeared to be cruising toward victory with a 5-1 lead, but that's when Bernie Carbo's home run cut the deficit to 5-3. Evans, whose exceptional defense often overshadowed his bat, followed with a two-run blast in the ninth off Reds relief pitcher Rawley Eastwick, and the game was tied. An already memorable game was about to become unforgettable.

Caesar Geronimo led off the bottom of the 10th with a single for Cincinnati. Manager Sparky Anderson called for pinch hitter—and bunt specialist—Ed Armbrister to bat. He squared to bunt, and as he hit the ball and Fisk jumped up to try and grab it, the Boston catcher and the Reds runner became entangled. Fisk's throw to second sailed into center field, sending Geronimo to third, and Armbrister to second. The Red Sox manager, Fisk, and the rest of the Boston players screeched at home plate umpire Larry Barnett to call interference, but he refused, and the play stood. A Morgan sacrifice fly won it for the Reds, leaving the Sox to fume in the clubhouse afterwards.

Fisk likened trying to field the ball to "smashing into a linebacker." Pressed for an explanation of his call, the umpire Barnett

(Right) Carlton Fisk waves fair his home run in Game 6 of the 1975 World Series. (Associated Press/ Harry Cabluck)

(Facing page) Boston's Carlton Fisk jumps on home plate after hitting the homer that won the sixth game of the World Series with Cincinnati in the 12th inning at Fenway Park, Boston, Oct. 21, 1975. Teammates and fans cheer him. (Associated Press/J. Walter Green)

insisted there was no "intent to intefere." Drago dismissed the explanation, claiming Fisk had tagged Armbrister, and therefore he should have been out anyway. "It's terrible to have people who don't give a damn running something 60 million people are watching," he groused.

As his teammates vented, Tiant, calmly puffing one of his signature Cuban cigars, promised, "We'll take care of this on the field." And so he did. Tiant threw 163 pitches in Game 4, gutting out a 5-4 win that was preserved by Lynn's superb over-the-shoulder catch in the ninth on a Griffey fly ball that ini-

tially looked to be out of the park. The series was tied 2-2.

Cincinnatti roughed up Reggie Cleveland in Game 5, while relying on Gullett to shut down the Sox hitters. Tony Perez, who had done little for the Reds to that point, belted two homers to account for the 6-2 win, and the Red Sox were down 3-2 again, just like in '67.

Game 6 was postponed three times because of poor weather. Lee was scheduled to pitch, but when the rain afforded Tiant the extra rest, Johnson re-jiggered his rotation and went with his hot hand.

A three-run shot by Lynn staked Boston an early lead, but that's when the Big Red Machine kicked into gear. Griffey, Morgan and George Foster all delivered big hits, and in the top of the eighth, when Geronimo snuck a home run just inside the Pesky pole, the Reds were on top, 6-4.

The Red Sox dugout was quiet, yet hardly downtrodden. Carbo, who had thrived in the postseason, came on to pinch hit with two out in the eighth. He knocked a two-run homer into the center-field bleachers, and the Fenway fans exploded. It was 6-6. The Reds made a bid to end it in the 11th, when Morgan clocked a deep shot to right, but

Evans, who would go on to win eight Gold Gloves, chased it down and made a stunning grab. Anderson said afterward, "That's the greatest catch I've ever seen."

With the score still knotted 6-6 in the bottom of the 12th, Fisk stepped up to the plate. He took the first pitch for a ball, then cranked the next pitch toward left field. The ball appeared to be lazily curving foul, but as Fisk stood on the first base path, he motioned wildly with his arms, attempting to coax it fair. The ball clanked off the foul pole. Home run. The Sox were 7-6 winners in one of the most exciting and dramatic World Series games ever. Organist John Kiley immediately

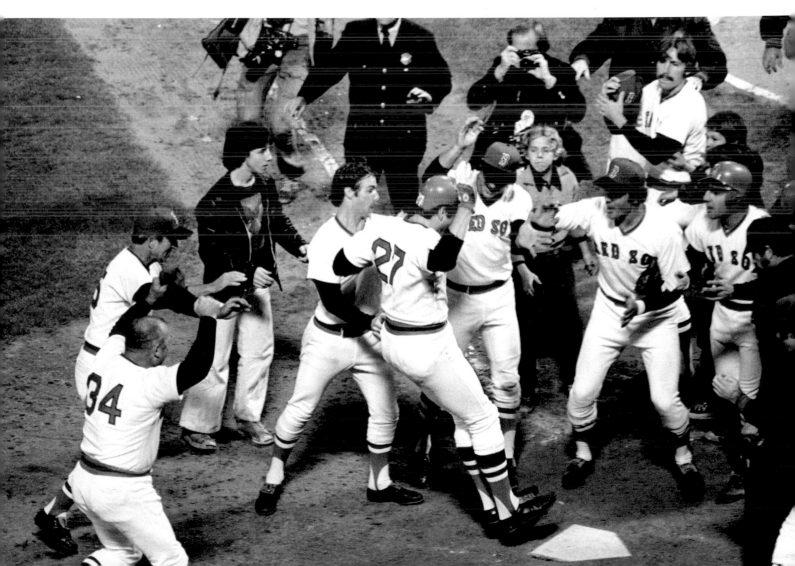

played a rendition of the Hallelujah Chorus, and the fans poured onto the field to meet Fisk at home plate. Pete Rose, who was on the *losing* end of the score declared, "This is the greatest game in World Series history and I'm just proud to have played in it."

The Boston Globe • October 22, 1975

CARBO HOMER TIES IT IN 8TH EVANS CATCH SAVES IT IN 11TH FISK'S HR IN 12TH BEATS REDS, 7-6

By Peter Gammons, Globe Staff

And all of a sudden the ball was there, like the Mystic River, suspended out in the black of the morning.

When it finally crashed off the mesh attached to the left field foul pole, one step after another the reaction unfurled: from Carlton Fisk's convulsive leap to John Kiley's booming of the "Hallelujah Chorus" to the wearing off the numbness to the outcry that echoed across the cold New England morning.

At 12:34 a.m., in the 12th inning Fisk's histrionic home run brought a 7-6 end to a game that will be the pride of historians in the year 2525, a game won and lost what seemed like a dozen times, and a game that brings back summertime one more day. For the seventh game of the World Series.

For the game to end so swiftly, so definitely, was the way it had to end. An inning before, a Dwight Evans catch that Sparky Anderson claimed was as great as he's ever seen had been one turn, but in the ninth a George Foster throw ruined a bases-loaded, none-out certain victory for the Red Sox. Which followed a dramatic three-run homer in the eighth by Bernie Carbo as the obituaries had been prepared, which followed the downfall of Luis Tiant after El Tiante had begun with the help of Fred Lynn's three-run, first-inning homer, as a hero of unmatched emotional majesty.

So Fisk had put the exclamation mark at the end of what he called "the most emotional game I've ever played in." The home run came off Pat Darcy and made a winner of Rick Wise, who had become the record 12th pitcher in this 241-minute war that seemed like four score and seven years.

. . .

So, if the honey and lemon works on the throat and Alka-Seltzer does the same for the heads, Fenway will not be alone tonight. She has one drama, and it is perhaps sport's classic drama.

Bill Lee and Don Gullett, the Cincinnati Reds and the Boston Red Sox, and a long night's journey into morning; a game suspended in time as Fisk's homer was suspended beyond the skyline, a game that perhaps required the four-day buildup it got.

Summertime has been called back for just one more day—for the seventh game of the World Series. ■

In Game 7, Lee, still emotionally bruised from being passed over in Game 6, pitched five shutout innings for a 3-0 lead before Rose, who batted .370 in the Series, touched him for a single, and Perez hit a two-run shot. Lee was forced to leave with a blister in the seventh, giving way to relievers Roger Moret and Jim Willoughby, who had been reliable in relief. In the bottom of the eighth, with the game tied 3-3 and nobody on, Johnson pulled Willoughby for pinch hitter Cecil Cooper. Cooper struck out, but more significantly, Willoughby was out of the game, leaving rookie Jim Burton to pitch the ninth.

Burton walked Griffey, and Geronimo sacrificed him to second. Dan Driessen grounded out, with Geronimo going to third. Burton had two strikes on Morgan when the second baseman, planted in his signature stance, with his elbow high and twitching, whacked Burton's slider to right field. The Reds took the lead, 4-3. That margin held when Yaz, with two outs in the ninth, flied out to end the most popular World Series ever. More than 75 million viewers had watched the Red Sox lose a heartbreaker.

* * *

Mindful of pushing forward, the team added veteran pitcher Ferguson Jenkins in 1976. The first Yankees-Red Sox series, predictably, was marred by a fight. On May 20 in the Bronx, New York outfielder Lou Piniella came charging home on a single to right. Evans gunned him down with a perfect throw to Fisk, who was blocking the plate. Piniella and Fisk collided, hit the dirt, then came up swinging. Both benches emptied, and Lee, who forgot the unwritten baseball rule that pitchers never enter the fray, wound up in the middle of the pile. New York third baseman Graig Nettles tossed Lee to the ground, and the lefty landed awkwardly on his shoulder. He left the stadium in a sling, and would not pitch again for two months. Manager Darrell Johnson vowed Boston would exact revenge by overtaking New York in the standings, but they were eight games back on July 9 when Tom

Yawkey, their longtime owner, died without realizing his goal of a baseball championship.

As the Yankees continued to flourish the next two seasons, Boston floundered while officials haggled over Yawkey's estate. A new ownership group that included Yawkey's widow, Jean, as well as, Haywood Sullivan and former trainer Buddy LeRoux eventually took control of the team. Sullivan immediately fired O'Connell. Johnson, meanwhile, had already been replaced by third-base coach Don Zimmer, a short stocky man with a marine buzz cut and a huge wad of tobacco crammed into his mouth. Zimmer was often ridiculed by his own players. Lee called him "the gerbil," in reference to Zimmer's pudgy cheeks. He, Jenkins and Wise resented the manager's constant meddling, and were alternately in and out of Zimmer's doghouse.

Sullivan gave Zimmer some new options by signing free agent (and Yankee) pitcher Mike Torrez, trading for the speedy Jerry Remy to play second base, and acquiring Dennis Eckersley, a young free-spirited pitcher with long flowing hair, and a nasty repertoire of pitches. The nucleus of Rice, Lynn, Fisk, Evans and Yaz remained intact. Tiant was also still pitching, and the 1978 Red Sox plowed their way atop the division by May. By June 15, they were an astounding 26-4 at home. They delighted in beating up a Yankees team that had taken a nosedive under the mercurial manager Billy Martin. When baseball paused for its All-Star break, the Red Sox had posted a 57-26 record and held a comfortable nine-game lead over Minnesota. New York? The Yankees were a complete afterthought.

New York owner George Steinbrenner had seen enough. Martin was fired and replaced by Bob Lemon. The managerial change was just what the Yankees needed. They certainly had the talent, led by slugger Reggie Jackson, who bickered incessantly with Martin, and the best pitcher in baseball that year, Ron Guidry. The Yankees surged under the calming influence of Lemon, and by August, New York was within six games of the Boys in Boston.

The Red Sox, conversely, were slumping. On August 26, Remy broke his wrist. Three days later, Evans was beaned by Seattle pitcher Mike Parrot, and would be plagued with nauseating dizzy spells for the remainder of the season. Third baseman Butch Hobson struggled with painful bone chips in his elbow that made every throw an adventure in the final weeks of 1978, yet Zimmer stubbornly refused to pull him from the lineup.

By the time the Yankees strutted into town on September 7th, the Red Sox lead had deteriorated into a shaky four-game margin. The Red Sox players dutifully discussed the importance of the series and the need to put enough distance between themselves and New York to end it.

Then they went out and lost 15-3. New York rocked its former pitcher, Torrez, for 15 hits and 12 runs. Willie Randolph had 5 RBIs while Hobson committed two errors. By the time Torrez was mercifully pulled, down 12-0 in the bottom of the fourth, fans were pouring out of Fenway. Those who stuck around saw Drago bean Munson in the sixth, yelling as the ball left his hand, "Look out!"

Zimmer downplayed the lopsided score, and promised his team would come to the park with a new focus the following day. He was rendered speechless after his team got thumped, 13-2. The panic in the Red Sox clubhouse was evident. Boston wasn't just los-ing, it was being humiliated in its own park. Eckersley and his 16-6 record got the nod for the third game of the homestand, but the lefty Guidry retired 18 in a row, fanned the side in the 5th, and took away a 7-0 shutout victory. The Red Sox held a team meeting to clear the air. Lee lobbied to pitch the final game of the series, but his antagonistic relationship with Zimmer squashed any chance of that. The manager went with left-handed rookie Bobby Sprowl, who didn't get out of the first inning. New York won 7-4 to sweep the series, and was now tied with Boston in the standings.

The debacle was quickly dubbed the Boston Massacre. The Red Sox had been outscored 42-9, and had committed 11 errors. *Boston Globe* columnist Ray Fitzgerald opined, "What happened to the Red Sox should have qualified them for federal aid." Four days later, Boston limped into New York and lost two out of three. They trailed by two games with 14 to go.

An angry Fisk challenged his teammates to make a final run. "We're not done yet," he snapped. "Don't make the mistake of counting us out."

The proud catcher struck a chord. The Red Sox ripped off eight wins in a row. On the final day of the season, Tiant pitched a two-hitter to beat Toronto, and the city of Boston engaged in collective scoreboard watching. The Yankees were playing Cleveland. If they beat the Indians, they won the pennant outright. They lost, 9-2. The Yankees and the Red Sox had finished the season with identical 99-63 records.

A one-game playoff would determine the winner. This time, Zimmer did not hand Sprowl the ball, but he couldn't give it to Tiant, either. He had shot his wad the day

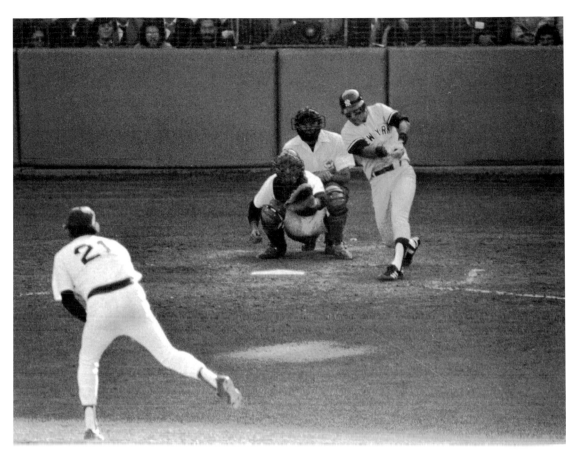

Bucky Dent hits his famous homer over the Green Monster in Fenway Park. (Associated Press)

before. That left Torrez, who had lost 8 of his 9 final starts, and the pitching matchup seemed cruelly one-sided. New York would be coming at the Red Sox with a rested Guidry, who would win the Cy Young that year with a 24-3 record.

Yaz struck first with a solo shot in the second inning, then a Burleson double, Remy sacrifice and Rice RBI in the sixth upped their cushion to 2-0. Torrez, meanwhile, was handling his old teammates. The mood at Fenway became festive. As the game headed into the seventh, there was reason to believe the unthinkable might occur—Boston could be headed for a playoff berth *and* beat the Yankees at the same time.

But Torrez, pitching on three days' rest, finally wore out in the seventh. Chris Chambliss and Roy White banged out back-to-back singles. With two out and two on, the job of keeping the Yankees rally alive rested in the hands of shortstop Bucky Dent. Dent was

a decent fielder with no bat. He had hit only .140 over the final 20 games of the season, and was not a power threat. He looked overmatched by Torrez, falling behind 0-2 in the count, including a foul ball that bounced off his foot, and nearly drove him from the game. As he tried to shake off the painful injury, his teammate, Mickey Rivers, gave the ball boy his bat and told him to swap it with Dent's.

Torrez went after Dent with his fastball, but, as he would confess later, he left it "up just a little bit." Dent plopped a 3-run homer into the left-field screen. Had the game been played at Yankee Stadium, it would have been a routine out. But in Boston's little band box, Dent's fly ball signified the latest strain of Fenway agony. As Boston fans looked on incredulously, hits by Munson and Jackson obliterated their fantasy. There was no longer any lead. The Yankees had taken control, 5-2.

The Red Sox refused to give in. Key hits by Remy, Yaz, Fisk and Lynn left them down, 5-

4, in the ninth. The pinstripes called for their top reliever, Rich "Goose" Gossage to finish off their nemesis. Gossage found himself in a jam, with Remy on first and Burleson on third with two outs, and Yaz at the plate. Gossage threw him a fastball, and Yaz jumped on the pitch, but slammed his bat in the dirt in disgust as the ball popped up harmlessly to third base. Nettles secured his ball in the glove, and the Fenway faithful filed out quietly, cursing that Bucky "bleeping" Dent.

A devastated Yastrzemski said softly that he hoped the Yankees would win the World Series. Zimmer and Torrez did not share his sentiments. They paid for the latest Red Sox failure, and became the favorite targets of bitterly disappointed fans. Both would soon be gone from the club. The painful loss had cast a pall over the city, one that was even recognized by Humbert Cardinal Medeiros. In a speech to the people of Boston, the Cardinal noted, "The city has been saddened twice in one week. We just lost a pope (John Paul I), which is sad. And now we lose to the Yankees, which is also very sad."

The fallout from the '78 collapse was swift. The Red Sox refused to re-sign Tiant; he went to the Yankees. Lee was traded to Montreal, and even though Boston led the league in home runs the following season, they finished fourth, fired Zimmer, and traded Burleson and Hobson. Yet the worst was yet to come. Sullivan and LeRoux, in a clerical snafu, failed to tender Lynn and Fisk a new contract offer by the required date of December 20th. That allowed both players, who were insulted by Boston's lowball offers in negotiations, to become free agents. Lynn agreed to a trade to California that netted Boston pitcher Frank Tanana and infielder Joe Rudi, two players

that were past their prime. A bitter Fisk, meanwhile, simply walked away, signing a contract with the Chicago White Sox. On October 12, 1983, Carl Yastrzemski retired with more career hits (3,419) than anyone else who had ever worn a Red Sox uniform. He choked up just a little as he ran around the field, slapping hands with the Fenway fans. He thanked the Yawkeys, then disappeared into the tunnel leading to the clubhouse with the realization his dream of winning a championship was over.

* * *

Another era of Red Sox heartbreak had come to a close, but down in Houston, where a big right-hander was throwing heat, a new one was already beginning to unfold. Pitcher Roger Clemens joined the Red Sox organization in 1983, and soon came to symbolize the furtive hopes of a new generation of Sox fans. He was a hard-throwing, fearless competitor who spoke with a Texas twang in a stream-of-conscious jumble of unfinished sentences. His first big league season in 1985 was dampened by shoulder problems, but when Clemens pulled on his 21 jersey in spring training the following February, he was tanned, fit and healthy.

"I'm ready to go," the big Texan declared. "It's going to be a great season."

Manager John McNamara, never one for hyperbole, felt the same way. With Clemens, Bruce Hurst, and Dennis "Oil Can" Boyd in his rotation, he felt confident his team could compete for the division title. Hurst was a solid lefty with strong legs and a nasty breaking ball. He could also throw the fastball, and was working on a forkball in 1986 that enabled him to go 5-0 with a 1.07 ERA in

September. The Can was a combustible talent whose reed-thin frame was deceiving. He threw hard when he needed to. Boyd's biggest obstacle was often himself. He was too emotional and too unreliable, and was unpopular with many of his teammates, who believed he got special treatment.

Third baseman Wade Boggs was one of them. He had toiled in the Sox minor league system for years before coming up to the big leagues for good in 1982, and didn't appreciate the slack guys like the Can received. Boggs was a hard-working, fastidious, superstitious baseball man who ate chicken before every single game. He, like Boyd, was known to speak about himself in the third person, but nobody cared, because he could hit.

Boston needed a respected clubhouse presence to balance off such volatile personalities, and they gained one when then they swapped Mike Easler for New York first baseman Don Baylor. It was the first deal between the Red Sox and the Yankees since the Cater for Lyle fiasco. With the cerebral Marty Barrett at second base, and Evans and Rice still aboard, the lineup looked set. The only lingering question mark as the team headed north was its relief corps. As if on cue, closer Bob Stanley blew a lead on Opening day to a chorus of boos.

On April 29, the same day the Celtics were hosting the Atlanta Hawks in the NBA playoffs, Clemens struck out the side in the first inning of a game against the Seattle Mariners. By the time he jogged off the mound in the second inning, having knocked out five of the first six batters he faced, there was an air of anticipation enveloping Fenway. Something special was happening. As Clemens racked up strikeout after strikeout, with bleacher fans dutifully posting K's on the back wall, his

teammates gave him a wide berth, allowing him to maintain his focus alone in the dugout between innings. Clemens knew he was having a terrific day, but later admitted, "I threw so many strikes, I kinda lost track for a while."

His no-hitter was broken up by his former college teammate (and future Red Sox infielder) Spike Owen in the fourth. And, when Gorman Thomas tagged Clemens for a solo homer, suddenly his magnificent performance was in jeopardy of being all for naught. The Mariners were ahead, 1-0, and Clemens looked alternately stunned and furious.

Evans set things right with a three-run homer. As Clemens approached the final innings, still throwing in the nineties, the ballpark was abuzz with the possibility of him breaking the major league record for most strikeouts with 19. That record was held by Tom Seaver, Steve Carlton and Clemens's boyhood hero, Nolan Ryan. With his mouth parched, and his legs cramping, Clemens unleashed three straight fastballs to Phil Bradley. All three were strikes, the last one a called K that propelled Clemens into the record books.

Clemens became an overnight national celebrity. His work ethic was touted as unparalleled. Camera crews followed Clemens and his friend and fellow pitcher Al Nipper as they jogged along the Charles River for their off-day workouts. What the cameras didn't capture was the times they stopped to play pickup basketball with the UPS drivers who engaged in a daily game at lunch. Soon, fans were following Clemens home from the ballpark, forcing the pitcher to ask toll collectors on the Mass Pike to purposely slow up cars by counting out their change so he could escape undetected.

Roger Clemens breaks the major league record for most strikeouts in a game, fanning 20 Mariners on April 29, 1986. (Stan Grosfeld/*The Boston Globe*)

While Lonborg and Tiant before him had provided considerable thrills for Red Sox fans, neither had done it with the pure power Clemens demonstrated on the mound. His dominance was contagious. After his 20-strikeout performance against Seattle, his team won 19 of its next 24 games.

General manager Lou Gorman added a veteran arm when he traded for the 41-year-old Seaver, who was headed for the Hall of Fame, but wanted to bring one more World Series ring along with him. Clemens greeted Seaver enthusiastically in the clubhouse. The young pitcher was 14-0 and wondering if anyone would ever hit him again. Clemens earned the

honor as the American League starting pitcher for the All-Star game. At that point, Boston led its division by 9 games.

There was only one problem: The Can, who had posted an 11-6 mark to that point, was left off the AL All-Star squad. He greeted the news with a tantrum in the Red Sox clubhouse, throwing his clothes and cursing out his teammates and his manager before peeling out of the players' parking lot. When Boyd calmed down, he returned to Fenway, but was denied entrance. He was suspended for three days, then checked into the UMass Medical Center in Worcester to undergo an evaluation, including, according to the team, drug testing. The team slumped to 3-10 in his absence. Stanley lost his job as the closer, with McNamara handing it over to the untested Calvin Schiraldi. By the time Boyd returned to a standing ovation from his patient fans, Boston's lead had evaporated to three games, and the Yankees, Blue Jays, Orioles and Tigers were all giving chase.

Clemens further established himself as the leader of the team in the stretch run. When his team needed a win to stop their slide, Clemens provided it. Seaver, meanwhile, injured his knee in the final week of the regular season, and never pitched again for the Red Sox. Oil Can had regained enough trust from the organization to be on the mound the day Boston clinched the title with a 12-3 victory.

Boggs was leading the league in hitting at the time, and in the final days of 1986, found himself in a close race with Yankees first baseman Don Mattingly for the title. Boggs had boosted his average up to a healthy .357 when the Yankees came to town for the final 4 games of the year. Mattingly was at .350. Boggs announced he had suffered a hamstring injury, and would sit out the last series. That meant Mattingly, who was at .350, would have to go 9-12 against Boggs's teammates to take the title.

New York's players and fans screamed foul. They were convinced Boggs was faking to protect his numbers. A tabloid headline screeched, "Chicken!" But Boggs would not pick up the bat. Mattingly went 3 for 5 in the first day, but wound up as the runner-up with a final average of .352.

Boston turned to Clemens to set the tone against the California Angels in the ALCS. Instead, he gave up five early runs, watched Angels pitcher Mike Witt retire 17 in a row, and the Red Sox lost 8-1. Boston rebounded with a 9-2 flogging of its own in Game 2, but when they dropped both Games 3 and 4, they were down 3-1, and their World Series hopes were in jeopardy.

Witt was on the mound for California, and built a 5-2 lead. Sox outfielder Tony Armas sprained his ankle running down a fly ball in the second inning and had to leave the game. In the ninth, Sox first baseman Bill Buckner singled, and a Baylor two-run homer gave Boston new life. Witt coaxed Evans into a harmless pop-up, and with two down, Angels manager Gene Mauch decided to pull Witt and bring in reliever Gary Lucas to pitch to Boston's lefty catcher, Rich Gedman. Lucas hit Gedman on the hand.

Mauch then signaled led for Donnie Moore, a tested veteran who had battled shoulder problems in the second half of 1986. Outfielder Dave Henderson, who replaced Armas after his injury, stepped up to the plate and took two horrible swings. Moore worked the count to 2-2, then threw Hendu a forkball, low and away. Henderson whalloped the pitch into left-center field for a home run, leaping into the air for a 360 degree spin as he ran toward the bag. Sox 6, Angels 5. Even though California tied it in the bottom of the ninth, the Red Sox—for once—played the role of the spoiler. The charmed Henderson ended it in the 11th with an RBI liner, and Boston had won, 7-6.

The shell-shocked Angels never recovered. Boston blew them out in the final two games, 10-4 and 8-1. Although Barrett was the MVP on the strength of his .367 average and his error-free play at second, the new Sox legend was Henderson, the affable center-fielder who was a reserve for most of 1986. Henderson enjoyed a magical postseason run that continued as Boston turned its attention to its World Series opponent, the New York Mets.

The Mets were not nearly as distasteful as their Yankee neighbors, but they were still from New York, and possessed a certain measure of arrogance that comes along with winning 108 games and running away with your division by 21 games. Buckner, who had played in the National League, warned his teammates about their power. Boston's veteran, limping from an an Achilles injury he suffered in the California series, declared himself ready to play.

Game 1 proved to be a gritty pitcher's duel between Hurst and Mets righthander Ron Darling, who had gone to high school in Massachusetts. Boston escaped with a 1-0 win, with the one run unearned. Jim Rice walked in the seventh, moved to second on Darling's wild pitch, then scored when Mets second baseman Tim Teufel booted a Rich Gedman grounder. Schiraldi came on in the ninth to record the save, and admitted afterwards, "I was as nervous as I've ever been." Buckner, who had been replaced in the eighth by Dave Stapleton for defensive purposes, expressed his disappointment to Barrett, who told him McNamara did the right thing. "We're up, and Stapes can make plays you can't," Barrett said bluntly.

Any semblance of another pitching showdown disintegrated in the early innings of Game 2. Mets star Doc Gooden gave up six runs in five innings, and Clemens, the Cy Young and MVP winner, was gone midway through the fifth. Bob Stanley pitched three strong innings of relief, and Boston won easily, 9-3. The Mets were pressed to explain their anemic hitting. They had batted only .189 against Houston in the National League Championship Series, and they were feeling the pressure from the New York media. Boyd, who would pitch Game 3, boldly predicted he would "master" the Mets.

Boyd was nearly late to the ballpark when he drove to Logan Airport and picked up his family from Mississippi. The Sumner Tunnel, which exits the airport, was jammed with traffic, and the excitable Can was getting nervous. His brother poked his head through the sunroof of the car and implored the motorists to let his brother through. On cue, the cars parted and gave Boyd a clear lane to Fenway.

New York roughed Boyd up for four runs in the first inning, including a leadoff home run by Lenny Dykstra, who sniffed after his team's 7-1 victory, "The only one who was mastered tonight was him." The Mets winner was Bobby Ojeda, who had pitched for the Red Sox just one year earlier. After the Sox loss, McNamara said he would go with Nipper in Game 4, so Hurst could pitch on four days' rest. Nipper, one of the most likable players on the team, was carting around a bloated ERA of 5.38. He gave up three runs in the fourth inning. Suddenly, hitting was no longer a problem for the Mets. Catcher Gary Carter hit two home runs, and Dykstra also connected on a long ball. Boston's meat of the order, meanwhile, had problems of its own. Boggs went 0 for 5 in Game 4 and was hitting just .212 for the Series. Rice (1 for 4) and Buckner (0 for 5) were not faring much better.

With the Series now tied 2-2, the Red Sox enlisted legend Ted Williams to throw out the first pitch. Boston chased Gooden again with big hits from Rice, Henderson and Evans, leaving the young Mets star winless in the

1986 World Series. Hurst, meanwhile, chalked up a complete game in the 4-2 win. McNamara exhibited just a glimmer of a smile after the game, and why not? Boston would trot out Clemens for Game 6 on five days' rest. His record with that much time off between starts: 6-0 with a 2.29 ERA. The Mets, conversely, would be asking Ojeda to pitch on three days' rest for the first time all season.

As the Series went back to Shea Stadium, McNamara was asked if he was considering replacing a struggling Buckner (he was hitting .174 and wearing special high-top shoes to protect his achilles) with the veteran Baylor at first. "I think it will be Buckner," deadpanned McNamara. "He was hobbling at 100 percent today."

After Paul Simon sang the national anthem, Boston provided Clemens with a 2-0 lead on RBI singles from Evans and Barrett. The Mets got two back in the fifth on RBI singles from Ray Knight, Wilson and a rare Evans error. As Clemens came off in the seventh with a 3-2 lead, he showed McNamara a developing blister in his middle finger. He had already thrown 135 pitches, and McNamara replaced him with Schiraldi in the eighth. A Carter sacrifice fly tied it 3-3 and Clemens, like Gooden, would not record a W in the '86 Series.

In the years that followed, it became a matter of debate whether Clemens asked to come out, or whether McNamara pulled him. Both the manager and the pitcher had different stories on that critical decision, one of many in this now legendary game.

The game went into extra innings. In the top of the 10th, Henderson homered to left, poised to be the postseason hero again. Boggs added a two-out double, and Barrett singled him home. 5-3 Red Sox.

As Schiraldi coaxed both Backman and Keith Hernandez into fly balls in the outfield, Red Sox personnel were busy in the bowels of Shea Stadium, wheeling carts of champagne into Boston's clubhouse. Attendants peeled the foil off the bottles, and carefully laid a T-shirt proclaiming the Red Sox "World Champions!" over each player's chair. Balloons were hung from the ceiling. Some Red Sox officials debated whether to head down from the luxury box to the clubhouse, while Jean Yawkey sat stoically in her seat. She had seen it all before. She knew it wasn't over until the final out.

She was right. Schiraldi yielded singles to Carter and Mitchell. He got two quick strikes on Knight, and was one away from nailing down the World Series when Knight rapped an RBI single, cutting the lead to 5-4. McNamara pulled the kid and brought in the veteran Stanley to end it. Admitted Schiraldi afterwards, "I didn't do the job. I don't deserve any more chances."

The portly Stanley, who had endured the wrath of his fans all season, worked the count to Mookie Wilson to 2-2. He, too, was just one strike away from winning it. But when Stanley came back with another fastball, it tailed away and grazed off Gedman's glove. It was scored a wild pitch, but Bostonians argue to this day whether Gedman should have been able to block the ball. Mitchell ran home from third and the score was tied, 5-5.

Stanley bore down. His heart skipped hopefully when Wilson hit a weak ground ball toward first. It should have been the play that enabled Stanley to escape the jam. Instead, Buckner, who had not been replaced by Stapleton this time, failed to rush the ball. The ball bounced three times, skipped under

Bill Buckner's error allows the winning run to score in Game 6 of the 1986 World Series. (Stan Grosfeld/*The Boston Globe*)

his glove, and through his legs. Fans all throughout New England sat in utter disbelief as Knight scored from second with the winning run. The Sox clubhouse crew quickly snapped up the championship T-shirts, popped the balloons, and wheeled the champagne away. Torrez, the goat in 1978, was seen running through Shea Stadium shouting, "I'm off the hook! I'm off the hook!" In a brief interview with Boston television commentator Clark Booth, Torrez looked straight into the camera and said, "I can really honestly say Boston can't blame me anymore for Bucky Dent."

Buckner retreated to the showers and did not come out for thirty minutes. When he did, he courageously faced the hordes of reporters and said wearily, "The ball skipped. I thought I had it. Nobody feels worse than I do."

The next day, torrential rains forced the postponement of Game 7, leaving the Red Sox

to revisit their demons for another 24 hours. The added day off did have its benefits, though. It allowed McNamara to pitch Hurst, who was 2-0 with an ERA of 1.06 in the series. Boyd, the scheduled pitcher, wept bitterly when he was informed he would not be given the chance to save the season.

Hurst submitted another heroic outing. The Sox spotted him three runs, and he pitched a one-hitter through five innings. But Hurst had only pitched on three days' rest a handful of times. Mets hitters Lee Mazzilli and Keith Hernandez tagged him for key hits in the sixth, and by the time the inning was over, the game was tied 3-3, and Boston's most reliable postseason pitcher was gone.

McNamara brought Schiraldi in to pitch the eighth. Knight homered. McNamara tried relievers Joe Sambito and Stanley, but the bullpen couldn't hold, and New York pulled ahead 6-3. They won their World Championship by an 8-5 score, and in the funereal Red

Sox clubhouse, Nipper cried, Boyd cursed and Evans insisted, "I don't believe in luck. I don't believe in history either, but maybe I'm starting to. Sixty-eight years (without a championship) is a long time. It does make you wonder."

The Boston Globe • October 28, 1986

THE METS TAKE IT, 8-5

. . . and Boston is Mudville once again

By Dan Shaughnessy, Globe Staff

New York—The taste is so very bitter. When the Red Sox get to the seventh game of the World Series, the other team uncorks champagne while the Sox uncork wild pitches.

What is it like to live in a city that wins a World Series? Call your out-of-town friends and ask. Generations of Bostonians may never know

The New York Mets beat the Boston Red Sox, 8-5, in the seventh game of the 1986 World Series last night, and Boston is Mudville once again.

Somebody will rise up and say that the Sox did well to get this close. They'll say that if they told you in spring training that the Red Sox would win the American League East and the AL pennant, you'd be delighted.

But you are not delighted. The Red Sox took you to the edge again. They made you fall in love and they broke your heart. Again.

The Sox had every opportunity to win their first World Series since 1918, but they failed. They found new ways to miss the mark. They penned another macabre chapter in the region's longest-running horror story.

. . .

But they couldn't finish it off, and that is what Boston fans will remember when they think of the '86 Sox.

Ninety-two-year-old Bostonian Dick Casey saw all the Boston Series games when the Red Sox beat the Cubs in 1918. Before Game 6, he told NBC-TV, "I pray to God I don't die until I see another winner. This is my year. I must be gonna die pretty soon."

Not yet, sir. Stick around a while longer. ▪

The city held a parade the following day for their beaten team, but it was sparsely attended. The Red Sox legacy of losing was nothing to celebrate.

Boston has not been back to the World Series since 1986, but Clemens, Boggs and Zimmer have. Each of them won their championship rings wearing the uniform of the New York Yankees.

CHAPTER SIX

Destiny and Dent

by Harvey Araton of The New York Times

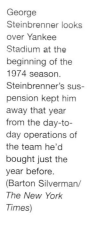

George Steinbrenner looks over Yankee Stadium at the beginning of the 1974 season. Steinbrenner's suspension kept him away that year from the day-to-day operations of the team he'd bought just the year before. (Barton Silverman/ *The New York Times*)

Late on the Sunday afternoon of July 9, 1978, Lou Piniella dropped into the seat next to me on the Yankees' team bus after an 8-4 pounding in Milwaukee's County Stadium and unwittingly saved my budding journalism career.

Absurdly inexperienced and, worse, an inveterate Yankee fan, I had set out on the ultimate candy-land adventure and wound up in unimaginable misery. Attempting to make sense of a dysfunctional three-ring circus starring Billy Martin, Reggie Jackson and George Steinbrenner was the rookie reporter's equivalent of facing an agitated Clemens or Pedro in his first big-league at-bat. The Yankees dropped four of five on a road trip to Hell to fall 11½ games behind the hated Red Sox in the American League East, on the way to digging themselves into a now immortalized 14-game hole.

The games were the least of it, but for the record, one was lost in Texas when a kid second baseman, Damaso Garcia, failed to cover first on a sacrifice bunt. In the opener of the three-game weekend series in Milwaukee, the majestic Ron Guidry was beaten for the first time after 13 wins. The next night, Rich Gossage surrendered a decisive two-run homer to Larry Hisle in the eighth inning. Sunday, Don Gullett blew his shoulder out. Billy benched Reggie. Reggie blasted Billy. Imbibing into the wee hours, Billy could barely open his eyes in the light of day and, for his part, the volatile Piniella couldn't stand the sight of what was happening to the defending World Series champions.

Sweet Lou vented his frustrations to reporters, a tirade I happened upon in the clubhouse only as it was ending—a potentially disastrous lapse, considering my employer

was Rupert Murdoch, the Steinbrenner of daily journalism. No one on this cutthroat beat was about to bail out the rookie from Murdoch's scandal sheet but fortunately for me, Piniella didn't choose another seat on the post-game bus from which to resume his pregame rant. Everyone was sick of Steinbrenner, he complained, adding that the Yankees' chances of catching the Red Sox were roughly equivalent to Billy and Reggie sharing the Nobel Peace Prize.

Admittedly, this was gourmet food for the belching back-page New York City tabloid beast, but all professionalism aside, Piniella's practically conceding to the Red Sox a day before the all-star break was a dagger to the inner child in the seat next to him whose first vivid recollection of any baseball happening was Roger Maris's 61st home run in 1961—off the Red Sox' Tracy Stallard. To the boy whose first live game at Yankee Stadium occurred July 20, 1965, made historically noteworthy by Mel Stottlemyre's grand slam, inside-the-park home run—off the Red Sox' Bill Monbouquette.

I can still conjure up the delightful sight of all those Yankees circling the bases as the ball scooted into Death Valley between Carl Yastrzemski in left field and Jim Gosger in center in the pre-reconfigured Stadium. Just another indelible Yankee-Red Sox memory, treasured like the ticket stub a new girlfriend once produced from a Dave Righetti no-hitter on July 4, 1983—against (who else?) the Red Sox. (I gained permanent possession of the Righetti stub through marriage in 1985.)

Often raised question: Why do we romanticize a rivalry that for the better part of a century has been so discriminately one-sided, arrogance versus impotence, in the context of birthing World Series championships? Each generation has its motivation, its emotional bonding mechanism. Speaking for baby boomers, many of us were born too late to revel in the dynastic Yankees of the Fifties and early Sixties. We watched with wide-eyed curiosity as they dominated the American League through 1964 but the chronological truth of the matter is that we were barely old enough to distinguish between Mickey Mantle and Superman, the Yankee rotation and the Fantastic Four. By the time I was a Babe Ruth leaguer, the Mick was a hobbled has-been.

To me it always seemed preternaturally cruel that 1965, the year I took my first No. 4 subway line ride to Yankee Stadium, happened to be the first of 11 pennantless seasons. The Yankees' descent to the bottom of the American League standings and to virtual insignificance resulted in their purchase by Steinbrenner in 1973 from the CBS company and my own rude adolescent awakening in the age of Vietnam to harsh political and social realities: America wasn't omnipotent and all that's pure. The Yankees, my Yankees, were downright pitiful.

But the times sure were a changin' as Steinbrenner took control by making the soon-laughable promise to remain apart from daily baseball operations.

The New York Times — January 4, 1973

C.B.S. SELLS THE YANKEES FOR $10-MILLION

By Joseph Durso

The Columbia Broadcasting System said yesterday that it was selling the New York Yankees to a 12-man syndicate headed by Michael Burke, now president of the team, and George M. Steinbrenner 3rd of Cleveland.

The price is $10 million in cash, which is $3.2 million less than C.B.S. paid for the franchise in 1964, the last year the Yankees won the American League pennant. Mr. Burke, who has been running the club for C.B.S., will continue to direct it for the self-styled "absentee owners," and the Yankees, he said, will remain in New York.

The paying public probably will not be affected by the change in ownership, both men conceded. But Mayor Lindsay said in a statement that the city welcomed the news "as the landlord of the Yankees" and he promised that the city's $24-million program to buy and modernize Yankee Stadium would "continue in full force."

The only partners in the syndicate who appeared at Yankee Stadium for the announcement were Mr. Burke and Mr. Steinbrenner, 42-year old chairman of the American Ship Building Company and part owner of the Chicago Bulls basketball team. No other partners were identified—except as "prominent business executives and sportsmen"—though the Yankees said they would be introduced in person here next week.

· · ·

"As landlord of the New York Yankees," Mayor Lindsay said in his statement, "the city welcomes today's news. The city has made firm plans and appropriated funds to refurbish completely the stadium and its environs by 1975. These plans, appropriations and all agreements continue in full force and effect. For the Yankees, which are such an integral part of the Bronx and the whole city, we know the best is yet to come."

In its statement C.B.S. said "the $10-million purchase price substantially recoups the original C.B.S. investment of $13.2 million, taking into account consolidated financial results during the period of ownership. The purchase price is well in excess of the value carried on the C.B.S. books."

"We plan absentee ownership as far as running the Yankees is concerned," Steinbrenner said. "We're not going to pretend we're something we aren't. I'll stick to building ships." ■

The dormant Yankee-Red Sox rivalry of the late sixties was reignited by their young, emerging catchers, the squat Thurman Munson and the statuesque Carlton Fisk. They played with attitude. They didn't like each other. During Steinbrenner's first year as principal owner, the '73 season, Munson and Fisk collided at home plate on a failed Yankee suicide squeeze. Punches were thrown. Positions were hardened. There was no longer doubt that Steinbrenner's Yankees would fight. But could they win? We waited for a sign, any sign, and it came during the second week of September 1974, fittingly enough at Fenway Park.

On the strength of a stunning late August surge and a proverbial Boston swoon, the Yankees arrived in Boston tied for first place with the Red Sox, who had since May been the sole occupier in the A.L. East. These were the Red Sox of Yaz and Fisk, of the young Fred Lynn and Jim Rice, and of the Cuban magician, Luis Tiant, who already had 20 wins in the bank when he took the mound against Pat Dobson, the Yankees ahead by a game on the strength of their first victory at Fenway in 13½ months the previous night.

My Yankee-loving friends and I huddled

around the television as we would four years later for a one-game playoff, for Mike Torrez's date with destiny and Dent. The 1978 game would become our seminal baseball event but what we watched on Sept. 10, 1974 qualified as an indisputable Yankee-Red Sox classic, far more for its qualitative drama than its historical significance. For the hope it engendered that our childhood mythology was soon to become our young adult reality.

The details have been checked for accuracy but what true baseball fan can't re-create a dozen games, recall them like a favorite poem? So it was, the Sox scored a run in the first inning but Dobson proceeded to match Tiant zero for zero, into the ninth when, with one out, Piniella drew a walk. "BALL FOUR!" bellowed the Scooter, Phil Rizzuto, in the Channel 11 booth, somehow knowing that Tiant's largesse foretold breathtaking events.

Sure enough, Bill Virdon, the Yankees' manager, pre-Martin, sent out a swift pinch runner, Larry Murray. Chris Chambliss, who would in two years win a pennant with one cathartic swing, laced a low line drive to the dirt track in right field. While Dwight Evans gave chase, Murray scored, Chambliss wound up on third. Evans, however, contended that a fan had reached over the low fence, touched the ball, and that the runners should be returned to third and second. While an argument ensued, Chambliss, standing at third, suddenly felt a prickly pain in his right arm, below the shoulder. He couldn't believe what he saw: a steel dart imbedded, cutting the skin right through the gray road shirt.

"When I looked back toward the stands behind third, there were darts all over the grass," said Chambliss, still appalled when I mentioned the episode almost three decades later. "I could have been hit right in the eye."

The run stood. The game went into extra innings. Dobson survived a bases-loaded jam in the ninth. In the 11th, the Yankees were saved by a sprawling stop by their second baseman, Sandy Alomar, and a Silly Putty stretch by the first baseman, Bill Sudakis. The stage was set for one of those archetypal Yankee moments that have, across the decades, defied competitive logic.

Arriving early that morning after a deal with Texas was one Alex Johnson, a strange and surly slugger joining his seventh team in 11 years. Facing Diego Segui in the 12th, Johnson hit a drive to right center that carried into the bleachers. He circled the bases, head down, without so much as an acknowledgement of the uproar in the Yankee dugout. In another time, another race, such a blow would have carved him a special place in New England infamy but a late September surge by Baltimore snatched the division from Boston and New York.

Springtime in Steinbrennerville had obviously come, though. The Yankees were no longer rotting at the core. Munson and Piniella were the new anchors, with Bobby Murcer, Roy White and Sparky (stolen from the Red Sox in 1972) Lyle. Graig Nettles came over from Cleveland to play an acrobatic third base in 1973, traded to the Yankees by Gabe Paul, who followed several months later to become the Yankees' team president. Chambliss, another Indian, was on his way. However suspicious all this was, Steinbrenner's reaching back to his hometown for the man who suggested he buy the Yankees in the first place was perhaps the most astute baseball decision he's made.

"People always think of the Yankees as players who George buys but the 1970s team was really the work of Gabe Paul through a number of very smart trades," said Marty Appel, the team's public relations director during those years. No deals were more ingenious than the two Paul made in the winter before the 1976 season. First Bobby Bonds, who had come from the Giants for Murcer and spent one injury plagued season in right field, was sent to the Angels for the eccentric and electric center fielder, Mickey Rivers, and Ed Figueroa, a dependable sinker ball pitcher. The acquisition of Figueroa allowed Paul to dispatch Doc Medich to Pittsburgh for a package of players that included the pitcher Dock Ellis and a rookie second baseman from Brooklyn, Willie Randolph. A plodding lineup was infused with youth, speed and defense up the middle. Matched with the combustible but canny managing of Martin, the Yankees returned from their two-year stay at Shea Stadium to a remodeled Yankee Stadium and won 97 games.

Chambliss hit a walk-off, pennant-clinching home run in the ninth inning of a deadlocked fifth game of the ALCS against Kansas City's Mark Littell but the Yankees were outclassed, swept in the World Series by the same Big Red Machine that had upstaged Fisk and the Red Sox the year before. Piniella, Munson, et al. believed they were only lacking experience for baseball's grand stage, and that they were on their way, especially with Guidry developing into one of baseball's premier pitchers. Steinbrenner wasn't taking any chances. In the emerging system of player emancipation known as free agency, it was now his turn at bat, his opportunity to wield his wallet like 40 meaty ounces of Louisville Slugger.

Announcing himself as an eager participant for decades to come, as a system-changer and the best friend the players' union ever had across the ideological street from Marvin Miller and Donald Fehr, Steinbrenner had already signed Catfish Hunter on New Year's Eve for the 1975 season.

The New York Times — January 1, 1975

YANKEES SIGN UP CATFISH HUNTER IN ESTIMATED $3.75-MILLION DEAL

By Murray Chass

Jim (Catfish) Hunter signed a five year contract estimated at $3.75 million with the New York Yankees last night, ending the most celebrated bidding war in American sports history. The total value of the pact sets a record for baseball.

The Yankees, trying to regain the glory that was theirs until the last decade, landed the 28-year-old right-hander, considered by many experts to be baseball's premier pitcher, with an assist from Clyde Kluttz, a club scout. Kluttz signed Hunter to his first professional contract with the Kansas City A's in 1964.

The signing, announced at a New Year's Eve news conference, took place at the Yankee offices in the Parks Administration Building in Flushing, Queens, where intricate negotiations wound up after Hunter and his lawyers flew here from North Carolina earlier in the day.

Gabe Paul, the Yankees president, refused to

disclose monetary terms but it was believed to be a $3.75 million package.

· · ·

The decision, which Finley is contesting in court, created a unique situation in baseball history. While football, basketball and hockey have been subjected to costly bidding wars in the last 15 years because of the birth of competing leagues, baseball has never had that problem.

Before baseball adopted its free-agent draft, major league clubs competed for young prospects and frequently paid upwards of $100,000. But a free agent of Hunter's experi-

ence and status was unheard of.

And when it came time for the American League's 1974 Cy Young Award winner to make his choice, he was swayed not by the money but by Kluttz's involvement and the Yankee image.

· · ·

Nor, Hunter said, would all the money dilute his desire to win. "In the last World Series," he said, "I had a card in my pocket that said, 'Winning isn't everything, but wanting to is.' I always want to win."

Hunter, a major leaguer for 10 years, tied for the most victories in the majors last season with

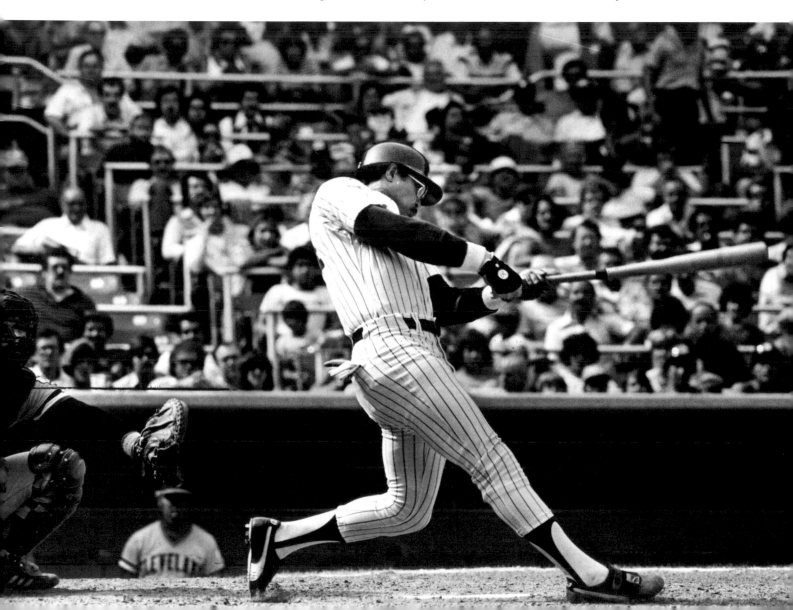

25. He lost 12 games and had a 2.49 earned-run average. He won 21 games in each of the previous three seasons, while losing only 23, giving him a four-year record of 88 victories and 35 defeats. He also won four times without losing in the World Series.

This was the pitcher who was the object of the affections and treasuries of teams that sent a constant stream of representatives to the tiny town of Hertford where Hunter has lived all of his life and the tiny town of Ahoskie where the law firm of Cherry, Cherry and Flythe has its offices.

Hertford and Ahoskie had never seen anything like it and now the Yankees hope Hunter will help them see the things they always used to see—pennants.

Reggie Jackson hit everything for the Yankees in 1978—from singles to home runs. He was George Steinbrenner's prize. (*The New York Times*)

For '77, Reggie was his prize, the home run slugger that Gabe Paul's sturdy lineup of contact hitters lacked, the self-proclaimed straw to stir the drink. The Yankees won another pennant and flattened the Dodgers in the Series with Reggie clouting three Yankee Stadium home runs in the clincher on a luminous South Bronx night. Mr. October was born. The Yankees were all the way back.

Yet for all of Reggie's theatrics, Martin's bluster and the quintessential professionalism of the Munson-Piniella-Chambliss cabal, it was Steinbrenner, the Boss, who defined these Yankee teams, who created and cultivated a bellicose environment, setting the precondition that judgment day was every day, and that failure in any form would be met with disgust and disdain. Steinbrenner's Yankees of the mid-to-late 1970s permanently changed

the tone of sports coverage, the perception of failure, in New York City. Condemnations of his tactics were widespread but you could never get away from the underlying acknowledgment, however grudging, that he produced what Yankee fans had long been waiting for.

Infected with Steinbrenner's expectations and emboldened by Martin's pugnacity, the Yankees carried on like a remake of the Bowery Boys. Not surprisingly, there was another brawl with the Red Sox in 1976, this one involving Piniella and Fisk, and leading to a free-for-all that left Boston's lefthander, Bill "Spaceman" Lee with a separated shoulder, never quite the same again. When the Sox couldn't be lured into battle, the Yankees turned on each other, as Martin and Jackson nearly came to blows one afternoon in the visitors' dugout at (where else?) Fenway Park.

Like New York, a city in fiscal and social upheaval, reeling from a 1977 summer blackout and a terrifying shooting spree by the killer known as Son of Sam, these Yankees were always on the edge but the ultimate survivors. They won three straight cliffhanger playoff series against a Kansas City team laden with worthy opponents like George Brett, Amos Otis and Fred Patek. They tormented Tommy Lasorda's talented Dodgers in successive World Series. And amid all those achievements, a run that carried the Yankees far beyond the limits of divisional enmity and reestablished the blighted Bronx as the center of the baseball universe was forever encapsulated in, yes, Boston on Oct. 2, 1978. On a sunny Monday afternoon, a season for the ages was reduced to a one-game playoff, a memory most easily accessed by the mere mention of a man who choked up like an undersized little leaguer begging to get his bat on the ball.

At the intersection of fate and Fenway, Bucky Dent hit a slider from Torrez high and deep, over the Green Monster. Bucky Bleeping Dent, for those in New England still keeping score, carrying old grudges.

The New York Times — October 2, 1978

RED SOX WIPED OUT ON DENT'S MIGHTY HOMER OVER THE WALL

By James Tuite

Boston—Somehow, it all defied logic. After more than 300 hours of baseball in 162 games spanning half a year, the season was distilled into 172 minutes on a sunny October afternoon.

Yet, here was the reductio ad absurdum: the New York Yankees, torn by bitterness and 14 games out of first place a month ago, sat atop the American League East on Monday, headed for a pennant confrontation with the Kansas City Royals.

"I've been dreaming of this," said Bucky Dent, of the seventh-inning homer he hit over the left-field wall. "You know you dream about things like that when you're a kid. Well, my dream came true."

He was talking about a looping drive that cleared the formidable rampart by at least five feet and sent Chris Chambliss and Roy White scurrying home ahead of him. That sent the Yankees two runs ahead of the Boston Red Sox and proved to be the mightiest blow of their 5-4 victory.

A double by Thurman Munson that scored Mickey Rivers provided another Yankee run in the seventh, this one off Fred Stanley. He had replaced Mike Torrez after the Yankees put a Dent in their former teammate. A Reggie Jackson homer in the eighth put the game away.

The record books will probably find it difficult to explain that Rivers and a bat boy deserve asterisks for Dent's home run. After Dent was struck on the ankle, Rivers handed a bat to Tony Sarandrea, the 18-year-old batboy.

"Give this to Bucky," said Rivers. "Tell him there are lots of hits in it. He'll get a home run."

Dent switched to the new bat and gave lie to Hemingway's observation that "a man can be destroyed but not beaten." That may apply to old fishermen but not to the Yanks: they defeated the Red Sox without destroying them.

For the record, Boston, still on a natural high after winning 12 of their last 14 games and eight of them in a row, gallantly fought back. Their partisans among the 32,925 noisy viewers here saw them make a game effort with two more runs in the eighth but only after the Yanks had collected a decisive one on a looping homer to centerfield by Jackson.

"It was a fastball right over the plate," said Jackson, who detoured on his way back to the dugout to shake the hand of his part-time adversary and Yankee president, George Steinbrenner.

· · ·

As for Don Zimmer, the Red Sox manager, he headed for Florida and a good night's sleep. "Usually these things don't bother me," said the old Brooklyn Dodger, "but I didn't sleep the last two nights."

Now he can settle down at the Holiday Inn that overlooks Calder racetrack and watch the morning workouts without worrying about his lineup against the Royals. Like Robert Browning, he will seek "a privacy, an obscure nook, to be forgotten even by God."

The Yankees left for Kansas City Monday night, wondering whether they can maintain their fine edge or whether they have been depleted of their energy. "Who knows," said Nettles, "it could go either way."

Dent was not worried about his injured foot. "A little ice and champagne will fix that," he said, smiling. "We'll just have to play solid, aggressive baseball against the Royals," he said. "We've got to concentrate on cutting down their base hits."

Dent, like the other Yanks in the clubhouse before the game, paid little heed to a voice blaring from a portable radio. It was Paul Harvey, the Chicago broadcaster, telling of the things that will come about in 100 years, like a pill that will raise IQ's and of doorlocks that will open automatically at the sound of a particular voice. He didn't say anything about the Red Sox ever beating the Yankees.

Where were you when the Yankees were batting in the top of the seventh inning, trailing 2-0, Chambliss and Roy White on base and the handsome shortstop stepping in against Torrez, who, speaking of curses, had won two 1977 World Series games for the Yankees before joining the Sox as a free agent? For Yankee fans, and especially those of us born in the 1950s, what followed was baseball's version of the first moon landing. For New Englanders, Dent's home run was athletically akin to the Kennedy assassination, at least for another eight Octobers, until 1986.

That afternoon, I nervously sipped beers and chewed fingernails in the cramped apart-

ment of Phil Mushnick, a *Post* colleague as well as a childhood friend growing up on Staten Island. We didn't have to worry ourselves with professional conflicts of interest that day, of going to work at all. Just weeks after my brush with journalism mortality in Milwaukee, the newspaper labor wars, as volatile as baseball's, shut down New York City's three major dailies. We were free to pursue full-time engagement as baseball fanatics.

In fact, many of the 1978 Yankees came to believe that the sudden halt of screaming headlines was instrumental in the charge back from 14 games. The reality was that the Don Zimmer–managed Red Sox contributed mightily by going into a dreadful slump and by the time of the newspaper strike a major source of the Yankees' divisiveness had been expurgated. In late July, Martin spent too much time in an airport bar and proceeded to serve up unsavory characterizations of Jackson ("a liar") and Steinbrenner ("convicted") to the very sober Murray Chass of the *New York Times* and Henry Hecht of the *Post*. Under fire, Martin resigned and the more staid Bob Lemon stepped in to ride the historic wave that carried the Yankees from their nadir of 14 games out on July 17 to within four games of the Sox as the Yankees went into Boston for a four-game series on Sept. 7.

Oh, to be young, on strike and fortunate enough to have a colleague willing to sign you in on picket duty. Free of marching for better dental coverage, I gassed up my cranky Honda Civic and headed north with a couple of buddies to score center-field bleacher seats, to prove that I could have the time of my life while having beer cups and assorted debris hurled at my Yankee-helmeted head. At least the natives weren't exploding firecrackers, an occurrence that had already convinced Rivers

Ron Guidry was virtually untouchable in 1978, with the Yankees winning 30 out of his 35 starts. (*The New York Times*)

he was best suited in center in his trusty batting helmet. Anyway, the Yankees celebrated the occasion of my first-ever visit to Fenway by sweeping the Sox by the combined score of 42-9. We attended three games of what is now remembered as the Boston Massacre, including a 15-3 rout of Torrez and the Red Sox bullpen in the opener and a 13-2 blowout the following night when Jim Beattie carried a shutout into the ninth. Jim Bleeping Beattie!

How different, I wonder, might that October have turned out had the Sox been able to even split at home, maintain a four-game lead? How many baseball lives would have been recast had they, not the Yankees, won it all that year and established themselves as New York's competitive equal for the decade at two World Series and one championship apiece? How would the lifting of the so-called Curse of the Bambino have affected the next quarter-century? Would a team that was free of its inglorious past no longer feel

obligated to live inside it? Would antiquated Fenway have already come down, replaced during the 1990s wave of retro ballpark construction fueled by Clinton-era prosperity?

Watching the Red Sox strand 12 runners and get swept out of the playoffs at home by Cleveland one fall night in 1995, it occurred to me that perhaps their curse was not the Babe but the beloved ballpark itself. Forever, it seems, Ye Olde Town Team has been tailored to antiquity, wailing at the Wall while taking one base at a time. Go back to '78: the Red Sox may very well have survived Dent's home run and the additional two the Yankees tacked on for a 5-2 lead after 7½ innings had they been more adept at manufacturing runs.

Symbolism is an inevitable part of history but the roots of the Red Sox' more spectacular failures typically went much, much deeper. Bill Buckner was run out of Boston for his impersonation of a wicket on Mookie Wilson's ground ball, but the sixth game of the 1986

Rich Gossage fires pitches against the Red Sox at Yankee Stadium on Sept. 10, 1978 helping to tie the game. (*The New York Times*)

World Series was blown by the bullpen, not Buckner, and always overlooked was the 3-0 lead surrendered two nights later in Game 7. Likewise, the Red Sox had every opportunity to win the '78 playoff before the seventh inning, and after. The Yankees, as usual, were the superior fundamental and more opportunistic baseball team.

Start with Guidry, who had been virtually untouchable that season, 25-3 (including the Oct. 2nd playoff victory), with a 1.72 earned-run average. In June, at Yankee Stadium, he struck out 18 Angels. He threw nine shutouts, tying a Babe Ruth record. The Yankees won 30 of his 35 starts and in September Guidry had pitched consecutive two-hit shutouts against the Red Sox. But the playoff had been forced by Boston on the final day of the regular season, leaving Lemon no choice but to pitch Guidry on three days' rest. Guidry, whose lightning left arm belied his slender, unimposing figure, did not have his overpow-

ering stuff. A lineup he later called the toughest he ever faced might have feasted in this park on a sub-par southpaw. The best the Sox could do was a Yaz homer in the second and a single run in the sixth.

By the home seventh, with one out and the Red Sox stirring, Lemon went to Goose Gossage, his closer, these being the days before quiche-eating, one-inning wonders. By the time Gossage reached the ninth with a precarious 5-4 lead, he was practically working on fumes. With one out, Rick Burleson was on first, Jerry Remy at the plate. Here, Piniella made what was one of the most fortunate plays in baseball history or what I have come to believe was the best illustration of divergent destinies: before and beyond Bucky, all the way to Aaron Bleeping Boone.

It was a play that in the blink of a sun-blinded eye demonstrated the champion's resourcefulness the Red Sox couldn't quite match, that didn't show up in the box score or receive its proper airtime compared to the Dent home run or the ceremonial squeezing of the final out. One of those freaks of circumstance on which the principals involved never quite reach a circumstantial unanimity. A quarter-century later, with all due respect to Dent, Piniella was sure his moment in the sun was the difference between historic heartbreak and "a team winning the pennant."

Remy hit a Gossage fastball on a line to right. Burleson took off from first. Had he reached third, the tying run would have been 90 feet away with only one out.

"I remember sitting on the bench in the seventh inning and telling Lem that I was going to be in big trouble if the ball was hit to me out there on a line," Piniella said. "You couldn't see a thing. The sun was sitting up there behind the press box like a huge fireball. When the ball was hit, I saw it coming off the bat. Then it disappeared."

Willie Randolph was injured that day, sitting in the dugout. He remembers Piniella "kind of groping around out there, then suddenly grabbing the ball with his bare hand."

Actually, Randolph was informed, it was Piniella's glove hand.

"Okay," he said, "the glove hand."

Burleson, rounding second, screeched to a halt. When Jim Rice flied out to Piniella to deep right-center, Burleson tagged up and took third—as it turned out, one out too late. Red Sox fans had more reason than ever to curse their team's station-to-station attack. Worse, they had to endure the suggestion that Piniella, the same hothead who sat on the bus in Milwaukee nearly three months earlier and, far from a pennant, ran up a white flag, had decoyed Burleson, duped the Red Sox out of the tying run.

"When the play happened, I didn't actually see much because I was running with my head down," Remy, now a Red Sox broadcaster, recalled. "But I've seen it a couple of times on film. Burleson got ripped up here for not taking third but if you watch it closely, you'll see that Piniella not only made a great stop but that he also made a quick throw in. That was the key. Did he decoy? I don't see how."

Did he decoy?

"Yeah, I actually did," Piniella said. "See, because I knew the sun was bad, I was almost expecting something like that. So when I saw the ball leaving the bat, I started backing up, backing up, pounding the glove like it was coming right at me. If Burleson was looking out there, and he had to be, that's what I wanted him to think. But once I lost the ball, I never saw it again until the last second. Stuck the glove out, made a strong throw to third. If it gets past me, we probably lose. No excuses."

The Red Sox had none either, given all the chances they had, right down to the great Yastrzemski stepping in against Gossage, strength against strength. Once, reflecting on '78 while relaxing in the Yankees' spring training clubhouse, Gossage told me that the night before the playoff he had closed his eyes and drifted off to sleep imagining this very game-ending scenario: tying and winning runs on, late afternoon shadows crossing the field, him on the mound, Yaz in the box.

That Gossage was even with the Yankees was an example of Steinbrenner's commitment to excellence or excess, depending on one's allegiance. Lyle had barely finished celebrating winning the 1977 Cy Young Award when he learned that Steinbrenner had signed Gossage, a fireballing right-hander, a mustachioed Mariano Rivera, as a free agent. Lyle was so befuddled that he answered the telephone one winter morning at his New Jersey home and told me, a complete stranger and office clerk on rewrite tryout, that he wanted to be traded. My first back-page "*Post* exclusive" made no headway with Steinbrenner, who said he needed righty and lefty closers. Lyle knew there was only room for one. Months later, sitting in the Fenway visitors' bullpen, he was sure he could get Yaz, the southpaw slugger with his bat cocked high, out with his trademark slider, down and away. Lemon never gave him a look. The game rested with Gossage, weakened as he was.

"I was scattered that whole day," Gossage said. "The pressure was so great that by the time Yaz came up, I was all over the place. Breathing heavy, heart pounding. It was about then that I had this conversation with myself. I said, 'This is what you wanted, what you dreamt about. The worst that can happen is that you'll be home in Colorado tomorrow. It's not life and death.' Then it was like this eerie calm came over me. I was relaxed. I mean, really relaxed, with this amazingly controlled aggression. I looked in at Yaz and actually told myself: 'This is fun.' And when I got him to pop up and the game was over, Munson told me I had about a foot more on that fastball than any other pitch I'd thrown that day."

Years later, passion still came to Gossage's voice as he spoke of the moment when Yaz lifted the ball tamely in the air and Nettles squeezed the Yankees' 32nd pennant. His eyes narrowed, a fist clenched. The barrel chest and cheek-to-cheek mustache completed the picture of intimidation that captured his closer's credo: "You've got to want to bury them, put your foot on their throat."

In October of 1978, the Yankees left the Red Sox under a mountain of frustration. A decade that had been the Yankees' least productive since before the 1920s was closing with a flourish, with New York's sense of proper order restored. But then came 1979, a tragedy in the family, a shocking death even those who reviled the most decorated team in baseball would mourn. In the South Bronx, a dynasty was at half-staff, and it would be years before the Yankees would raise a World Series banner again.

* * *

The plain truth was that something was lost from Munson and the Yankees even before he crashed his Cessna Citation airplane, while practicing takeoffs and landings at Akron-Canton Regional Airport on Aug. 2, 1979. Only months earlier, in the eighth inning of Game 3 of the '78 ALCS, the Yankees trailing by a run, Munson walloped a mammoth two-run homer into the left-field bullpen off the Royals' Doug Bird. Though no one's idea of a slugger, Munson was on that day positively Ruthian, larger than life.

And then he was gone, paying the ultimate price for wanting better access to his family, for learning to fly. Munson had even considered asking the Yankees to trade him to Cleveland. By '79, he was wearing down after years of taking a beating behind the plate. He became the personification of a team that resembled an aging boxer following his most brutal war, Ali after Frazier. Even when Martin replaced Lemon in Steinbrenner's often-preposterous game of musical managers, the Yankees seemed tired. After Munson perished, they were emotionally spent.

Steinbrenner, predictably, moved quickly to

retool his roster. The Yankees were potent enough to make the playoffs in 1980, but the Royals finally beat them and the Boss blamed and fired his manager, Dick Howser, who had won a mere 103 regular-season games. In the strike-torn season of '81, the Yankees reached the World Series but succumbed in six games to the Dodgers.

With every failure he construed as embarrassment, Steinbrenner grew more strident, more meddlesome. When Winfield, his newest and richest free agent, struggled in the '81 series, Steinbrenner cruelly dubbed him Mr. May and issued a public apology no one had asked for. By the mid-eighties, the Mets had nurtured a formidable young pitching staff. They took figurative ownership of New York, a humbling turn for Yankee fans, most of whom I knew rooted for the Red Sox in the '86 World Series. Even the power of positive thinking from fans grown accustomed to winning couldn't pull the Yankees' long-tormented American League cousin through against the junior side from New York, New York.

In the eighties, Yankee fans had Winfield, a superb player, and the emerging Don Mattingly to cheer for but season after season was undone by a lack of pitching, by an organizational blueprint consistently undermined by the owner's chronic intolerance. My own rooting proclivities had by then waned, complicated by career demands, ethics and exposure to Steinbrenner. Any journalist who spent time around the Yankees invariably came to realize the true horror of what it meant to be an employee in the path of Hurricane George.

Never will I forget the summer afternoon I sat in a Triple A ballpark in Omaha, Nebraska, hearing Bobby Meacham and his wife, Gari,

tearfully speak of how a promising career had been derailed, arguably destroyed, by an ogre of an owner who would flip the switch on the trap door to the minors when his young shortstop made a costly error, who would rage that Meacham's strong religious beliefs had made him too accepting of his mistakes. Once, while Meacham was on the disabled list, Steinbrenner ordered his dressing stall stripped bare. His equipment was packed into a bag and thrown against a wall. Teammates Mattingly, Dave Righetti and Mike Pagliarulo propped open an old trunk, stood it upright, and in it placed Meacham's clothes, his spikes, a poster and a bottle of champagne.

As the years passed, many Yankee fans had to dichotomize their allegiance, make a clear separation between church (the Stadium) and state (the Boss). Never was this easier than when Joe Torre became manager in 1996 and what ultimately may be recalled as the most gracious Yankee core of champions in the history of the franchise embarked on a remarkable run of four World Series titles in five years, six Series appearances in eight.

My own two sons have cut their teeth as casual baseball fans on Torre's Yankees, while I have gone off to cover games as a columnist for the *New York Times*, explaining that because Dad editorializes, he does not root. Well, most of the time, that is. Occasionally, understandably, there is bound to be a tug on those deep-rooted memories tracing all the way back to 1961. Really, how could Maris and Stottlemyre and, yes, Alex Johnson be suppressed when the Yankees psychologically socked it to Boston again, snatching Game 7 of the 2003 ALCS late in the New York night.

Watching with my family at home, I crossed one of those generational thresholds of contentment when the 14-year-old, for whom baseball's slow pace had always been a major source of irritation, described the tension of the extra-inning marathon as unbearable. Giddily, we waved Derek Jeter and Hideki Matsui bobble head dolls at the television screen as the Yankees rallied and Grady Little surrendered to Pedro's competitive conceit. As the game stretched toward the familiar conclusion Yankee fans and Red Sox fatalists would, as usual, attribute the outcome to some baseball authority much higher than the commissioner's office.

Such abstract explication inevitably short-changes the Red Sox' dogged pursuit of the Yankees. It undervalues the inspiring dynamic that has forced the Yankees to be even better than the sum of their very capable parts and has exposed the most human qualities of a franchise that was once compared to U.S. Steel.

Men of steel? I don't think so. All the way back in 1974, Chris Chambliss took a dart in the arm at Fenway Park, and proved that real Yankees do cut.

For Red Sox Nation, it only matters if they bleed.

Fenway Park and Yankee Stadium

By Jack Curry of The New York Times

They are two aging baseball stadiums that are really more friendly ballparks than stadiums to their fans, two ballparks that are just as much landmarks as ballparks and two landmarks that are as hallowed as two cathedrals that have each been standing for close to a century.

The religion practiced in the ancient cathedrals known as Yankee Stadium and Fenway Park is universal, the religion of baseball. It is impossible to think about the New York Yankees without linking them to the Stadium and just as impossible to dwell on the Boston Red Sox without linking them to Fenway Park.

Some people love cozy Fenway for the Green Monster in left field and love the much more spacious Stadium for the short porch in right field. Some people loathe them for the same reasons. But, anyone with a sense of history keenly understands how pivotal they have been while housing two of the most storied franchises in professional sports.

The Stadium and Fenway have framed the greatest rivalry in baseball, like two grand, green stages, separated by a mere 206 miles. The ride from the Bronx to Boston can be navigated in three and a half traffic-free hours, which is about how long it takes the Yankees and the Red Sox to play another possibly thrilling game and add another sliver of history to an endlessly entertaining pile.

Who has walked into Fenway, stared at the

The Green Monster, Fenway Park's famed left field wall, during an All Star batting practice in 1999. While the Monster may have made the Red Sox more vulnerable on the road, it works in their favor at home. (Associated Press)

37-foot Monster looming so close in left and not dreamed of slapping one off the wall? Not even over it. Just off the wall would be enough. Who has strolled into the Stadium, peered toward the 314-foot sign on the right-field fence and not dreamed of smacking one over it? It does not look that deep in right, right? It is those daily dreams, shared by so many Jeter and Garciaparra wannabes, that add to the allure of these parks.

Like all good cathedrals, the parishioners who inhabit them are what makes them so special. From the players to the fans to the vendors, these parks that moonlight as cathedrals have more than 170 combined years of history scattered from one corner to another and then back again, thousands of memories filling sunny days, dark nights and long winters waiting for those days and nights.

"You've had grandfathers who have taken their sons and then taken their grandsons to see games over the years," said Whitey Ford, the Hall of Fame Yankee who actually pitched his first major league game at Fenway on July 1, 1950. "Maybe they all want it to be that way forever."

Still, with all of the nostalgia that permeates the rivalry and the two settings, there is also a cold reality. The cold reality is that the Stadium has played host to teams that have won 26 World Series titles while Fenway has played host to teams that have won only four of Boston's five titles and none since 1918. The Yankees have excelled in their home while the Red Sox have evaporated in theirs.

No matter how charming fans think Fenway is as a place where they almost feel as if they can reach across a row of seats and touch Pedro Martinez's arm and a place that has hardly changed in almost seventy years, it remains a place that has not been home to a champion in 85 seasons and counting.

FENWAY PARK

Fenway was born on April 20, 1912, five days after the *Titanic* sunk, and is the oldest and smallest ballpark in the major leagues. It was considered more of a pitcher's park while the Red Sox won four championships in Fenway's first seven seasons. The Red Sox were a formidable force in their quirky home, a place with support beams obstructing the views from some seats and fans so close to the field that they might as well have been sitting in their own backyards.

Everything about the Red Sox changed after they sold Babe Ruth, their premier player, to the Yankees for $100,000 and a $300,000 loan in 1919. Everything. The Red

Sox have not won a title since losing Ruth and their drought has been blamed on curses, misfortune, poor timing, poor personnel decisions, bad luck, bad pitchers, bad hitters, bad fielders and, of course, the Monster. It has been part of this ignominious streak, too. How big a part is debatable.

Tom Yawkey, the owner, added the wall before the 1934 season, a fence built of metal and steel and a fence that immediately became the focus of the park. Wrigley Field has its ivy, Yankee Stadium has its famous facade, but no stadium has anything like the Monster. The fence was so big that it made the already small park look even smaller. With such an inviting fence in left and scant foul territory down the outfield lines, Fenway evolved into a hitter's paradise.

Ted Williams, the greatest Red Sox hitter of all time, disliked the Monster, saying it skewed the balance of a game. Williams frowned upon anything that gave the pitcher or the hitter an unfair advantage and he felt the wall allowed a weak hitter to hit a pop fly to left that could clear the fence and demoralize a deserving pitcher. The last man to hit .400 did not grouse, though, when the Red Sox moved the bullpens to right field in 1940. That brought the fence 23 feet closer to the plate to cater to the power of their remarkable left-handed hitter.

Dom DiMaggio, Williams's teammate and the bespectacled gentleman who roamed center at Fenway, disagreed with Williams about the Monster. DiMaggio, a right-handed hitter, enjoyed pulling the ball and knowing, if he lifted it in the air enough, it was sure to rattle off the wall. The fence became all green in 1947. Before that, it was blanketed with advertisements.

"My admiration for the wall is for the fact that the wall treated me so well," said DiMaggio. "The wall and I got along beautifully. I bounced enough shots off it, I'll tell you."

But the wall also influenced the Red Sox to crowd their lineup with right-handed hitters and its presence helped boost the home statistics of its players. Usually these right-handed hitters were slow-running sluggers, meaning the Red Sox fielded teams who tried to pound the wall while not being skilled in bunting, stealing or hitting with runners in motion.

That approach worked at Fenway, but it made the Red Sox a much more vulnerable team on the road for half of their games. The managers who did not make many strategic decisions at home because they were used to waiting for a player to smash a timely homer at Fenway, something that could happen at any time and from any player in the lineup, waited forever for the huge homer on the road.

For far too long, the Red Sox were a team built for Fenway, but burdened by it away from the park. The Yankees have a 482-483-7 all-time record in Boston (not all games at Fenway) while the Red Sox are a much worse 381-565-7 in New York (not all games at the Stadium).

"It appeared we were always overloaded with right-handed power hitting," said DiMaggio. "In the later years, they realized you had to win games on the road, too."

DiMaggio said a lack of consistent pitching, not the Monster, is what has contributed most to the failure of the Red Sox to win a title. But Whitey Ford, while remembering how he shuddered before facing Boston's stellar lineups with Williams, Bobby Doerr and Johnny

Pesky, also thought the wall had handicapped the team.

"It seems like it's hurt them," said Ford. "Everybody remembers the Bucky Dent homer."

Indeed, they do. That one hurt. Hurt so badly. Dent was a puny shortstop, a puny Yankee, who quieted Boston in a 1978 playoff for the American League East title by poking a homer over the Monster. People in Boston rarely utter his name without adding an expletive between Bucky and Dent. In that one game, the wall, both lovable and laughable, destroyed the Red Sox.

Obviously, pitching at Fenway has been torturous for left-handers. Mel Parnell is the last Red Sox lefty to win 20 games, doing it in 1953. Over the last half century since Parnell did it, the Yankees, whose Stadium favors lefties because of the spacious left center and center, have received eight 20-victory seasons by lefties.

"Left-handers were a no no for us at Fenway," said DiMaggio.

Ford, who never minded when Casey Stengel skipped him in the rotation at Fenway, said a lefty could be successful there if he had a good sinker or slider and kept the ball in on right-handed batters' hands. While ground-ball pitchers are seemingly better suited for Fenway, Roger Clemens and Martinez combined for six Cy Young Awards as Red Sox and both are hard-throwing righties who generate a lot of fly balls.

"Those two," explained Ford, "would be successful anywhere."

Fenway is not just generous to right-handed hitters. Left-handed hitters, including Williams and Wade Boggs, a perennial batting champion, also learned how to adapt to the dimensions of the park. Boggs peppered doubles off the wall and once hit .418 at Fenway across a whole season.

The latest version of the Red Sox is an offensive force as they led the major leagues in runs scored and set an all-time record for total bases in 2003. Of course, the Red Sox love to hit homers at Fenway, especially into the new seats atop the Monster. But the organization emphasizes having players with high on-base percentages because that leads to the most chances to score runs.

In addition, with Martinez, Curt Schilling and Derek Lowe, Boston has three pitchers in its 2004 rotation who have been 20-game winners. Schilling agreed to a trade to the Red Sox because they showed him recent statistics proving Fenway is not as much of a homer haven as he believed. All three starters are righties as Boston was not expected to have a lefty in the rotation. At Fenway, that is not a terrible thing. Maybe that is a good omen for the Red Sox and their ballpark. Finally.

YANKEE STADIUM

Amazingly, it took only 248 days to build Yankee Stadium. And, when it was built, they came. The fans, that is. There were over 74,000 spectators in the Stadium when the Yankees beat the Red Sox, 4-1, in the first game there on April 23, 1923. Ruth clubbed a three-run homer, one of what would become hundreds of reminders of the mistake the Red Sox made in dealing him to the Yankees.

The Stadium immediately became known as the House That Ruth Built because everyone understood Ruth's drawing power as the most impressive slugger the sport had ever seen made the new stadium a reality. The

Let WHITE Build it of CONCRETE

SECOND BASE

THE OSBOR
ARCHITE
CLEV

Yankees won their first World Series in the opening year of the Stadium and have since played host to 36 championships. Before 1923, they had shared the Polo Grounds with the New York Giants.

Unlike Fenway, which favored right-handed batters, the Stadium was Death Valley for them. The left-field foul pole sat a tempting 281 feet from the plate, but a hitter had to pull a ball down the line to take advantage of it or risk being robbed by the 395-foot fence in left. It only got worse for right-handed hitters as the distance was 460 in left center and an incredible 490 to center. The Yankees reduced the center-field fence to 461 in 1937. Joe DiMaggio, for one, lost a countless number of homers in the yards and yards of outfield grass.

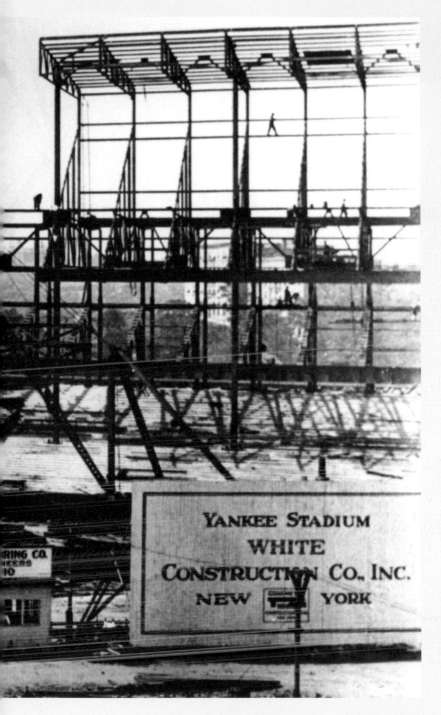

YANKEE STADIUM
WHITE
CONSTRUCTION CO., INC.
NEW YORK

But for left-handed hitters, like Ruth and Lou Gehrig, the right-field foul pole was a delightful 295-foot poke away and the fence was a reachable 370 feet to right. For Ruth, right field was an easy shot and he targeted the bleachers so often that the area in right became known as Ruthville.

The old Yankee teams filled their lineup with left-handed hitters and also wanted reli-

able lefties on the mound at the Stadium. Since most opponents had more right-handed hitters and right-handed pitchers, the Yankees usually had a sizable edge when they leaned to the left at home.

"I was left-handed and there weren't many left-handed hitters in the lineup against me," said Ford. "The right-handed hitters, unless they pulled it right down the line, had to hit it about 460 feet to get it out. For me, it was a great place to pitch."

Dom DiMaggio added, "If you look through Yankee history, they always had good left-handed pitching. That's a good thing to have. Left-handed pitchers are worth their weight in gold in Yankee Stadium."

That approach obviously worked for the Yankees with left-handed sluggers like Ruth and Gehrig and, later, Roger Maris and switch-hitter Mickey Mantle and, still later, Reggie Jackson. As much of an advantage as the Stadium is for left-handed sluggers, Ruth (32 of 60 in 1927) and Maris (31 of 61 in 1961) both had more homers on the road in their record-setting seasons. Joe DiMaggio is the only right-handed-hitting Yankee with more than 40 homers at the Stadium in a season.

Before Whitey Ford, the Yankees had Hall of Famers Lefty Gomez and Herb Pennock. After Ford, they had Ron Guidry, Andy Pettitte and even David Wells. Heading into 2004, the Yankees, like the Red Sox, were not expected to have a lefty in their rotation. That could be an ominous sign. The Yankees have not reached the playoffs with an all-righty rotation in 57 years, according to the Elias Sports Bureau.

General Manager Brian Cashman said, in theory, it makes sense for the Yankees to have

A panoramic view—actually a composite of three negatives—of New York's Yankee Stadium in 1949 during the World Series. Yankee Stadium has hosted 36 championships over its history. (Associated Press)

strong left-handed hitters in the lineup, as they currently do with Jason Giambi and Hideki Matsui and switch-hitters Bernie Williams and Jorge Posada, and reliable left-handed pitchers, which they do not have after failing to resign Pettitte. But Cashman added that he addresses specific needs on his roster and does not try to fill holes because a player hits or throws left-handed.

"I think it's great for discussions and debates, but I think it's all overrated," said Cashman. "Is it nice to have? Yes. Is it necessary? No. I wouldn't stay away from a top right-hander to sign a lesser left-hander" because of the dimensions of the Stadium.

But Cashman did stress the importance of another element of a spacious Stadium: having a centerfielder who can cover a vast area. There is something special about being the Yankee centerfielder. Always has been. Always will be.

From Earle Combs in the 1920s and '30s to Joe DiMaggio in the '30s and '40s to Mickey Mantle in the '50s and '60s to Bernie Williams in the '90s until now, the Yankees have often had stars patrolling that hallowed area. The fence sits a more realistic 408 feet from the plate today.

"If you want to have a good defensive team and support your pitching staff at our stadium, you need to have a guy who can go and get it," said Cashman. "You need someone who can cover a lot of ground."

Dom DiMaggio loved playing at the Stadium with the Red Sox because he viewed the area that he had to cover as a challenge. Plus, Joe, Dom's older brother, would trot past him after each half inning so that also made the games appealing. In one of Dom's earliest games at the Stadium, Joe went with brotherly love over team unity in dispensing some advice about playing center.

"He thought I was playing pretty close and he told me that, with the wind currents circling around, I should play deeper," said Dom. "I played about fifteen feet deeper, he hit a shot to left center and I got it. Had he not said anything, I wouldn't have caught it."

The Stadium underwent a remodeling after the 1973 season and the Yankees played their games at Shea Stadium for two years. The Yankees eliminated the original roof of the Stadium to enhance the sight lines for fans in the refurbishing, which almost forced them to lose the famous façade. But they were able to keep the look by putting a replica of the façade above the 560-foot-long scoreboard.

Like the first Stadium, the second Stadium also hosted a World Series in its first year of operation in 1976. Though the Yankees lost that series to the Cincinnati Reds, they rebounded to win titles in 1977 and 1978. Their best pitcher in those seasons was Ron Guidry, a lefty, and their best power hitter was Reggie Jackson, another lefty.

Like Fenway, one of the most popular tourist attractions in Massachusetts, the Stadium is a place visitors to New York want to see. By winning four more titles under Manager Joe Torre from 1996 to 2001, the Yankees ended one of their longest periods without a championship and returned to a rarified position atop the baseball world.

One day, Fenway, with its uncomfortable seats, and the Stadium, with its paucity of luxury boxes, might become extinct. George Steinbrenner clamored for a new stadium in the 1990s, but the principal owner has not been as vocal since the Yankees have exceeded 3.2 million fans for the last five years. The Red Sox have spoken of constructing a modern park near Fenway that would maintain some of the character of the old place, a change that some believe is inevitable.

One day, the homes for both teams might not be these landmark parks. But, until then, they will remain prized cathedrals, the places where the fans of the Yankees and the Red Sox happily go to watch games, adore their teams and worship according to the religion of baseball.

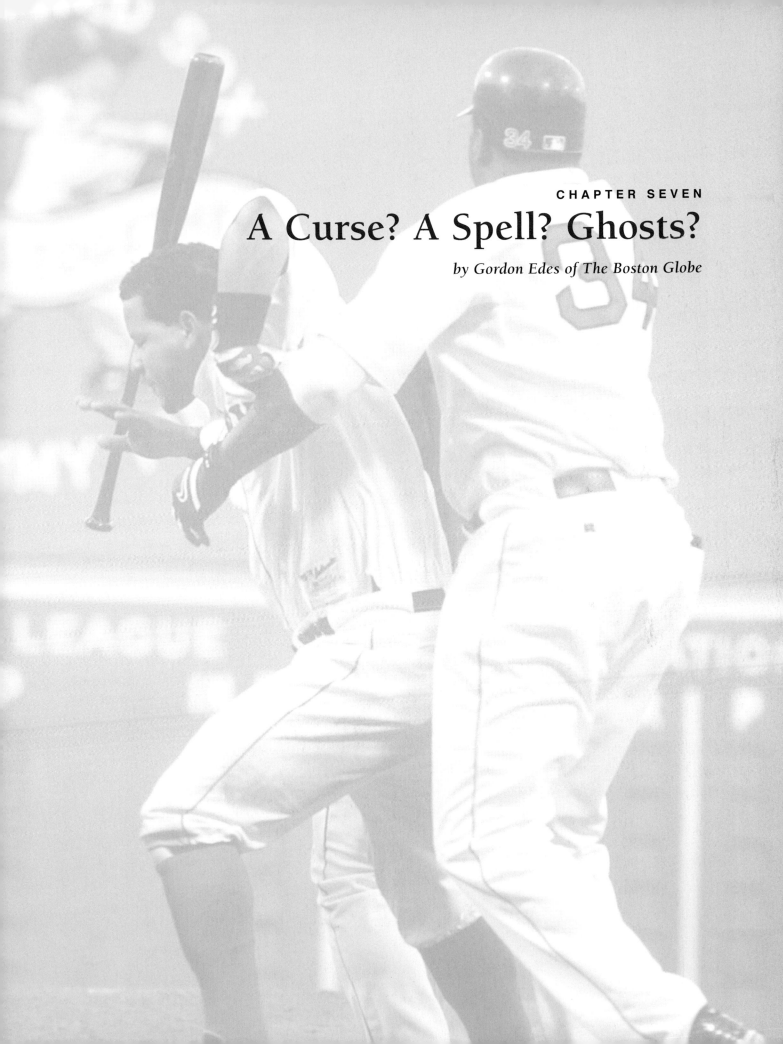

CHAPTER SEVEN

A Curse? A Spell? Ghosts?

by Gordon Edes of The Boston Globe

On Sept. 28, 1996, Roger Clemens pitched his last game for the Boston Red Sox. He gave up home runs to Mike Aldrete and Bernie Williams and lost to the New York Yankees, 4-2.

A crowd of 33,612 in Fenway Park rose to its feet as manager Kevin Kennedy took the ball from Clemens, who leaned over and scooped a handful of dirt from the mound as a keepsake. There was cheering from the visitors' dugout, too, an acknowledgment of the right-handed pitcher who would finish his career with the Red Sox tied with the legendary Cy Young for most victories in club history, 192.

"We had some guys on the bench, we had guys giving him a round of applause when he left," Yankees manager Joe Torre said afterward. "You appreciate somebody like Roger Clemens pitching."

Ten days earlier in Detroit, in a dramatic coda to his Red Sox years, Clemens struck out 20 Tigers, matching the major-league record he had set a decade earlier, when he was just 23 years old and the ace of a 1986 team that would go to the World Series, the last Red Sox team to do so.

"I've got some great pitchers on my staff," Yankees owner George Steinbrenner said two days after Clemens overwhelmed the Tigers, "but if there's one guy I'd want to give the ball to this time of year, it would be Roger Clemens."

As was so often the case for the owner whose lucrative cable-TV deal allowed him to spend dramatically more than most of his rivals, Steinbrenner ultimately would realize his vision of Clemens in pinstripes, although it did not come as soon as he wished. Clemens, who was famously declared to be in the "twilight of his career" by the then-Red Sox general manager, Dan Duquette, elected to sign with the Toronto Blue Jays as a free agent after the 1996 season, spurning a lesser offer from the Yankees, and did not become a Yankee until the eve of spring training in 1999, when he was acquired from the Blue Jays for left-hander David Wells, a one-time Steinbrenner favorite (who would later be welcomed back into the Bronx fold).

The Yankees without Clemens won 114 games in 1998 and swept the San Diego Padres in four games. But with Clemens a Yankee, and with Duquette outmaneuvering the Yankees (among others) to acquire 26-year-old Pedro Martinez as the gifted ace to take Clemens's place one season after his departure from Boston, the Red Sox-Yankee rivalry was about to be raised to a level of passion and intensity as white-hot as any era that preceded it.

It wasn't just about Clemens and Martinez, though their Game 3 matchup in the 1999 American League Championship Series would be billed as the Game of the Century. The teams dueled each other for the services of the same players in winter, trumpeted similar expectations in the spring, staged scintillating showdowns in summer, and took the measure of each other in the fall, with two Octobers (1999 and 2003) as the setting for the first postseason series between the two.

Only once before (Bucky Dent's winning homer in the 1978 playoff game), had the Sox and Yankees played each other for the right to go to the World Series. This time, there was skullduggery between scouts in Latin America, high-stakes auctions for free agents, beanballs and brushbacks, dueling superstar shortstops, fighting words between owners,

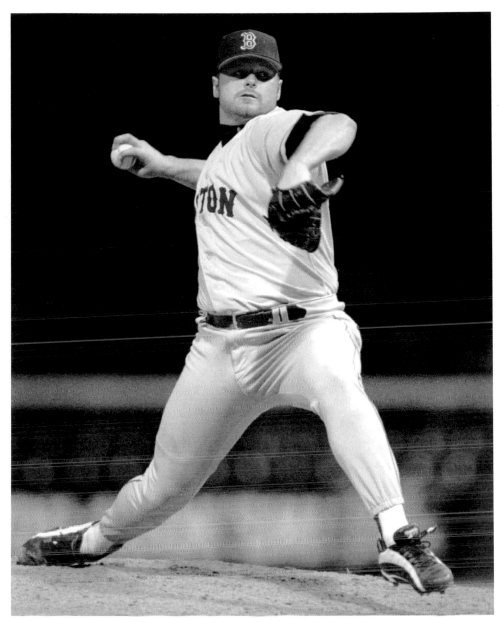

Boston Red Sox starting pitcher Roger Clemens delivers against the Detroit Tigers in the fourth inning Wednesday, Sept. 18, 1996, in Detroit. Clemens went on to tie his own major league record with 20 strikeouts in Boston's 4-0 win over the Tigers. (Associated Press/Tim Fitzgerald)

lights between players and a groundskeeper(!), trash-talking by stars and trash-throwing by fans, mocking nursery-rhyme words from a manager to an owner (Hello, Georgie Porgie), a tragicomic tiff between a 72-year-old coach and the superstar who brusquely toppled him to the ground, near-perfect feats and epic failures. And, in the end, there were Aaron "Bleeping" Boone and Grady Little, taking their rightful places next to names that had defined this rivalry for previous generations, Pesky and Buckner, Dent and John McNamara.

"There's no rivalry," Martinez had insisted after beating the Yankees in Fenway Park on May 23, 2002. "I love Bernie Williams. I love Derek Jeter. I love everybody. We just compete. We're not part of that Babe Ruth stuff. We don't have anything to do with it. I wasn't even born then."

Martinez would learn soon enough that the date of birth on his driver's license was not sufficient to keep him from being forever linked to the history he tried in vain to deny, even as it claimed him as its own. Another Martinez utterance would come to haunt Sox fans, one in which he tried to cast aside with one defiant statement a decades-long burden of disappointment.

"I don't care about damn curses," he had said in exasperation during the 2001 season. "Wake up the damn Bambino and have me face him. Maybe I'll drill him in the ass, pardon me the word."

The Yankees didn't need Ruth's ghost in the box to humble Martinez. One broken-bat single by Jorge Posada in an October eighth inning that will be replayed for years to come will suffice.

But eight years earlier, in 1995, the balance of power between the two clubs had taken a rare dip in Boston's favor. Dan Duquette, pride of Dalton, Massachusetts, and graduate of Amherst (archrivals to Steinbrenner's alma mater, Williams), had assembled a team that would win the American League East, its first division title in five years.

The new general manager wasn't shy about expressing his feelings toward the Yankees. As a teen, he'd been in the Fenway Park stands for the '78 playoff game. "I don't think 'hate' is the right word," Duquette once said. "I would never say I hated the Yankees. The emotion with me was disdain. I disdained the Yankees from the earliest time I could remember."

The Yankees finished second in '95, but not before denting Boston's confidence by sweeping the Red Sox three straight by a combined score of 26-8 in September.

This was the first year of the wild-card initiative and Don Mattingly, the Yankee first baseman, contemplated the possibility that for the first time, the Yankees and Red Sox could meet in a playoff series if the Yankees claimed the wild card. "That would be pretty cool," Mattingly said. "It wouldn't hurt the

rivalry any. There'd be a few deaths. . . just kidding."

It would not come to pass. The Red Sox were eliminated from their division playoff series in three straight games by the Cleveland Indians, while the Yankees fell in five games to the Seattle Mariners.

Earlier that summer, a mini-controversy had arisen over comments made by Mo Vaughn, the Sox slugger who was born in Connecticut and educated at Seton Hall, that suggested Vaughn had his sights set on playing for the Yankees. It foreshadowed a later controversy involving another Sox slugger, Manny Ramirez, a native of Manhattan's Washington Heights, who would tell TV interviewer Joe Morgan that he pined for pinstripes.

"It's unfair how I've come off in that," Vaughn complained. "That was a New York writer asking me about my hometown team. What am I supposed to say, 'No, I hate the Yankees and never want to play for them'?"

A large segment of Sox fandom would likely have been delighted with just such a response, but Vaughn, who would be elected the American League's Most Valuable Player that season, was keeping his options open. Vaughn was still in a Red Sox uniform a year later, when the Sox never overcame a 7-19 start and the Yankees in their first season under Joe Torre won the World Series over the Atlanta Braves.

It was another former Red Sox star who basked in his first World Series championship—Wade Boggs, the third baseman and hit machine who took a victory lap on the back of a police horse in Yankee Stadium. A few weeks before that ride, Boggs couldn't resist taking a shot at Lou Gorman, the former

Sox general manager, who had permitted Boggs to leave as a free agent. "He said I was just 'passing through,' Boggs said. "He said my number was nothing special. Things like that. But that's okay."

A new Yankee dynasty, one that would produce four World Series titles in five years and six pennants in eight years, was taking shape. The Sox, meanwhile, were about to take a major step backward with the departure of Clemens, whose mediocre won-loss record (40-39) in the previous four years was sufficient grounds to hold the line on a new contract.

Clemens was offended that the Sox' first offer included only $10 million in guaranteed payments. They eventually offered $22 million over four years with incentives, but Clemens took the Blue Jays' money ($27.5 million over four years) and fled for Toronto. A *Boston Globe* editorial on the day after he signed with the Blue Jays threw brickbats at neither side, though Duquette's hard-line stance with Clemens upset other Sox veterans, including Vaughn, who two years later would follow Clemens out the door after drawn-out negotiations awash in bitterness from both sides.

"Clemens and the Red Sox," the *Globe* editorial opined, "made sensible decisions in an uncertain universe."

Sox fortunes without Clemens spun into a black hole, at least for a year, despite the arrival of a rookie shortstop, Nomar Garciaparra, whose ritual toe-tapping and tugging of his batting gloves would soon be copied by starstruck Little Leaguers throughout New England. Under new manager Jimy Williams, the Sox finished in fourth place, 6 games under .500. They were officially eliminated

from the postseason on Sept. 16, when they dropped a doubleheader to the Yankees. One of the season's few highlights came on May 30, when Vaughn, who had made his big-league debut against the Yankees on June 27, 1991, hit three home runs in a Sox win over the Yankees managed by bench coach Grady Little, with Williams away attending his daughter's high school graduation.

"This isn't Beantown, this is Mo-town," Sox outfielder Darren Bragg crowed afterward.

Vaughn's days in Boston already were numbered, but in August of that summer, Duquette pulled off a deal with the Yankees, a rare exchange between the clubs, in which the Yankees acquired right-handed catcher and DH Mike Stanley for the stretch run in exchange for reliever Jim Mecir and a minor-league prospect named Tony Armas Jr. Mecir would never pitch for the Red Sox—he was lost to Tampa Bay in the expansion draft — and Stanley would return to the Sox that winter and contribute mightily to two Sox playoff appearances.

But it was Armas that Duquette used to maximum effect, pairing him with top pitching prospect Carl Pavano in a package he sent to Montreal for Martinez, winner of the National League's Cy Young Award for an Expos team that could no longer afford to keep him. Duquette, who had previously served as Expos GM, had traded for Martinez once before in a deal for which he had been roundly criticized, trading All-Star second baseman Delino DeShields to the Dodgers for Martinez, whom Dodger officials decided did not have the endurance to be a front-line starter, a spectacular misjudgment.

In Martinez, the Sox finally had a worthy successor to Clemens, who had made a dazzling return to Fenway Park by striking out 16 Red Sox batters in his first start against the Sox in a Blue Jays uniform.

Martinez did not disappoint, striking out 11 in Oakland in his Sox debut (and tying Clemens's team record for Opening Day K's) and winning 19 games while whiffing at least 10 batters in a game on eight occasions. The Sox made it to the playoffs, only to fall to the Indians again in the first round. The Yankees, meanwhile, had a season that many rank as the greatest ever in pinstripes, a record 124 wins combined (114 in the regular season, 10 in the playoffs). Their World Series title came at the expense of the San Diego Padres and their CEO, Larry Lucchino, who was highly aggravated by the lousy seats the Yankees doled out to Padres executives and family members for the first two games in New York.

Lucchino and Steinbrenner had been on the opposite side of numerous issues ever since Lucchino became CEO of the Baltimore Orioles in 1980, most of their conflicts revolving around the tensions between big-market clubs and small-market teams. Neither man could have known that in a little over three years, Lucchino would be in uncomfortable proximity to Steinbrenner as CEO of the Sox, and the designation of the Yankees as "the Evil Empire" would be born.

But it took the end of the millennium for the dawning of a new chapter in the rivalry, one which in 1999 would climax in the Yankees and Sox meeting for the first time in the American League Championship Series. With Vaughn leaving after the '98 season, Duquette mounted a stealth campaign to sign Bernie Williams, the Yankees' centerfielder who had won the AL batting title by two percentage points over Vaughn. But the Yankees

never lose one of their own to the Red Sox, and Steinbrenner intervened at the last moment, signing Williams to a seven-year, $91.5 million deal.

"The bottom line," Yankees GM Brian Cashman said, "is the Red Sox drove the price up."

Within an hour of Williams striking a deal with the Yankees, the Sox received notification that Vaughn had signed a six-year $80-million deal with the Angels. Duquette's countermove was to sign second baseman Jose Offerman to what many in the industry considered a vastly inflated, four-year, $26 million deal.

"We've got a lot of Chicken Littles who say the sky is falling," Duquette groused, "but we've got the core of our team back. You're going to see a competitive team."

Because Martinez had what arguably may have been the greatest single season by a pitcher ever, and with Garciaparra winning the first of two successive batting titles, the Sons of Jimy Williams, as they were called in the *Globe*, were more than competitive. They were playoff-bound. On Sept. 10, 1999, Martinez, who started the American League All-Star game in Fenway Park and struck out five potential Hall of Famers in a string of six batters (Barry Larkin, Larry Walker, Mark McGwire, Sammy Sosa, and Jeff Bagwell), pitched what may rank as the greatest game ever pitched by an opponent in Yankee Stadium.

Martinez struck out 17 batters, the most Yankees ever to go down whiffing, and did not walk a batter, He allowed just one hit, a second-inning home run by Chili Davis, who guessed right on a 95-mile-an-hour fastball and lined the ball over the fence. He retired the last 22 Yankee batters in succession. By game's end, a sellout crowd of 55,239 was standing and yelling in support of Martinez, especially a raucous group of Dominican fans in right field, and accorded Martinez a tribute unknown for a visiting pitcher: As the strikeouts mounted, they hung "K" cards to keep count.

The Boston Globe • *September 11, 1999*

THE ONLY KING OF HILL, MARTINEZ WHIFFS 17 IN ONE-HIT MASTERPIECE

Gordon Edes, Globe Staff

NEW YORK — There is a certain segment of the population that refuses to acknowledge the splendor of any artist, regardless how accomplished, unless they see it for themselves.

There is a name for these people, known throughout the land: New Yorkers. It didn't matter if you were the Beatles or Baryshnikov, your credentials were suspect until you showed what you had here.

Understand then, that last night in the Red Sox 3-1 win over the Yankees in Yankee Stadium, Pedro Martinez vaulted yet another threshold of greatness in his season for the ages by throwing his second career one-hitter while striking out a career-high 17, including 12 of the last 15 batters, the last five in succession.

What has been cause for a summer-long lovefest from Bar Harbor to Yarmouth was recognized finally by the world's toughest critics: Martinez, who allowed only Chili Davis's second-inning home run, is in a class by himself this year.

"I've never seen anyone pitch like he did tonight," said Martinez's older brother, Ramon, author of a no-hitter and 18-strikeout game himself, echoing a sentiment repeated by Red Sox manager Jimy Williams. "I've seen guys pitch perfect games, no-hitters. He's the best pitcher in baseball right now. Anyone knows that. Nothing would surprise me. I keep telling him he might break the strikeout record, he might pitch a perfect game, a no-hitter. Anything, at any time.

"Tonight all three of his pitches were working, he threw all of them for strikes. When he is like that, he can pitch with his eyes closed, and that's what he did tonight."

In a game that contained all the best elements October playoff baseball has to offer—a feverish full house, two ancient rivals, wire-to-wire high tension—Martinez showed yet again why the Red Sox believe that any time he pitches, they can beat anyone.

That includes the Yankees of this or any other year.

He believes it, too.

"We have good pitching," he said. "We could do anything with anybody in a short series. We can beat the Yankees. We just need a chance to get in the playoffs."

· · ·

"It was the best-pitched game I've ever seen," Yankee pitcher David Cone said afterward, "excepting my perfect game, of course."

The Yankees won the division, but for the second straight season the Red Sox qualified as the wild card, and this time beat the Indians after losing the first two games of their division series. In the deciding Game 5, Troy O'Leary, a Duquette waiver wire pickup, drove in seven runs with a grand slam and three-run home run, and Martinez, in a profile in courage that would win him the lasting respect and admiration of Sox fans, came out of the bullpen despite an aching right shoulder and, minus his trademark fastball, somehow held the Indians hitless over the final six innings of a 10-9 Sox win.

The joy that coursed through New England after the Sox eliminated the Indians paled by comparison to the anticipation of what was to come: the Yankees and Sox, for the first time, facing each other in the ALCS. Clemens vs. Martinez. Garciaparra vs. Jeter. At Babe Ruth's gravesite, in section 25 of the Gate of Heaven Cemetery in Hawthorne, N.Y., flowers covered the grave. Someone had also left a Nomar Garciaparra jersey, size extra-large. "Yeah, I believe in the Curse," said gravedigger Dave Santiago.

William Weld, the former governor of Massachusetts, had set up his law practice in New York, but wanted his allegiance known. "I'm a Yankees hater," he said.

Duquette showed up at Yankee Stadium wearing an ALCS cap, which bore the logos of both teams. A red circle with a slash through it had been taped over the Yankee logo. "My wife, Sharon, said, 'Let me fix that up for you,'" Duquette said.

The Yankees won the first two games, each by a run, the first game on Bernie Williams's 10th-inning home run to dead center field off Rod Beck, after umpire Rick Reed blew a call at second base in the top of the inning and ruled that second baseman Chuck Knoblauch had held onto a throw from third baseman Scott Brosius. Replays clearly showed the throw was dropped and a shaken Reed admitted as much in a press conference afterward.

"I hope they don't decide to take 81 years of frustration out on one call at second base, even though it was important at the time," he said.

But then came Game 3, which the *Boston Herald* cast in the form of a fight poster and billed it as "The Game of the Century," pitting Clemens against Martinez. A sign on Storrow Drive reading "Reverse Curve," had been altered to read, "Reverse the Curse." Around the ballpark, vendors were doing a brisk business selling bumper stickers proclaiming a matchup of "Cy Young vs. Cy Old." One anonymous fan bid $12,100 on an Internet site for four box seats.

On an unseasonably warm October afternoon in the Fens (73 degrees at game time, when Dominic DiMaggio, the former Sox great and brother of Joe, threw out the ceremonial first ball), leadoff man Jose Offerman hit Clemens's second pitch of the game into the right-field corner for a triple. On a 2-and-2 pitch, the next batter, John Valentin hit a ball into the net for a two-run home run.

The Sox scored two more runs in the second, and when Mike Stanley led off the third with a single, Torre took out the Rocket and brought in Hideki Irabu, who promptly gave up a two-run home run to Brian Daubach, making it 6-0, as the ballpark exploded in bloodlust.

"Where is Roger?" the crowd chanted. "In the shower," they screamed in response.

The final score was Red Sox 13, Yankees 1. Martinez, despite claiming he had "nothing," allowed just a run and five hits in seven innings. In Section 22, Debbie Clemens sat with her weeping sons.

"They treated him like dirt," she would later tell Globe columnist Dan Shaughnessy.

"...I think that's why they don't ever win in Boston. The fans have it backward. There is no sportsmanship in that town. It's mean. It's miserable and mean."

The next night, fan behavior took an even uglier turn. Frustrated by another terrible umpiring call—on Knoblauch's "phantom" tag of Offerman—manager Williams was ejected when he threw his cap to the ground while disputing another call by first-base umpire Dale Scott. Fans threw debris onto the field, causing play to be interrupted for several minutes.

The Yankees scored six runs in the ninth, when Ricky Ledee hit a grand slam off Beck, and Williams closeted himself in his office after the Yankees' 9-2 win.

He had plenty to say the next day, however, after learning that Steinbrenner had blamed him for inciting the fans.

"I've never worried about Georgie Porgie," Williams said. "He's never been in the trenches. When Georgie Porgle speaks, I don't listen."

The next night, the Yankees closed out the Sox and the series, Jeter setting the tone in the 6-1 win with a two-run home run off Kent Mercker in the first inning. In the series, the Sox made twice as many errors (10 to 5) as the Yankees, while the Bombers turned seven double plays to none by the Sox.

"We had our opportunities and we didn't capitalize," said Garciaparra, who batted .400 with two home runs but made four errors. "Am I going to go back and regret anything? No need to do that. Are you kidding me? No need to do anything. There's nothing for us to hang our heads about."

The Yankees went on to sweep the Braves for their third World Series title in four tries.

It would be four years before the Sox would return to the playoffs. By then, they would have new owners, a new general manager, a new manager--and the same outcome.

After the '99 playoff loss, Duquette made another major move, trading for center-fielder Carl Everett, a former No. 1 draft choice of the Yankees who harbored a long-standing grudge about his treatment in the lower minors.

"As long as I'm playing ball, it doesn't matter where I am, as long as it's not in a Yankee uniform. . . I never liked pinstripes," Everett proclaimed on his first day in camp.

Sports Illustrated put Martinez on its cover and predicted that the Sox would win it all in 2000. "Great," Clemens said sarcastically. "New century." Martinez would out duel Clemens in May, 2-0, in a game decided by a two-run home run by Trot Nixon in the ninth inning in Yankee Stadium, and would go on to win his second consecutive Cy Young Award, but three weeks later the Yankees pinned a 22-1 defeat on the Sox in Fenway Park, the worst Sox home defeat in franchise history.

Everett played well, hitting two home runs in his Fenway Park debut, but was suspended for 10 games after head-butting an umpire and had a falling-out with manager Jimy Williams that became an unsettling element in the Sox clubhouse. The Yankees would finish just 2½ games ahead of the Sox, but that was misleading. They all but wrapped up the division in early September, and beat the Mets for their fourth World Series title in five years.

"Pitching," Martinez said. "They are, dammit, better than we are."

Duquette targeted free agent pitcher Mike Mussina as the man most likely to close that gap, but Mussina signed with the Yankees instead. *Globe* columnist Bob Ryan wrote, "I have never seen anything to match the bitterness and anger that have permeated the Boston baseball off-season atmosphere since the Yankees signed Mussina."

Pressured to make a counterstrike, Duquette elected to sign free-agent slugger Manny Ramirez instead, giving him an eye-popping, eight-year, $160-million contract eclipsed only by the record-setting 10-year, $252-million deal Texas gave shortstop Alex Rodriguez. Ramirez made a terrific first impression, beating the Yankees' unhittable closer, Mariano Rivera, with an extra-inning base hit in an exciting April game.

But decimated by major injuries to Garciaparra, Martinez, catcher Jason Varitek and third baseman John Valentin, and with the clubhouse torn asunder by the Everett-Williams rift, which also led to irreconcilable differences between Williams and Duquette, the club imploded. "I thought the Bronx Zoo was something," said Cone, the former Yankee pitcher who made an ultimately futile attempt to come back from a sore shoulder with the Sox, "but this place takes the (expletive) cake."

Martinez, after brazenly saying he would drill the Babe in May, hurt his shoulder shortly thereafter, and didn't win another game for the rest of the season, and clashed with management over pitching while still hurt. Mussina, on a July Sunday night in Fenway Park, came within one batter of pitching a perfect game against the Sox, Everett ending his bid with a two-out pinch single in the ninth. Williams was fired in August, and the Sox proceeded to lose 21 of 26 games under

Joe Kerrigan after the pitching coach was promoted to take Williams's place.

On Sept. 10, the Sox were in New York and rained out of what would have been Clemens's bid for his 20th victory. That night, the team flew to Tampa. The next morning, terrorists flew two planes into the World Trade Center. With the Sox out of the playoffs, New England baseball fans found themselves in the unusual position of rooting for New York.

The Boston Globe • October 27, 2001

NEW BEST FRIENDS

Editorial

GO NEW YORK!

The cheer arises from an untapped well deep within the psyche of Red Sox Nation. The voice sounds strange but feels exactly right. The World Series begins tonight, and the Yankees must win their fourth-in-a-row enchilada grande.

Were this a normal year, they would have to lose, and swiftly, as Boston hissed every run scored against the Diamondbacks. An October of same-old, same-old baseball would fuel outrage against the aging trophy hogs and possibly the rending of garments in the street over the failure of Seattle perfection, or Oakland muscle, to triumph in the clinch and bring on a battle of young titans.

The "Oh, what might have been" chorus, as perennial as the golden leaves, would have extended to the Boston debacle, magnificence lost, and cursed karma.

But this October follows a September that has made much of life feel raw and alien, and ancient sports rivalries seem part of an America that is almost unreachable now. Would that the

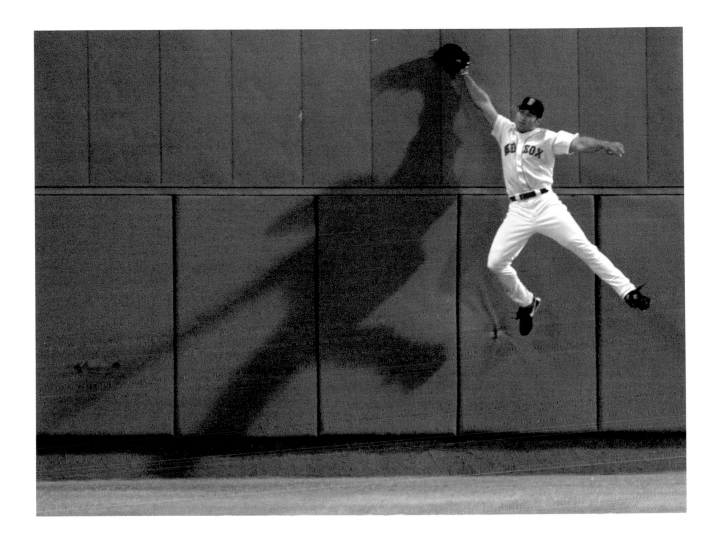

Red Sox Johnny Damon leaps for a deep fly to center at Fenway, but a fan grabs it in an early season game in 2002 against the Yankees. (Associated Press)

Yankees loomed as the tallest enemy on the horizon and New Yorkers were still the insufferably arrogant neighbors to the south.

Through the aching clarity of this transforming autumn, we see the Yankee greatness for what it is—the ever-solid team, whose members play better than they are as individuals when the effort counts the most.

Today they are also metaphor. Even Lou Piniella, manager of the Seattle Mariners, who lost the American League championship after getting creamed 12-3 in the fifth game in New York this week, could see the poetry. He told reporters: "You know, the amazing thing is that about the eighth inning when the fans were really reveling in the stands, the one thought that did come to my mind was: 'Boy, this city suffered a

lot, and tonight they let out a lot of emotions.' And I felt good for them in a way—not that we were getting beat, or not that we were getting beat up—but I felt good for them, I really did."

Feeling good for the Yankees and New York is feeling good for our country and ourselves. Sitting in the living room, we feel the sting of tears and cheer the unabashed Broadway shtick—flags waving, firemen and police officers singing "God Bless America," Mayor Rudy Giuliani hugging Yankees, manager Joe Torre hugging Giuliani, the crowd on it's feet screaming "RU-DY! RU-DY!" or "USA! USA!" and a tape of Frank Sinatra singing "New York, New York."

The show up in the Bronx says we will survive the horror still smoking in lower Manhattan. The Great American Pastime is now a symbol for

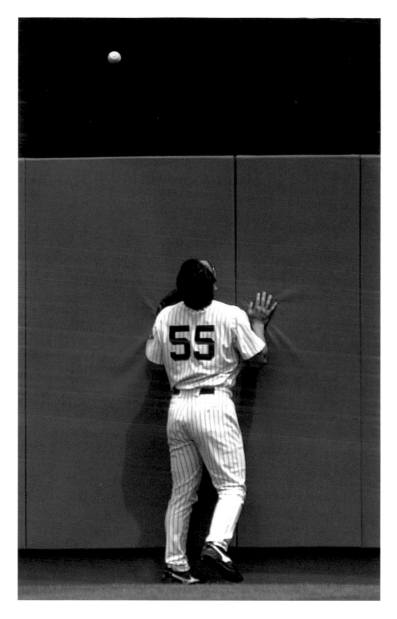

Hideki Matsui watches hopelessly as the first of two of Red Sox David Ortiz's homers clears the wall at Yankee Stadium on July 6, 2003. (Chang W. Lee/*The New York Times*)

America itself, and the Yankees are the team from ground zero. So, Diamondbacks: Fuh-GETaboutit! ▪

O n Dec. 21, 2001, in a Phoenix resort hotel, major-league owners approved the sale of the Red Sox to a new ownership group headed by John W. Henry, a billionaire moneymarket manager who previously owned the Florida Marlins and a one percent stake in the Yankees. His principal partners included Tom Werner, the TV producer

(*Cosby* and *Roseanne*) and former Padres owner, and Lucchino, Steinbrenner's long-time adversary.

Naturally, one of the first things the new owners did was address the rivalry with the Yankees.

"We have the resources to be competitive," Henry proclaimed. "We'll give the Yankees a real run for their money, starting next year."

Added Werner: "The curse of the Bambino? We prefer to think of it as a spell we intend to break."

Under a new management team—interim GM Mike Port and the laid-back Grady Little

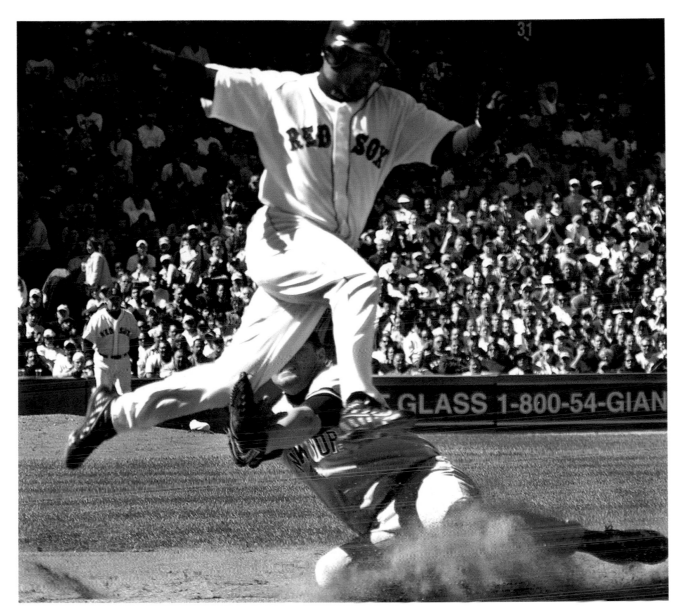

Roger Clemens slides to make a tag at first base on a leaping Troy O'Leary. April 19, 2001. (Barry Chin/ *The Boston Globe*)

as new manager—the Sox beat the Yankees five times in their first six meetings. Martinez, after beating the Yankees, 3-1, on May 23 in Fenway, said: "It was just curse, curse, curse, not even baseball. Who cares? I believe in God. I don't believe in curses."

But even with a lineup that featured seven All-Stars, including new centerfielder Johnny Damon, the Sox were overtaken by the Yankees. Wells and Mussina shut out the Sox in consecutive games in August, the first time since 1943 Yankee pitchers had accomplished that feat in Fenway Park. The losses dropped the Sox nine games behind the Yankees. The

Sox won 93 games and missed the playoffs. Little blamed—labor unrest—a strike was averted with a last-minute settlement—for distracting his team.

The Sox asked the Yankees for permission to interview Gene Michael, one of Steinbrenner's top assistants, to be their new general manager. Steinbrenner, furious, declined their request, and the Sox wound up hiring 29-year-old Theo Epstein, a Lucchino protege.

Epstein made Montreal pitcher Bartolo Colon a prime off-season target. So did the Yankees. When the Expos traded Colon to the

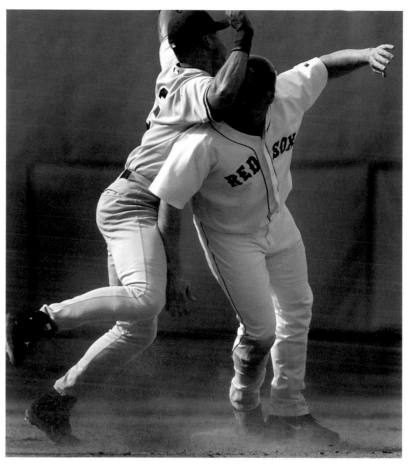

July 26, 2003. Jeremy Giambi is safe under the tag of Derek Jeter. (Barry Chin/*The Boston Globe*)

White Sox instead, Boston officials privately grumbled that the Yankees had rigged the deal behind the scenes so the Red Sox wouldn't get him.

But it was in pursuit of Jose Contreras, the Cuban defector, that the teams went to extraordinary lengths to outdo each other. Luis Eljaua, the Sox director of international scouting who had courted Contreras for months, checked into the Hotel Camp Real in Managua, Nicaragua, the same boutique hotel where Contreras and his agent were staying, and quietly bought up the other rooms in the hotel, to keep the Yankees out. Epstein flew to Nicaragua to oversee negotiations personally. The Sox thought Contreras would be theirs.

Yankee dollars said otherwise. On Christmas Eve, Steinbrenner signed off on a four-year, $32-million deal, $5 million more than Boston's last offer.

"It's very difficult to bid against a team with an unlimited budget," Henry complained afterward. Cashman, the Yankee GM, called that "sour grapes." Lucchino inveighed against the Yankees "Evil Empire," touching a nerve with the Boss, who fired back by calling Lucchino "baseball's foremost chameleon. . . He's not the kind of guy you want to be in your foxhole." Lucchino laughed and said that "on a list of top people with respect and affection for me, you will probably not find George's name there." This was getting personal. "The days of trying to shed your own problems by blaming the Yankees are over," Yankees president Randy Levine said.

Commissioner Bud Selig ordered the verbal volleying to end. As usual, the issues would be resolved on the field. As usual, the Yankees won in the end. Clemens hit Kevin Millar with a pitch in the hand in a July series, and said Millar should have gotten out of the way faster. Millar, who had originated "Cowboy Up" as a team rallying cry, said Clemens's comments were "stupid."

Two days later, Martinez hit two star Yankees, Alfonso Soriano and Derek Jeter, in the hands with pitches, Soriano while in the act of swinging. Steinbrenner popped off at Martinez.

"He'll probably buy the whole league," Martinez responded, "but not my desire and my heart. . . He's not going to put any fear in my heart."

On a July visit to Boston, Torre described riding the elevator at the Ritz-Carlton in which the team was staying. He encountered a couple of Boston fans from Concord, Mass. "They were kidding but you could still see an edge to it," Torre said, "They told me, 'If it came down to a choice between getting Saddam Hussein or beating the Yankees, we'd take beating the Yankees.' I think they were kidding."

On Aug. 31, Clemens pitched what at the time was believed to be his final game in Fenway Park, and Sox fans rose and saluted him as if he was still one of their own. Manny Ramirez inflamed the rivalry when he missed an important late-August weekend series against the Yankees because of a sore throat, and also missed a doctor's appointment the morning after socializing with Yankees infielder Enrique Wilson the night before. Ramirez refused to pinch-hit the next day in Philadelphia, and, in what was perhaps the watershed game of the season, the Sox won anyway on Trot Nixon's ninth-inning grand slam.

The Boston Globe • September 7, 2003

AN OLD '78 - PLAYED BACKWARD

By Dan Shaughnessy

NEW YORK - A quarter of a century has passed and now it is as if the hardball gods have conspired to settle an old score.

New England church bells are ringing, the skies are crisp and blue, and all the water tastes like wine. It is early September and the Red Sox have the Yankees on the run. How odd to type these words. It is as if Charlie Brown is finally ready to kick that football between the uprights.

The symmetry is downright scary. Today marks the 25th anniversary of the first day of the four-game Boston Massacre of 1978. On that fateful weekend, the Yankees came to Fenway trailing the Red Sox by four games in the American League East. Four days later, after sweeping by an aggregate count of 42-9, the Yanks left Boston tied for first. It was the centerpiece of the cataclysmic Sox collapse of '78, the colossal fall against which all others are measured.

Yesterday the 2003 Red Sox thrashed the first-place Yankees in the venerable Bronx ballyard. On the heels of Friday's 9-3 win, in which they led, 8-0, after three innings, the Sox routed Roger Clemens (how sweet is that?), taking a 7-0 lead in the fourth en route to an 11-0 triumph that moved the Sox within a game and a half of first place. Boston trailed the Yankees by 7½ games Aug. 20.

Yesterday's rout was on national television, and Fox reminded viewers that the Yanks hadn't been the victims of a double-digit shutout loss to the Sox at home since losing to Boston, 10-0,

Yankees Bernie Williams *(foreground)* loosens up before Game 3 against the Red Sox in 1999. The mythic Green Monster stands behind him. (Barton Silverman/*The New York Times*)

in the Polo Grounds on April 23, 1919. Babe Ruth homered for the Red Sox that day.

Can you stand any more?

. . .

Meanwhile, George Steinbrenner is walking around, threatening coaches' jobs, claiming he wanted David Ortiz all along, and referring to Theo Epstein as "Oppenheim." Could this be the fall of the Evil Empire?

Something happened to the Red Sox last week in Philadelphia and Chicago. Toppled by New York last weekend, rattled by the latest Manny Ramirez brain cramp, the Sox came together under their manager-without-a-contract-extension, Grady Little, and decided to forget all the sideshows and make a run for it. The six-run ninth in Philly, while Manny sat, put a new charge into this team and the Sox haven't lost since.

They still could get derailed and blow the whole thing, of course. And history has taught

us to beware. But at this hour it truly feels like the Yankees are the ones in second place. A quarter of a century later, the Red Sox are finally paying the Yankees back for all those decades of indignities.

The Yankees won the division, then quickly disposed of Minnesota in the first round of the playoffs. The Sox, winners of 95 games, won the wild card then came from two games down to beat the Oakland A's in their division series to set up not only Yanks-Sox ALCS redux, but another Clemens-Martinez Game 3 rematch in Fenway Park. The Sox and Yankees split the first two games of the series, Tim Wakefield's knuckleball prevailing in the 5-2 opener in Yankee Stadium, Sox-killer Andy Pettitte pitching the Yanks to a 6-2 win in Game 2.

The Red Sox' Manny Ramirez is held back by teammate David Ortiz as he tries to get to Yankees pitcher Roger Clemens during a fourth inning fight. (Jim Davis/*The Boston Globe*)

In Game 3, Martinez, roughed up for a couple of early runs, threw a pitch at Karim Garcia that hit him in the shoulder, then pointed a finger at his head while yelling at Posada, the apparent implication being that he would be next. When Clemens threw an eye-high fastball to Ramirez, a pitch that nonetheless was over the plate, Ramirez took exception and headed toward the mound. The benches emptied, leading to the astonishing spectacle of Don Zimmer, the Yankees' beloved bench coach and former Red Sox manager and coach, charging Martinez, fists upraised. Martinez sidestepped Zimmer and tipped him to the ground, an image that would flash across the country on TV and in newspaper photos.

When order was restored and play resumed, the often-excitable Clemens kept his emotions under control and left with a 4-2 lead. But bad blood surfaced again late in

the game, when a Fenway Park groundskeeper and two Yankees players, reliever Jeff Nelson and outfielder Garcia, became involved in a fracas in the Sox bullpen that eventually led to criminal complaints against all three men. Yankee president Randy Levine blistered Sox security and said that if the groundskeeper had been a Yankees employee, "he'd be gone or in jail."

The next day, despite a mandate from Selig not to discuss the incident, all three Sox owners were present at a press conference to tell their side of the story. A tearful Zimmer, meanwhile, also appeared briefly at a press conference to apologize, and later exonerated Martinez, who said he would "never, ever, ever, ever, ever. . . raise my hand to him." Baseball disciplinarians fined Martinez $50,000, Ramirez $25,000, Garcia $10,000 and Zimmer $5,000.

A month later, in Rhode Island Superior

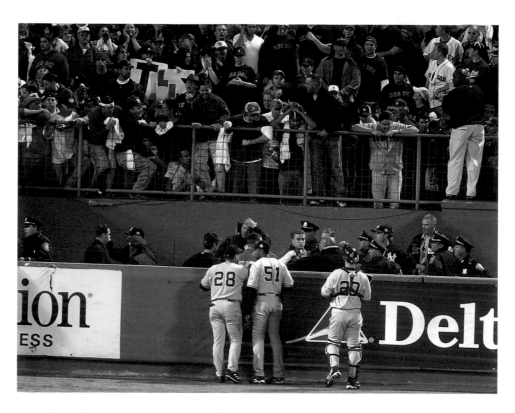

Court in Providence, 35 students from Woonsocket Middle School took part in a mock trial in which Martinez stood accused of assaulting Zimmer, whose Yoda-like presence next to Yankee manager Joe Torre had made him a national icon. The student jury, showing considerably less mercy than Zim, returned its verdict in less than five minutes: Guilty as charged.

Down two games to one, Werner invited his buddy Bill Cosby to visit the Sox clubhouse and loosen up the team before Game 4. Tim Wakefield, the knuckleballer whom Duquette had left off the ALCS roster in '99, beat the Yankees for the second time in the Series, but the Yanks prevailed in Game 5, Wells beating Lowe, 4-2.

The Sox returned to New York needing wins in each of the final two games to advance to the Series. They won Game 6, pounding Pettitte, 9-6. Game 7 would be Martinez-Clemens one more time. As Martinez warmed up in the Yankee bullpen before the game, New York policemen stood shoulder to shoulder along the bleachers to ensure his safety. The Sox got to Clemens for three runs early. By the eighth inning, it was 5-2. The Sox were five outs away from going to the World Series.

But Little left the ball in the hands of a tiring Martinez as the Yankees rallied. He visited the mound after Bernie Williams's single made it 5-3. "He asked me if I had enough left in the tank," Martinez said. "I said yes. I never say no."

Hideki Matsui followed with a ground-rule

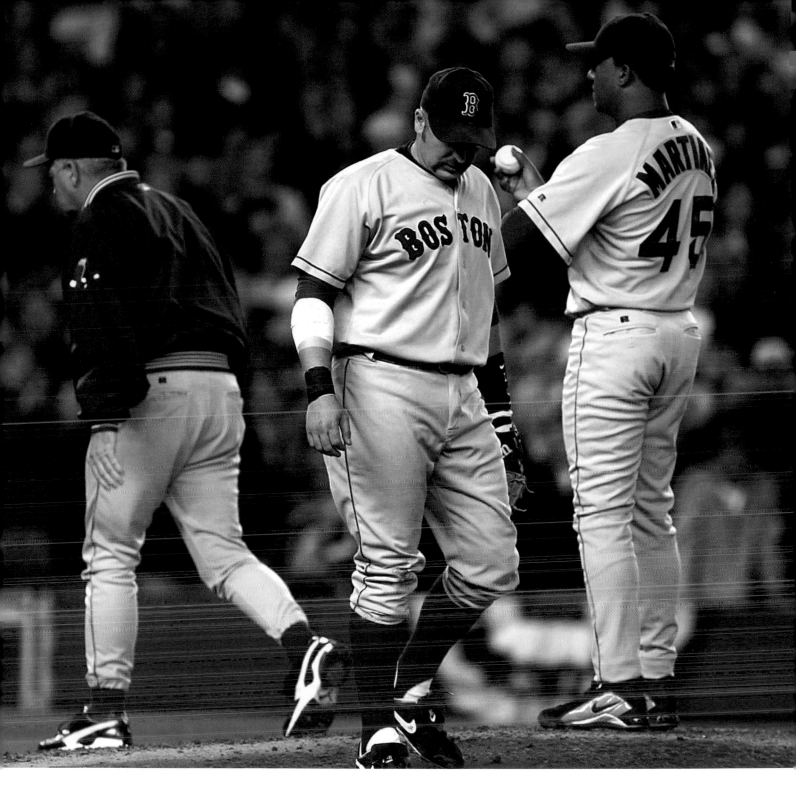

double, a broken-bat double by Posada tied the score, and in the bottom of the 11th, Aaron Boone went out to face Wakefield, but not before hearing this from Jeter: "Magical things happen here in the Stadium. Ghosts come out in October."

Boone hit Wakefield's first pitch for a home run, and a pain even sharper than the one left by Dent's shocking blow in '78 cut through Red Sox Nation. "It wasn't supposed to end this way," said a weeping Wakefield.

A villain was identified: Little, for sticking with Martinez when he could have turned to relievers Mike Timlin and Alan Embree, who had performed with great effectiveness in the postseason. "There's no reason to blame Grady," Martinez said. "If anyone wants to point a finger, point it at me."

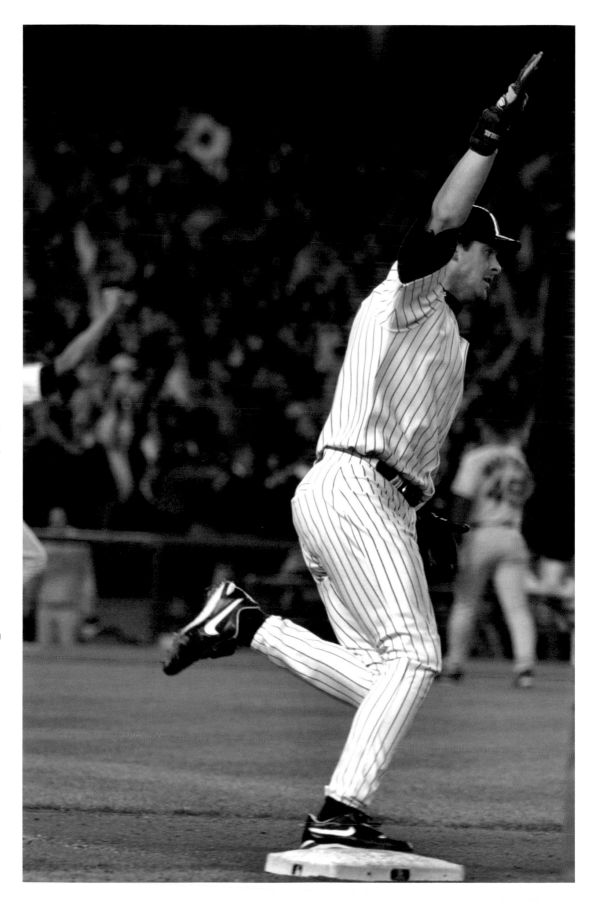

(Right) Aaron Boone signals "number one" as he hits first base on his home run jaunt after hitting the game-winning, American-league-pennant-clinching-home run off Red Sox pitcher Tim Wakefield *(49, walking off field, background right)*. (Jim Davis/*The Boston Globe*)

(Facing Page) Pedro Martinez, David Ortiz, Derek Lowe and John Burkett sit in the dugout after losing Game 7 of the ALCS. (Barry Chin/*The Boston Globe*)

No one, it seemed, listened. Within days of that devastating defeat, the Sox did not renew Little's contract. He saw that coming.

"Just add one more ghost to the list if I'm not there," he said, "because there are ghosts. That's certainly evident when you're a player in that uniform."

In November, the Red Sox succeeded in trading for ace Curt Schilling, the pitcher the Yankees had hoped would replace Clemens. "I guess I hate the Yankees now," Schilling said. The team also added the American League's premier closer by signing free agent Keith Foulke.

But their biggest off-season quest had begun just two days after losing Game 7 to the Yankees, when Tom Hicks, owner of the Texas Rangers, called Sox owners Henry and Lucchino and asked them whether they would consider trading Garciaparra, the face of the Boston franchise for the last seven years, for Alex Rodriguez, the 28-year-old shortstop widely considered the game's best player. Rodriguez, unhappy that Texas had finished in last place in his three seasons there, had signaled to Hicks his desire to play for one of two teams, Boston or New York. His real desire, he told friends, was to play for the Red Sox.

Henry and Lucchino were intrigued. The previous spring, Garciaparra had passed on their offer of a four-year, $60 million contract extension, and they had doubts whether Garciaparra, eligible for free agency at the end of the 2004 season, really wanted to remain in Boston. But in order to take on the remaining seven years of Rodriguez's 10-year, $252-million contract, the richest in sports, they decided they had to unload the bloated contract of Ramirez, of whom they'd grown weary despite his prolific hitting.

It did not help that Ramirez, who at $20 million a year was Boston's highest-paid player, had publicly expressed the wish to play for the Yankees, citing his roots, the Manhattan neighborhood of Washington Heights. Epstein took the rare step of placing Ramirez on irrevocable waivers after the season, hoping that the Yankees would be enticed. But the Yankees didn't bite, and the Sox made their counteroffer to Hicks: Ramirez plus a pitching prospect for Rodriguez.

After weeks of negotiating, which included Commissioner Bud Selig taking the rare step of allowing the Sox to deal directly with Rodriguez, the deal was declared dead two days before Christmas. The Sox were unwilling to satisfy Hicks's demand for additional millions to subsidize Ramirez's contract, and the players' union had rejected an agreement worked out between Rodriguez and the Sox that would have reduced the value of his contract by $28 million.

A young woman, a Red Sox fan, e-mailed Gene Orza, the union lawyer who had scotched the agreement on the grounds that it violated the collective bargaining agreement. "You've ruined my summer," she wrote, "and it's not even winter."

On the morning of Valentine's Day, February 14, Epstein was checking newspapers from around the country on his computer, as was his custom, when he came across a report that Rodriguez was about to be traded to the Yankees. Selig, in his Milwaukee home, heard the same report on the radio and laughed. Surely, it was just a rumor.

It wasn't. Days later, Rodriguez was in Yankee Stadium, trying on pinstripes. Henry, who had been out of the country on his yacht, was apoplectic, calling for Major League Baseball to implement a salary cap. It was, he said, the only "fair way to deal with a team that has gone so insanely far beyond the resources of all the other teams."

Steinbrenner pounced. "We understand John Henry must be embarrassed, frustrated and disappointed by his failure in this transaction," he wrote in a statement. "Unlike the Yankees, he chose not to go the extra distance for his fans in Boston."

And thus the battle was joined once again, for what Henry told Tyler Kepner of the *New York Times* was an "Arthurian quest."

Rodriguez, the newest centerpiece of this rivalry, already had a taste of what was to come. "It's like a passion that I've never seen before," he said, "and I can't wait to be in the middle of it and do my best."

CHAPTER EIGHT

Babe, Bucky, Buckner, Boone

by Tyler Kepner of The New York Times

It was the middle of December 2003 at Yankee Stadium, cold and wet and gray. The stands were empty, the infield grass torn up, battered by snowstorms. The only activity was inside, where Gary Sheffield tried on his new pinstriped jersey.

The scoreboard had a message that welcomed Sheffield, the slugger who for the moment represented the Yankees' counterpunch to Boston's opening winter jab. The Red Sox had snagged Curt Schilling in a trade with the Arizona Diamondbacks, acing out the Yankees for a pitcher George Steinbrenner craved. The high-stakes games never stopped. "They're a couple of prize-fighters just trying to one-up one another," said San Diego Padres General Manager Kevin Towers, speaking for the 28 fascinated teams taking it in from afar. "We're all kind of sitting here eating popcorn and drinking sodas, watching it."

After the Sheffield press conference, Joe Torre took a moment to reflect on what had happened two months before, when the field glowed as electricity flowed through the charged stands. The memory of an epic American League Championship Series had not dimmed for Torre, and neither had his conviction that the Yankees will always have an edge on the Red Sox.

"Boston," Torre said, "has something against them."

Torre is a rational man. The ability to think and act reasonably, to understand what is happening and not overreact, are the traits that made him the Yankees' longest-running manager under Steinbrenner. Torre would not seem likely to believe in the supernatural. But he does—to some extent, anyway. Torre believes there must be a heightened sense of doubt among Red Sox players, because their history stalks them. It repeats itself through the decades, rarely utter failure but never ultimate success, so often with the Yankees barricading the door.

"It's tough to ignore," Torre said. "I think that's part of the so-called psyche that not only works for us but works against them. If I sensed anything from them, it's been more frustration. You may have guys who want to keep fighting those demons, and yet when it's over with, will say, 'Maybe there's something to it.' It's just a body language, seeing that take place. I mean, Game Seven was an example. If they didn't win there, when were they going to win?"

A season of fierce baseball between the teams culminated with the stirring seventh game, which ended on Aaron Boone's 11th-inning homer to send the Yankees to the World Series. It was the first winner-take-all Yankees-Red Sox game since the 1978 American League East playoff, when a victorious Steinbrenner left town with Bostonians rocking his car. "They are very tough fans, very tough people up there," said Steinbrenner as he recalled the incident early this year. "They work hard."

They root hard, too, and from 1982 to 1995, Boston fans had much more to celebrate. The rivals had almost identical records over that 14-year stretch: 1,143-1,055 for the Yankees, 1,144-1,058 for the Red Sox. But Boston won four division titles and the Yankees won none. The Yankees' lows were also lower. While Boston only once lost more than 84 games in those seasons, the Yankees lost at least 86 games in each season from 1989 through 1992.

"We were kind of the doormat of the A.L. East," said Brian Cashman, the future Yankees general manager who was then just starting his career. "Their farm system was producing guys like Mo Vaughn, John Valentin and Roger Clemens. We were signing Dave LaPoint and Andy Hawkins and trading for Steve Trout."

The Yankees' four consecutive losing seasons, from '89 through '92, tied a franchise record for futility. The only other time the team had spent four seasons below .500 was from 1912-1915, a stretch that began before Babe Ruth started his career.

While the Yankees were losing, they had the added indignity of watching some of their own talent star for other teams. Steinbrenner had traded young players such as Fred McGriff, Doug Drabek, Willie McGee and Jay Buhner in the '80s and by the early '90s those players were exactly what the Yankees needed. The Yankees stumbled along with one star—Don Mattingly—and a host of faded veterans and young players of minimal talent.

The teams finished 1-2 in the division only twice in those seasons, in 1986 and '95, when the playoffs expanded and the Yankees made it as a wild card. As the continuity of the late '70s teams eroded, few players felt the rivalry acutely. "The way the game had changed, it wasn't quite there anymore," said Willie Randolph, then the Yankees second baseman. "Players viewed competition a little differently. They competed and wanted to win, but it didn't [tick] them off if the Red Sox came to New York and beat us, or vice versa. I didn't see the same edge. We didn't take it personally."

It bothered Randolph that animosity had turned to casual familiarity. He noticed more schmoozing around the batting cage, more handshakes and hugs. It didn't jibe with him.

Years later, as a Yankee coach, Randolph would still find himself sneering at his old combatants, Jim Rice and Dwight Evans, when they coached for Boston.

The Yankee renaissance began in 1996 and was the unexpected result of an unseemly episode. Steinbrenner had been banned from baseball by commissioner Fay Vincent in 1990, punishment for paying $40,000 to a gambler named Howard Spira who claimed to have damaging information on Yankee outfielder Dave Winfield. Steinbrenner did not return until March 1993, and while he was gone general manager Gene Michael held on to top prospects. By the mid-1990s those players—notably Bernie Williams, Derek Jeter, Andy Pettitte, Mariano Rivera and Jorge Posada—had become the foundation of a new dynasty.

The New York Times — August 5, 1990

RESTORING THE PRIDE OF THE YANKEES

By Claire Smith

When George Steinbrenner was ordered by Commissioner Fay Vincent to give up operational control of the New York Yankees last week, Americans who treasure baseball as the national pastime and those with a stake in the game as a business both had reason to feel relieved. One of the most demoralizing eras in a fabled franchise's history had ended.

Steinbrenner was barred from a role in the Yankees' management not because he was tyrannical or because his organization was inept. He was banished because he had consorted with a gambler, Howard Spira, to run a clandestine investigation of the outfielder Dave Winfield, Steinbrenner's nemesis. The Yankees owner admitted as much when he accepted Vincent's ban on Monday.

But while Vincent's action was aimed solely at protecting the sport from the taint of Steinbrenner's dealings, baseball will surely welcome an important side effect: an overhaul of the Yankees' image as a laughingstock and a renegade in the baseball world.

"They are one of the premier, recognizable sports franchises in the world," said John Schuerholz, general manager of the Kansas City Royals. "They still have that reputation, despite what has happened in the last several years or so. But definitely it's for all of our best interests to have the Yankees be a viable and competitive team. If they are, it can only be great for our game."

Baseball measures its well-being by the success of franchises in the major cities. And no team's aura has enhanced the game more than that of the Yankees.

"There are other teams asserting themselves, who stand on their own as far as being great draws," said Tom Grieve, general manager of the Texas Rangers. "The Toronto Blue Jays, the Oakland A's are doing very well. The Dodgers have always done well. But it would probably take a team like the Blue Jays or our Rangers 50 years' worth of winning championships to reach that plateau in terms of recognition."

Andy MacPhail, the grandson of a former Yankees owner, Larry MacPhail, and now general manager of the Minnesota Twins, agrees. "Undoubtedly there is some magic about the pinstripes," MacPhail said. "So it's important that the Yankees be at least representative, to take in as much of their share on the competitive

cycle as the game allows. They can't stay down or it hurts us all."

Television ratings, and the revenues they generate, rise when teams like the Yankees, Dodgers, Mets and Red Sox do well. Those teams are to baseball what the Celtics are to basketball and the Cowboys are to football— franchises vital to a sport's image, national appeal and viability as a business.

Steinbrenner came close to irreparably damaging the reputation of baseball's most lucrative franchise. His dictatorial dismissals, demotions and banishments left executives of other teams wondering whom on the Yankees they could deal with. A bemused official once asked, "Who do you call if you want to make a trade with the Yankees?"

Frank Robinson, manager of the Baltimore Orioles and president of the Baseball Network, a group of former players who have pressed baseball on affirmative action, was once asked if it bothered him that not one black or Hispanic candidate had been interviewed for the job of Yankees manager through 18 managerial changes in 18 years.

"Nah," he said. "We don't even consider them a part of baseball. That's a renegade team. George just keeps hiring and firing the same people over and over again." ▪

Torre replaced Buck Showalter as manager in November 1995, and the Sox began fielding consistently competitive teams in 1998, finishing second to the Yankees each year through 2003. It is the longest streak in baseball history of one team finishing second to another. Boston nearly signed Bernie Williams away from the Yankees before the

1999 season. But Steinbrenner never let it happen, and Williams was a hero that October, when the Yankees met the wild-card Red Sox in the ALCS. Williams drilled a walk-off homer off Rod Beck to win Game 1, and the Yankees took the series in five.

"The rivalry in '99 was already huge, off the charts," Cashman said. "The difference was that in '99, there was a lot more respect between the organizations. I think the organizations respect each other, but that respect was also publicly given in '99. In '03, the organizations themselves—from the players to the front office—seemed to get into verbal tussles much more. That raised it to a whole new level."

To Steinbrenner, there was one man to blame: his personal nemesis, Larry Lucchino, who became president of the Red Sox in 2002. The rivalry, Steinbrenner said, "is very intense, because of Larry Lucchino. He is a tough competitor. When he called us the Evil Empire, I didn't think that was very good. But so he did, and that caused a stir with the fans in Boston." Steinbrenner is friendly with John Henry, the Red Sox' principal owner and a former limited partner of the Yankees, but there may be no one in baseball he despises as much as Lucchino.

Lucchino and Steinbrenner had clashed in 1997 over a Japanese pitcher, Hideki Irabu. Lucchino, then the president of the Padres, held the negotiating rights to Irabu, who wanted to pitch for Steinbrenner instead. The teams grudgingly worked out a trade. Another international pitching star heightened the rift in 2002, when the Yankees and the Red Sox pursued Jose Contreras, a hard-throwing Cuban defector. Both teams showed up in Nicaragua in late December when open bidding began.

"We knew the Red Sox were very, very interested," said Gordon Blakeley, then the Yankees' vice president of international scouting. "I knew their general manager had flown in. You don't fly in unless you're really, really intent on doing something. That obviously put pressure on us." Theo Epstein, the Red Sox' general manager, offered four years and $27 million, $1 million short of the maximum he had been authorized to spend. As Blakeley and a scout, Carlos Rios, negotiated with Contreras at their bungalow at the Hotel Campo Real in Managua, Epstein watched the door from a hotel bar, just 40 feet away.

After three hours, Contreras emerged from the room with Blakeley, Rios and agent Jaime Torres, the deal done. In an interview with Murray Chass of the New York Times on Dec. 24, Lucchino made his famous putdown, using a "Star Wars" reference. "The Evil Empire extends its tentacles even into Latin America," Lucchino told Chass. (The Fenway Park organist would play music from Star Wars whenever the Yankees took batting practice in Boston in 2003.)

The next week, in the New York Daily News, Steinbrenner ripped back. "That's how a sick person thinks," he said. "I've learned this about Lucchino: he's baseball's foremost chameleon of all time. He changes colors depending on where he's standing. . . . When he was in San Diego, he was a big man for the small markets. Now he's in Boston and he's for the big markets. He's not the kind of guy you want to have in your foxhole. He's running the team behind John Henry's back."

It was a personal feud at full blast.

"It's a very, very bad rivalry," Steinbrenner said about a year later. "It is not good for anybody, for Lucchino or for me. But that was an ill-timed comment. I think the commissioner should have taken action there, and he didn't."

Steinbrenner had won Contreras, but as usual, he wanted more. In January, the Red Sox pursued David Ortiz, a left-handed-hitting first baseman. The Yankees already had two of those—Jason Giambi and Nick Johnson—but when he heard that Ortiz might sign with the Red Sox, Steinbrenner ordered Cashman to get him. Cashman did not, and he would hear about it often as Ortiz punished the Yankees during the season.

The Red Sox' moves brought them closer to the Yankees in talent, and the teams would become extremely well acquainted. Game 7 of the ALCS marked their 26th meeting in 2003. Thanks to the unbalanced schedule and the full slate of playoff games, it was the first time that two teams had ever played each other as many as 26 times in one season. The Yankees won the regular-season series, 10 games to 9, surviving several blowouts by the thunderous Boston offense. The Red Sox dazzled their fans, and Cashman noticed for the first time that Boston fans made up a sizable chunk of the crowd when the Red Sox played in the Bronx.

But when the Yankees needed a victory— to save face, maintain a comfortable division lead or keep Steinbrenner from boiling over— they usually got it. Five of the six regular-season series in 2003 ended with a Yankee victory, including one in July that moved Steinbrenner to tears. The only series that did not end with a Yankees victory came at Fenway Park in late July. The next day, Steinbrenner issued a missive through his publicist, Howard Rubenstein.

Steinbrenner first told Rubenstein to give reporters a relatively tame statement: "We didn't play well in Boston, but I'm not getting down on anyone. It's a long season and a long way to go." Minutes later, Steinbrenner could not resist a zinger. He had Rubenstein call back reporters with a jab at the Red Sox: "They haven't won anything yet." Naturally, it spiced the next day's sports pages.

The Red Sox stayed on Steinbrenner's mind. As the trading deadline approached, Boston traded for relievers Scott Sauerbeck from Pittsburgh and Scott Williamson from Cincinnati. Epstein's father, Leslie, expressed glee to the The Record of Hackensack, N.J., delighted that his son had snagged two pitchers that Steinbrenner—whom he called "Darth Vader, the convicted felon"—had wanted.

Steinbrenner admits that he cares about Boston's moves "a lot." "Sure," he said, "because we have to go against them. They made some very brilliant moves." Nevertheless, he added, "They had a bunch of players [who had] the seasons of their lives, and we still were able to overcome." The Yankees left their July series at Fenway with a one-and-a-half-game lead in the division. In their next series, in Boston, in late August, they won two of three games, capturing one after falling behind to Pedro Martinez, 3-0, in the first inning.

As the pennant race tightened, a fan approached Torre in the lobby of the Yankees' Boston hotel, the Ritz-Carlton on Newbury Street. "We're Red Sox fans," the fan said, "and if it was between catching Saddam Hussein and beating the Yankees, I'd take beating the Yankees." Torre laughed—and shuddered— as he told the story. The competitor in him also must have been satisfied to know that the fan did not then get his wish, even though he came close.

In consecutive games at Yankee Stadium on Sept. 5 and 6, the Red Sox won by scores of 9 3 and 11-0, cutting the Yankees' lead back to a game and a half. Steinbrenner raged to the *New York Post* during the first game of the series, imploring Torre to take a tougher approach. During the next day's blowout, a more composed Steinbrenner told the *Times* that he supported Torre, despite differences. "Look, I may not be everything he wants, and he may not be quite everything that I want in some ways," Steinbrenner explained. "Nobody is perfect. I just know I believe in Joe, I believe in the team and I believe that we are going to win."

The Red Sox were bringing out the best and worst in Steinbrenner, the ranting uber-boss and the passionate fan. "They make me very intense," he said months later. "I'm a really hard loser in a lot of ways. I don't like to lose, and they make me an intense competitor. I always have been and I always will be. There's nothing wrong with that."

The Yankees won the final regular-season meeting, and they took the division by six games with Boston capturing the wild card. In the division series, the Yankees dispatched Minnesota in four and the Red Sox survived a five-game set with Oakland. Torre picked a rested Mike Mussina as his Game 1 starter, while Boston chose the knuckleballer Tim Wakefield to lead an exhausted staff.

Wakefield was stingy, allowing two hits over six innings, and Ortiz, Todd Walker and Manny Ramirez homered off Mussina. Boston won Game 1, and after Andy Pettitte's victory the next night, the series shifted to Fenway for a dream matchup: Martinez against Roger Clemens.

It only seemed as if Clemens had come directly from the Red Sox to the Yankees. His career had detoured to Toronto for two Cy Young Award-winning seasons in 1997 and 1998, and the Blue Jays traded him to the Yankees in February 1999. But the 13 years Clemens spent in Boston made him a natural enemy of the Yankees' fans, and his gunslinger attitude on the mound made teammates wait before embracing him. In Boston, fans largely regarded him as a traitor, first for leaving, then for where he ended up.

Clemens shrugs off such talk. He said New York fans loved him even when he played for other teams, and he sniffed at the idea that Boston fans disliked him. "It's just nonsense," Clemens said in May 2003, a few days before a series at Fenway. "I enjoy the city still, to the fullest. You always want to play with the first team you came up with, but in reality, it's not always going to happen. But that city and that team will always be a part of my history. That's where I performed, and I performed greatly."

Clemens had three vintage Fenway performances left in him. He won his 299th game there on May 21, staying in to finish the sixth inning after taking a hit off his hand. On Aug. 31, Clemens won what seemed to be his final start in Boston, leaving in the seventh to a most improbable sight: a standing ovation in Fenway Park for a Yankee. By Game 3 of the ALCS, it was back to traditional roles. Clemens was hated, Martinez was hailed. But the Yankees had made a habit of handling Martinez as no other team could, always believing that their starter would pitch evenly with him and their hitters would tire him by working long at-bats. The Yankees also believed that Martinez was a headhunter.

In the July 7 game that left Steinbrenner teary, the Yankees stars Alfonso Soriano and Derek Jeter had to leave after being hit by pitches from Martinez. Randolph, the Yankees' third base coach, was particularly incensed. The spirit of the '70s churned inside him. "I was fuming," Randolph said. "I wished I was playing that day, because I thought, 'They're trying to take my guys out.' I was steamed. I just wanted to get somebody."

Roger Clemens, a veteran of intimidation, pitches in the second inning of Game 3. (Barton Silverman/*The New York Times*)

The New York Times — July 8, 2003

STEINBRENNER'S TEARS OF RAGE AND JOY

By Jack Curry

GEORGE STEINBRENNER was clutching a metal railing with both hands in the auxiliary press box yesterday, waiting for the tension of another Yankee-Red Sox game to finally dissipate. He paced, he perspired, he clapped, he pontificated. The Yankees loaded the bases against the always welcome Byung Hyun Kim in the ninth inning, and Steinbrenner, like everyone else, waited.

A dramatic game that featured a terrific duel between Pedro Martinez and Mike Mussina, and two Martinez pitches that caused hand injuries to Alfonso Soriano and Derek Jeter, ended with a 90-foot grounder by a player who had been a Yankee for four days. Curtis Pride's tapper glanced off Todd Walker's glove and enabled Hideki Matsui to scamper home and give the Yankees a 2-1 victory on a steamy day at Yankee Stadium.

Apparently, it also gave Steinbrenner the freedom to cry. The tears were visible beneath his sunglasses soon after Pride delivered for the second straight game. Steinbrenner depicts himself as a tough guy and a tough owner, a man who has avoided tears after winning some World Series titles. But on this emotional day in an emotional rivalry, when two of his best players wound up at a hospital for X-rays, Steinbrenner turned softer than pudding.

"I'm just proud of the way Mussina pitched," Steinbrenner said. "You know, I'm getting older. As you get older, you do this more."

But the soft side of Steinbrenner disappeared when he was asked about Martinez, who hit Soriano and Jeter with 2 of his first 11 pitches. Was Martinez retaliating for Kevin Millar's being hit by Roger Clemens on Saturday? Was Martinez simply establishing his game plan of throwing inside?

When Steinbrenner was asked if he thought Martinez had targeted his infielders, who both had bone bruises, he said: "It looked like that to me. I can't say what was in the man's mind."

A few minutes later, Steinbrenner, his emotions twisting from grandfatherly to godfatherly, added, "If indeed, and I'm not saying he did, but if he threw at them to try to deliver a message, he delivered the wrong message, in my opinion."

Another Yankee coach would have similar ideas in Game 3—and act on them. In the top of the fourth inning, just after losing the lead, Martinez plunked Karim Garcia on the upper back. Garcia then slid hard into second on a double play. The Yankees were furious and jawed at Martinez, who pointed to

(Right) Boston's Manny Ramirez ducks after Roger Clemens throws a high pitch to Jorge Posada in the fourth inning of Game 3. This was the pitch that ignited the brawl. (Associated Press)

(Facing Page) Clemens's pitch in Game 3 at Fenway leads to Pedro Martinez, left, throwing Yankees coach Don Zimmer to the ground. Zimmer was so angry by Martinez's reaction to the pitch that he marched out onto the field and tried to attack him. (Barton Silverman/The New York Times)

their dugout, then to his head.

Clemens, a veteran in the art of intimidation, knew that Ramirez would expect retaliation as the leadoff hitter in the bottom of the fourth. Fifteen years earlier, Clemens might have hit Ramirez. But he was savvier at 41 years old, and he fired a pitch level with Ramirez's head but directly over the plate.

Clemens could rightly claim that he had no intention of hitting Ramirez. But with nerves raw, Ramirez blew up, stalking toward Clemens with bat in hand. The benches emptied, and Yankee bench coach Don Zimmer—the manager of the doomed 1978 Red Sox—went hunting for Martinez.

Spotting Martinez alone near the first base

dugout, the 72-year-old Zimmer lunged at him, fist flying. Startled, Martinez grabbed Zimmer by the ears and flung him to the ground. It was an unforgettable image— Zimmer's body rolling to a stop, 34,000 people training their eyes on his pink, bald head. In a flash, the episode was lampooned on *Saturday Night Live*, an instant national joke. (Zimmer apologized tearfully the next day.)

Clemens had skillfully unnerved the Red Sox without throwing at anyone, and the Yankees held on for a 4-3 victory—but not without more bloodshed. In the ninth inning, Garcia and reliever Jeff Nelson brawled with a groundskeeper in the right-field bullpen. Nelson's complaint: the groundskeeper was waving a towel and cheering for the Red Sox. It was another outrageous example of a rivalry gone wild, and afterward the Yankees' president, Randy Levine, chastised the Red Sox for promoting an "attitude of lawlessness." After a day of rest on a rainy Sunday, the teams put away the riot gear for the rest of the series.

Boston won Game 4 behind Wakefield, and David Wells stifled the Red Sox in Game 5. Back in the Bronx, Boston staged a seventh-inning comeback to win Game 6. The season would come down to one game. For the Yankees, loaded with stars who sometimes did not seem to fit together, Game 7 became a shining example of teamwork. Martinez had a 4-0 lead in the fourth inning, and the Yankees knew the odds.

"It's Game 7, it's Pedro, we're down, there's no chance," Boone later recalled. "It ain't looking good. We were going to have to scratch and claw."

Clemens had nothing. That night, the American League's career strikeout king got just four swinging strikes out of 63 pitches, and trailed by 4-0 when Mussina relieved him with no outs and runners at the corners in the

fourth. The deliberate Mussina, who often struggles if he breaks from his routine, had made no relief appearances in his 430 professional games.

"Mike Mussina, who'd never done this before, puts a tourniquet on it, not even a Band-Aid," Torre said. "And all of a sudden, things turn." Mussina, who had lost his two starts in the series, struck out Jason Varitek. He got Johnny Damon to ground sharply into a double play. Then he threw two more scoreless innings.

The slumping Giambi had nudged along the offense with bases-empty homers in the fifth and seventh innings. But it was 5-2 Red Sox in the eighth, and Boone was stewing on the bench, feeling helpless. The night before, his brother Bret, the Mariners' second baseman who was analyzing the series for Fox, had a blunt conversation with Aaron. He had not seen much from his younger brother, and he told him he stunk. "But you never know," Bret added. "You get a big hit, everyone for-

gets about the bad at-bats."

True enough, but Boone could not contribute unless he played, and he was out of the lineup. In fact, since his trade from the Reds on July 31, Boone had been a major disappointment offensively. "It was going to be a very, very difficult off-season for me," he said.

Then, suddenly, he had hope. Jeter had been the quiet contributor in the ALCS, making big defensive plays at shortstop and bashing a homer off Martinez in the Yankees' one-run Game 3 victory. Now, with one out and the bases empty in the eighth inning of Game 7, he drilled a double over Trot Nixon's head in right field.

A rally was on. Williams singled Jeter home, and it was 5-3. With Hideki Matsui coming up, Red Sox Manager Grady Little came to the mound to see Martinez and returned to the dugout without him. It was a fateful decision: Matsui doubled to right, and Jorge Posada blooped a two-run, broken-bat double into center. Tie game. "I didn't think he was losing it," Posada said of Martinez. "He made some tough pitches. With one out, I couldn't strike out. I've got to put the ball in play, and that ball found a lot of grass."

With two outs, Ruben Sierra batted for Wilson and drew an intentional walk. Boone entered the game as a pinch runner, and he suddenly had a chance to make history. The week before, Randolph had passed Boone in a hallway outside the Yankees' clubhouse. "I just got a funny vibe about him," Randolph said. He stopped Boone and looked him in the eye. "You're my sleeper," Randolph told him. "Before this is all over, you're going to come up big for us."

It was hard to see how. Boone had batted .254 in two months with the Yankees, then .200 in the division series. He was 2 for 16 in the ALCS, and in the 10th inning, the Red Sox brought in Wakefield—more bad news. "I haven't faced that many knuckleballers, maybe one a year, but I had faced Wakefield," Boone said. "We probably faced him, including the postseason, maybe four starts, and I did not have real success against him. I think I had one hit, and that was pretty much it. He was a guy I did not enjoy facing."

Boone's memory was accurate: in four games against Wakefield, he was 1 for 11 with a single. But when Randolph saw Boone headed for the bat rack before the bottom of the 11th inning, he imagined something better. He could see Boone stroking a leadoff single, stealing a base and scoring the winning run. Randolph remembered his prediction, and he found Boone. "This is your time," he said.

Boone listened, but he was mostly concerned with Wakefield, wondering how to connect off such a confounding pitcher. Often, Boone recalled, he would take what

seemed like a good swing at Wakefield's flutterball, thinking he would crush it. Inevitably, he would tip the ball, or dribble a nubber somewhere, or miss it entirely. Boone had struck out in his last two at-bats against Wakefield in Game 4.

"When I went up to the plate, I actually considered taking a pitch," Boone said. "Then I said, 'Forget it. Get a good pitch to hit. Get something up and out over the plate and try to put a good swing on it.'" This time, when it mattered most, Boone did. This time, there was no doubt. At 12:16 a.m., two hundred thirty-six minutes after Clemens's first pitch, Boone lifted a high fly ball down the left-field line. Immediately, he knew it was a homer, knew that the Yankees had again slain their enemy and were going to the World Series.

Boone smiled wide and raised his arms in triumph, his eyes going first to the Yankees' bench, his mind instantly grasping what he had done. "I remember running around the bases and consciously telling myself to look around, look around, try to remember this and savor what's going on, focus on the moment," Boone said.

"Usually when I hit a home run or whatever, I never really look around. But I remember running around the bases, telling myself to look at people, look in the stands, look at the dugout. But in hindsight, honestly, I don't remember much. I just remember—wow. I remember floating around the bases." His teammates swarmed from the dugout to greet him at home plate, pushing and hugging each other until Boone leaped in and touched off the party. But one Yankee was not among them—Mariano Rivera, the most valuable player in the series.

Rivera was the Yankees' last pitcher in all

four of their victories. He worked two-inning saves in Games 3 and 5, and in Game 7 he went three innings, his longest stint in three and a half years. Rivera, a deeply religious man who had spent his whole career as a Yankee, sprinted for the mound and knelt there, flopping to the dirt with his chest, kissing the ground, sobbing. The base coaches, Lee Mazzilli from first and Randolph from third, rushed to him.

"He was crying like a baby, giving thanks to God," Randolph said. "All that emotion just poured out, like someone just totally shocked at what they were seeing, like a release of all this energy. Lee tried to pick him up, but Mo was so overwhelmed. Lee left him and I went over to grab him, and then the pile just kind of hit us, and it got a little crazy after that." In the delirious clubhouse afterward, Rivera said that the victory ranked as the greatest of all in his Yankee career. In the interview room— around the time that Clemens, Wells and pitching coach Mel Stottlemyre were toasting

the Babe Ruth plaque in Monument Park with open beer bottles—Torre said the same thing.

"To play them 26 times and beat our rival like we did, it couldn't be more satisfying," Torre said. "This has to be the sweetest taste of all for me."

When the World Series started, about 44 hours after Boone's homer, it seemed somehow anticlimactic. Yankee Stadium was filled for Game 1 against the Florida Marlins—a 10-year-old franchise—but even the players noticed that a certain kind of energy was missing. The Yankees would lose in six games.

Boone left town after the World Series and said he never had time to digest the New York reaction to his homer. But he knew he was the latest link in a chain of Red Sox infamy: "Babe, Bucky, Buckner, Boone," as the T-shirts say. Boone expects to hear about it forever. "As much as you try to ignore everything going on around you, you realize the passion in those games, and I guess the hatred a lot of the Boston people have for you because you're wearing the Yankee uni," Boone said. "And hatred, I don't think, is too strong a word. Those people, they're crazy, man."

Speaking three months later, Boone said people often looked at him in a funny way. It's the homer, he knows, and he can usually spot the gawkers' allegiance. After the season, Boone was relaxing outside the Los Angeles Coliseum before a U.S.C. football game. From 30 yards away, he said, some tailgaters noticed him and cursed him. Boone went over to meet them anyway. "They were these Boston guys," Boone recalled. "And actually, they ended up being really cool. They brought me into their tent. They were like, 'C'mon, have a sandwich —you suck!'"

Boone is the brother, son and grandson of

major leaguers. He lives in California and has played in the Midwest and Northeast. He named a few other rivalries—Lakers-Celtics, Browns-Steelers, Michigan-Ohio State–and said nothing compares to the Yankees and the Red Sox.

"The way baseball is now, the Red Sox and the Yankees are going to continue to be major players and always have at least a chance to be really, really good every year," Boone said. "Couple that with the fact that, back in the Northeast, you're born Yankees or Red Sox. It's bred into you. They wake up, and it's the most important thing. It's life or death, almost. I was talking to a guy out here, and he was asking me how I liked New York. I told him, 'It's not like out here. It's a whole differ-

Mariano Rivera kneels on the mound whooping for joy, comforted by an unidentified teammate, while Aaron Boone (not shown) circles the bases after his homerun hit in the eleventh inning. (Associated Press)

ent level of fan.'"

The Yankees lost the 2003 World Series on a Saturday, and within hours, the Red Sox were back on their minds. Officials from the Texas Rangers called Cashman before noon the day after the Series ended, asking him to meet with them at their Manhattan hotel to discuss a possible trade for Alex Rodriguez. The Red Sox would be another bidder. Cashman passed, annoyed at the timing and believing that Rodriguez would not fit anyway, with Jeter on the team. But the Rangers' strategy was obvious: play the enemies off each other.

The next month, when Pettitte became a free agent, the Red Sox made the richest offer: four years, $52 million. One Red Sox official said the team never expected Pettitte to take it, but they wanted to make things interesting for him away from New York. The Yankees' final proposal guaranteed just two years and

$26 million. The Houston Astros' winning bid was for three years and $31.5 million.

The Red Sox offer dwarfed anything else Pettitte got, but Pettitte, a Yankee for nine years, never considered Boston. Even as he was negotiating his departure from the only team he had played for, Pettitte remembered his place in the rivalry. "I couldn't do that to the organization," he said. "I wouldn't be able to do that to my teammates."

Pettitte's snub was not quite as bold as Jackie Robinson's, who chose to retire in 1956 rather than accept a trade from Brooklyn to the hated New York Giants. But, still, it was something.

Pettitte, a Texan, opted out of the rivalry at a time when others were clamoring to join. Schilling was excited about going to the Red Sox, but he would have been just as energized about joining the Yankees. Rodriguez told the Rangers that if they wanted to trade him, he would go to Boston or the Bronx.

The Red Sox spent more than two months trying to land Rodriguez for Ramirez, but their deal hinged on restructuring the remaining seven years and $179 million on Rodriguez's contract. The players' union considered the Red Sox's plan a reduction of the contract's value and vetoed it; Lucchino blasted the union when the deal fell apart.

But Boston never counted on another strike from Boone. On the night of Jan. 16, about three weeks after the Red Sox's Rodriguez deal collapsed, Boone was sitting at home in Newport Beach, Calif., and he was bored. He went to a gym nearby, and made a fateful decision: instead of running on a treadmill to work up a sweat, Boone entered a pickup basketball game.

As Boone chased a ball out of bounds, another player barreled into him, crushing Boone's left knee. Boone had torn his anterior cruciate ligament, jeopardizing his $5.75 million contract and leaving the Yankees with no established third baseman. Soon after, Cashman started dreaming of Rodriguez.

With the Boston deal dead, Rodriguez decided to encourage the Rangers to trade him to New York, where he would cede the shortstop position to Jeter and move to third base. On Feb. 16, the Yankees and Rangers completed a stunning deal, with Rodriguez (and $67 million) coming to the Bronx and Soriano and a prospect heading to Texas.

It was a body blow to the heart of Red Sox Nation, and two days later, Henry blasted the Yankees, advocating a salary cap in an e-mail message to reporters. "(T)here really is no other fair way to deal with a team that has gone so insanely far beyond the resources of all the other teams," Henry wrote, adding later, "Baseball doesn't have an answer for the Yankees."

At the Yankees' spring training complex in Tampa, Florida, Steinbrenner was livid. He issued a broadside at Henry in a statement: "We understand that John Henry must be embarrassed, frustrated and disappointed by his failure in this transaction. Unlike the Yankees, he chose not to go the extra distance for his fans in Boston. It is understandable, but wrong that he would try to deflect the accountability for his mistakes onto others and to a system for which he voted in favor. It is time to get on with life and forget the sour grapes."

Commissioner Bud Selig quickly ordered Henry and Steinbrenner to quiet down, but Selig's edict was destined to be futile. Boston and the Bronx had become baseball's hot spots, home of free-spending teams, seething bitterness and plenty of pulsating action. The Red Sox fight the Curse and the Yankees fight to protect it, with history always at stake.

But what if there really is no curse? The most powerful Yankee of all would rather not believe it.

"I don't think there are curses," Steinbrenner said. "It certainly appears that way, and you could make a lot out of it. But if there is a curse, God let it continue to live."

Maybe Steinbrenner is right. Maybe there is no curse. But why, then, does one team have 26 championships since the sale of Babe Ruth, and the other team have none? How does he explain that? For once Seinbrenner chose understatement. "We have made kind of a habit of handling them in tough spots," he said.

Victory . . . and defeat.

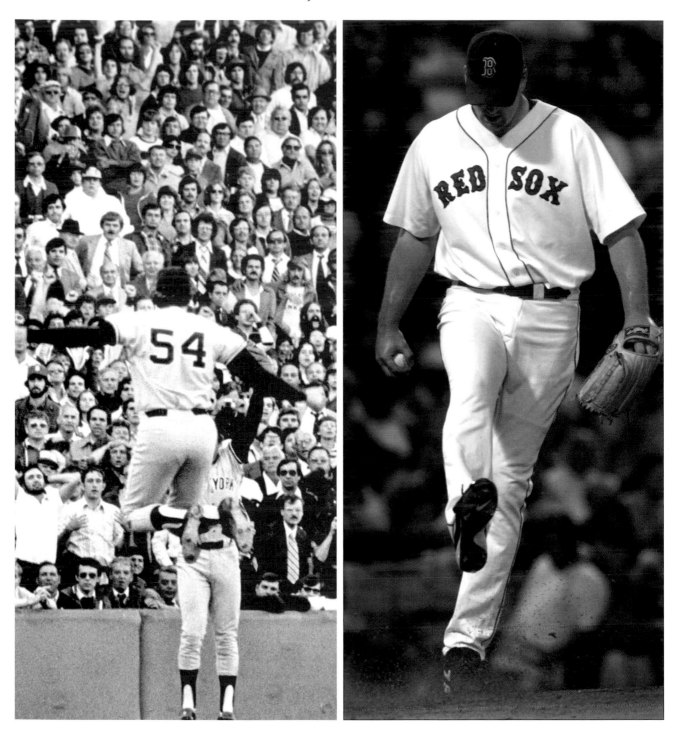

The Story of the Yankees and Red Sox throughout the years.

List of Illustrations

162. Hideki Matsui watches hopelessly as the first of two of Red Sox David Ortiz's homers clears the wall at Yankee Stadium on July 6, 2003. (Chang W. Lee/*The New York Times*)

163. Roger Clemens slides to make a tag at first base on a leaping Troy O'Leary. April 19, 2001. (Barry Chin/*The Boston Globe*)

164. July 26, 2003. Jeremy Giambi is safe under the tag of Derek Jeter. (Barry Chin/*The Boston Globe*)

166. Yankees Bernie Williams (*foreground*) loosens up before Game 3 against the Red Sox in 1999. The mythic Green Monster stands behind him. (Barton Silverman/*The New York Times*)

167. The Red Sox' Manny Ramirez is held back by teammate David Ortiz as he tries to get to Yankees pitcher Roger Clemens during a fourth-inning fight. (Jim Davis/*The Boston Globe*)

168. The fight in the Yankee bullpen before the 9th inning of Game 3 of the ALCS. (Matther J. Lee/*The Boston Globe*)

168. Yankees bench coach Don Zimmer (*left*), meeting with reporters to discuss his brawl with Pedro Martinez in Game 3. Manager Joe Torre is in the background. (Jim Davis/*The Boston Globe*)

169. In a non-move that would go down in Boston history, and ultimately cause the Red Sox to decline to renew his contract, manager Grady Little (*left*) came out to talk to struggling starter Pedro Martinez (*right*) in the eighth inning, but decides to leave him in the game. First baseman Kevin Millar is in the middle. (Jim Davis/*The Boston Globe*)

170. Aaron Boone signals "number one" as he hits first base on his home run jaunt after hitting the game winning, American league pennant clinching home run off Red Sox pitcher Tim Wakefield (*49, walking off field, background right*). (Jim Davis/*The Boston Globe*)

171. Pedro Martinez, David Ortiz, Derek Lowe and John Burkett sit in the dugout after losing Game 7 of the ALCS. (Barry Chin/*The Boston Globe*)

172. Pitcher Curt Schilling (*center*) holds up his new Boston Red Sox jersey with Red Sox President and CEO Larry Lucchino (*left*) and General Manager Theo Epstein, after a press conference in Scottsdale, Arizona, November 28, 2003 announcing a trade between the Red Sox and Schilling's former team, the Arizona Diamondbacks. (REUTERS/Jeff Topping)

183. Roger Clemens, a veteran of intimidation, pitches in the second inning of Game 3. (Barton Silverman/*The New York Times*)

184. Boston's Manny Ramirez ducks after Roger Clemens throws a high pitch to Jorge Posada in the fourth inning of Game 3. This was the pitch that ignited the brawl. (Associated Press)

185. Clemens's pitch in Game 3 at Fenway leads to Pedro Martinez, left, throwing Yankees coach Don Zimmer to the ground. Zimmer was so angry by Martinez's reaction to the pitch that he marched out onto the field and tried to attack him. (Barton Silverman/*The New York Times*)

186. & 187. In the 2003 game 7 at Yankee Stadium, Manny Ramirez catches Enrique Wilson's line drive in the second inning. While some may claim that the 1978 game against Boston was the greatest ever played, those who were there for Game 7 in 2003 might dispute that. (G. Paul Burnett/*The New York Times*)